TANGLED SOULS

TANGLED SOULS

LOVE AND SCANDAL AMONG THE VICTORIAN ARISTOCRACY

JANE DISMORE

Also by Jane Dismore:

The Voice from the Garden: Pamela Hambro and the Tale of Two Families Before and After the Great War
Duchesses: Living in 21st Century Britain
Princess: The Early Life of Queen Elizabeth II

First published 2022

The History Press
97 St George's Place, Cheltenham,
Gloucestershire, GL50 3QB
www.thehistorypress.co.uk

© Jane Dismore, 2022

The right of Jane Dismore to be identified as the Author of this work has been asserted in accordance with the Copyright, Designs and Patents Act 1988.

All rights reserved. No part of this book may be reprinted or reproduced or utilised in any form or by any electronic, mechanical or other means, now known or hereafter invented, including photocopying and recording, or in any information storage or retrieval system, without the permission in writing from the Publishers.

British Library Cataloguing in Publication Data.
A catalogue record for this book is available from the British Library.

ISBN 978 0 7509 9662 4

Typesetting and origination by The History Press
Printed and bound in Great Britain by TJ Books Limited, Padstow, Cornwall.

Trees for Life

Contents

Glossary of Main Characters

Late Victorian Britain was fascinated by an unconventional, mostly aristocratic, group of men and women, dubbed 'the Souls', who came together as friends in the 1880s. Writers, politicians, artists, intellectuals and creatives, they were dominant in political and cultural life. Many Souls were married, a few were single, and some were siblings. Others admired or envied them from the fringes, mixing with them but never becoming a part of them.

At the centre of this book is Harry Cust, one of around forty Souls; most are mentioned, although not all of them play a major part. The purpose of this glossary is to serve as a brief guide to those who feature most prominently and give some clarity to family relationships. Those Souls whose spouses were also part of the group are indicated in bold print, with occasional reference to their emotional entanglements. Mention is also made of those grand country houses in which the Souls gathered for 'Saturday to Mondays' to talk, play and love.

Families

The Custs and Brownlows

Harry Cust (Henry John Cockayne Cust, 1861–1917). Born into a family of distinguished politicians, lawyers and churchmen, Harry was handsome and clever, a poet, editor and MP, predicted at school to become prime minister. Lover of and loved by many women, he was the biological father of Lady Diana Cooper (née Manners) and perhaps others. In 1884, he inherited Cockayne Hatley in Bedfordshire from his father, Henry Francis Cockayne Cust, and later became heir to his second cousin, Earl Brownlow. In 1893, circumstances forced his marriage to **Emmeline 'Nina' Welby-Gregory** and the resulting scandal compromised his career and reputation.

Nina Cust (Emmeline Mary Elizabeth, née Welby-Gregory, 1867–1955). A poet, artist, sculptor and linguist, she was the quiet, intellectual and lovely daughter of Sir William and Lady Victoria Welby-Gregory (née Stuart-Wortley) of Denton Manor, Lincolnshire. Nina was related to the Duke of Rutland and, distantly, to **Harry Cust**, whom she had long loved. In 1893 they married after she told him she was carrying his child.

3rd Earl Brownlow (Adelbert Wellington Brownlow Cust, 1844–1921). Harry Cust's second cousin, a Conservative politician and courtier. His wife was the **Countess Adelaide**, née Talbot. The Brownlows entertained at their country estates, Belton (Lincolnshire) and Ashridge (Hertfordshire), and at their London house at 8 Carlton Terrace. Older than most Souls, Lord and Lady Brownlow were supporters of the arts and close friends of the Prince and Princess of Wales (later Edward VII and Queen Alexandra).

Lady Brownlow's sisters included **Gertrude**, 'Gity', wife of **George Herbert, 13th Earl of Pembroke** (1850–1895), who was ten years his senior. The Pembrokes entertained the Souls and other society figures at Wilton, their Wiltshire estate.

The Tennants

A family of eleven children, whose father was the wealthy industrialist and Liberal MP, Sir Charles Clow Tennant. The family home was The Glen in Peeblesshire. In London, they lived at 40 Grosvenor Square. The youngest two of his six daughters, intelligent, amusing and dismissive of social convention, were the vital force in the formation of the Souls, favouring friendship over political differences:

Laura Tennant (1862–86). Gifted, mercurial and enchanting, after rejecting other suitors, in 1885 she married the budding barrister, cricketer and future Liberal politician **Alfred Lyttelton** but died in childbirth a year later, after which the group of friends drew together more closely.

Margot Tennant (1864–1945). Original, witty and socially bold, her unlikely friendship with the older Arthur Balfour, a Conservative MP, led to regular gatherings at The Glen of politicians of all persuasions and other interesting people. Some became close friends and were known as the Souls. In 1894, she married widower **Herbert Henry Asquith**, Home Secretary in William Gladstone's government, and drew him into the group. In 1908 he became prime minister. She and Harry Cust enjoyed a long and enduring friendship.

Other Tennant sisters in the Souls were:

Lucy Graham Smith (1860–1942). An accomplished watercolourist and talented rider, she married Thomas Graham Smith, a landowner and horse fanatic, when she was too young, and they lived at Easton Grey in Wiltshire. It was not a happy marriage and she fell in love with Harry Cust. She became increasingly afflicted by crippling arthritis.

Charty (Charlotte) Ribblesdale (1858–1911). Considered to be the most beautiful of the Tennant sisters, in 1887 she married **Lord Ribblesdale (Tommy)**. A former soldier, keen hunter and archetypal English gentleman, dubbed by Edward VII 'the ancestor', he suffered intermittent ill health. Charty found strength in Harry Cust, with whom she was very close. The Ribblesdales' country home was Gisburne in Lancashire.

The Wyndhams

An aesthetically aware family of three girls and two boys headed by the Hon. Percy Wyndham (son of Lord Leconfield) and his wife Madeline, a follower of the Pre-Raphaelites. At their Wiltshire home, Clouds, they entertained artists and writers and gave intellectual and physical freedom to their children. Aristocratic by upbringing and bohemian by inclination, three of them became quintessential Souls:

Mary Elcho (1861–1937). Free-spirited and spontaneous, the eldest of the Wyndham siblings had wanted to marry Balfour but in 1883 was persuaded to marry **Hugo Charteris.** They shortly became Lord and Lady Elcho when he became heir to his father, the 10th Earl of Wemyss and 6th Earl of March, whose estates included Gosford in Scotland. A Conservative MP with a sharp wit, Hugo was also a gambler and womaniser, whose affair with the Duchess of Leinster had lasting consequences. Mary became known for her parties at their Gloucestershire house, Stanway, and maintained a close and lifelong relationship with Balfour, although she was not immune to other admirers. In 1914, Hugo inherited his father's title, becoming 11th Earl and Mary, the Countess.

George Wyndham (1863–1913). The second of the five siblings, the former soldier was a politician and poet, dark-haired and handsome. In 1887 he married the older widow, **Sibell, Lady Grosvenor**, who kept her title at the insistence of her former father-in-law, the 1st Duke of Westminster – her first husband was his son, the Earl of Grosvenor, by whom she bore the heir to the dukedom. The Wyndhams lived at Saighton Grange, Cheshire. George inherited his family's home, Clouds, in 1911. His political career began with his appointment as Balfour's private secretary in Ireland; his marriage, however, was less successful.

Pamela Tennant (1871–1928, later Grey). The youngest of the Wyndham siblings, she was literary, musical and self-centred. After her romance with Harry Cust was abruptly curtailed upon his marriage to Nina, in 1895 she married Sir Charles Tennant's son, Edward, a Liberal politician and businessman (soon created Lord Glenconner). They made their home at Wilsford in Wiltshire, but Eddy was not enough for her needs, and she turned elsewhere.

The Lytteltons

A family headed by George William, 4th Lord Lyttelton, Baron of Frankley, who had twelve children with his first wife, Mary Glynne; the children's uncle was William Ewart Gladstone, four times Liberal prime minister. The Lytteltons' eleventh child, May, was Arthur Balfour's first love, who died in 1875.

Alfred Lyttelton (1857–1913). The youngest of the twelve Lytteltons, a barrister, Liberal and a brilliant cricketer, Alfred was a good friend of Balfour's. He married **Laura Tennant** in 1885 but was widowed eleven months later. In 1892, he married **'DD' (Edith) Balfour** (no relation to Arthur) and followed a political career, becoming Colonial Secretary.

Other Lyttelton siblings and their spouses also appear in the book, not as Souls but as players in the lives of Harry and Nina Cust:

Reverend Arthur Temple Lyttelton: vicar of Eccles, married to (Mary) Kathleen (née Clive), a supporter of suffragist Millicent Garrett Fawcett.

Lavinia Talbot (née Lyttelton): married to Dr Edward Stuart Talbot, who was Vicar of Leeds and later a bishop. He was related to both Nina Cust and Lady Brownlow.

General Sir Neville Gerald Lyttelton: married to Katherine Stuart-Wortley, Nina's cousin.

Sybil Cust (née Lyttelton): born 1873 to their father's second wife and married to Sir Lionel Cust, Harry Cust's cousin.

Individuals

Arthur Balfour (1848–1930)

A philosopher and Conservative politician, his friendship with Margot Tennant led to the formation of the Souls and, respected and admired, he was at their centre. Balfour's uncle, Robert Gascoyne-Cecil, Marquess of Salisbury, was three times Conservative prime minister and gave Balfour his first Cabinet post as Chief Secretary for Ireland. Balfour himself became prime minister in 1902.

His sweetheart, May Lyttelton, died young, and he never married but maintained a lifelong and intriguing relationship with Lady Elcho (Mary, neé Wyndham). His family home was Whittingehame in Scotland, and his London house was 4 Carlton Gardens.

Wilfrid Scawen Blunt (1840–1922)
Poet, anti-imperialist and devotee of Egypt, his political stance was different from most Souls, yet their friendship largely endured. Some of the men were members of the Crabbet Club, which he founded. Blunt was also linked to the Souls by blood (as a cousin of the Wyndhams) and romantically, for despite being married (to Lady Anne née Noel, a granddaughter of Lord Byron), his infidelities were legion.

George Curzon (1859–1925)
Son of Baron Scarsdale of Kedleston Hall, Curzon suffered a harsh upbringing and was plagued by a spinal condition. Fiercely ambitious, he travelled across Europe and Asia, becoming an expert on foreign affairs. In 1895 he married American heiress Mary Leiter. In 1898 he was made Viceroy of India and created Baron Curzon of Kedleston.

Mary's death in 1906 left him with three daughters, after which he lived at Hackwood Park in Hampshire. His desire to serve another term as viceroy was thwarted, but he continued in politics. In 1911, he was created Earl Curzon of Kedleston (elevated to marquess in 1921).

Violet Granby (1856–1937)
A respected artist and unconventional even by the Souls' standards, Violet Lindsay married Henry Manners in 1882. In 1888 they became Marquis and Marchioness of Granby when his father became 7th Duke of Rutland. They lived at Belvoir Castle, Leicestershire, and in London, and shared a love of theatre, although Lord Granby favoured the actresses.

Violet fell in love with Harry Cust and in 1892 bore their daughter, Diana (who later became Lady Diana Cooper by marriage), which linked the pair inextricably, although Granby raised her as his own. In 1906, Violet became Duchess of Rutland when he became 8th Duke.

Ettie Grenfell (1867–1952)
Losing her brother and her parents at a young age, Ettie Fane was raised first by her grandmother, then her childless uncle and aunt, the Earl and Countess Cowper, who made her heir to their Hertfordshire estate, Panshanger. In 1887, she married Willie Grenfell, politician and sportsman, and at their Maidenhead home, Taplow Court, she became a noted hostess and confidante.

Ettie sought male attention and fascinated many, including some of the Souls. In 1905, she became Lady Desborough when Willie was created a baron.

Gay Windsor (1863–1944)
Christened Alberta but known as Gay, she was the creative and enigmatic daughter of Sir Augustus and Lady Paget, a German countess who influenced Gay's views on animal welfare and her choice of husband. In 1883, aged 19, Gay married **Lord Windsor (Robert Windsor-Clive)**, a talented architect, who designed their home Hewell Grange in Worcestershire; they also lived at St Fagans, near Cardiff.

In 1905, Gay became Countess of Plymouth when Robert was created earl. Seeing two unfulfilled marriages, Lady Paget did not discourage her daughter's relationship with George Wyndham.

PRELUDE

PRECIPICE

The afternoon of 12 August 1893 was still and humid in Hertfordshire. At Ashridge, the magnificent estate of the 3rd Earl and Countess Brownlow, at which Elizabeth I had lived as a child and where royalty still visited, a group of their friends had arrived for a 'Saturday to Monday' house party and were settling themselves in the glorious grounds. Some strolled lazily through the sweet-smelling Italian garden, others sought the coolness of the sunken grotto but most idled under the great cedar of Lebanon, for the lack of a breeze made anything other than talk too taxing.[1]

Besides, conversation was what they were good at, for several of them were part of a cultured set dubbed 'the Souls' by outsiders who envied their originality and wit. A largely aristocratic group of writers, artists and politicians, they had come together as friends nearly a decade earlier, sharing a disregard for the restrictions of Victorian upper-class etiquette: the dull drawing-room talk on 'acceptable' subjects; the separation of the sexes in social activities.

Although the Brownlows were half a generation older than most Souls, their patronage of the arts made them popular, and they often hosted the gatherings the group enjoyed at country houses, where they discussed an esoteric range of subjects and played clever word games. 'The only unforgivable sin was to be dull or stupid,' said Lady Cowper, aunt of Soul member, Ettie Grenfell.[2]

The weekend saw the start of the Brownlows' Silver Wedding Anniversary celebrations in Hertfordshire, a continuation of those already enjoyed with their tenants at their other estates, Belton in Lincolnshire and Ellesmere in Shropshire. As part of the festivities, the Brownlows were also marking an event of national interest, the recent marriage of Queen Victoria's grandson, Prince George, Duke of York, and Princess Mary of Teck, which they had attended at St James's Palace. The earl was part of the royal household and both he and the countess were regarded by the duke's parents, the Prince and Princess of Wales, as close confidants.

The Brownlows could chat about the wedding with one of their weekend guests, Arthur Balfour, who had also attended. Balfour, nephew of the former Conservative prime minister, Lord Salisbury, was now the Leader of the Opposition to Gladstone's Liberal government; within a decade of the gathering, he would himself become prime minister.

Attractive to women and admired by men, Balfour was at the heart of the Souls, a trained philosopher who believed that civilised discourse was possible among those of differing political views. At a time when the controversial issue of Home Rule for Ireland was threatening to divide the United Kingdom, such an ideal distinguished and elevated the Souls.

On that hot afternoon, as Balfour sat down and began to talk, not everyone wanted to be in his orbit; he could be intimidating to those who did not know him well. One such guest sat slightly apart, as she often did when in the company of the Souls. Nina Welby-Gregory, aged 26, an artist, poet and translator, knew they thought her too enigmatic, too quiet for their exuberant confidence.

Ashridge was more familiar to her than to many of the guests, for the Brownlows had known her since birth. In Ashridge House, so large that one visitor mistook it for a village, Nina knew her way through the 'endless chain of imposing rooms',[3] with their classical carvings and columns of fluted marble. The house had been exquisitely refurbished by Adelaide, the countess, with fashionable oak panelling and statues of Malta stone, while on every surface stood huge jars of roses from the garden. As an artist, Nina appreciated the earl's famed picture collection; his wife remained as striking now, at 49, as she was in Sir Frederic Leighton's portrait painted fifteen years earlier and still exuded an air of otherworldliness. To Nina's cousin, Susan Grosvenor, the Brownlows were one of the most handsome couples she had ever seen, 'They were both very tall and had a kind of impressive magnificence of air'.[4]

Nina had been at Ashridge on more than one occasion when royalty was present and the dining table gleamed with a mass of gold plate, some of it given to the Brownlows by their mutual godmother, Queen Adelaide, for whom the countess was named. She knew its bedrooms too, which could accommodate forty guests and their servants. That weekend, she was particularly interested in where her room was situated in relation to another of their regular visitors, the earl's second cousin, Henry John Cockayne Cust, known to the world as Harry Cust.

For all their wealth and privilege, one thing missing from the Brownlows' marriage was a child, but they were fond of Harry, now 32, whose parents were dead. Blonde and blue-eyed, with 'the profile of a Greek coin',[5] he had the Brownlow Cust good looks and, at over 6ft tall, their height. Blessed also with intellect and charm, and considered the best conversationalist of his time, he seemed to possess all life's gifts.

Early on, 'radiant with youth and spirits and early success',[6] he had discovered the effect he had on women, often older, married ones. The countess, seventeen years his senior, had a soft spot for him: Harry noticed she wrote to him, 'perhaps too lovingly', while he was abroad, 'saying how much she missed her dear boy'.[7]

Predicted at school to become a future prime minister, he had been Conservative MP for Stamford in Lincolnshire since 1890, his campaign supported by the Brownlows and other local grandees. Now he was also approaching the end of his first year as editor of a major evening newspaper, the *Pall Mall Gazette*, following the enthusiastic request of its owner, William Waldorf Astor. Being an MP was still an unpaid role and Harry was far from unusual in having another career.

Through his close family connection, Harry knew Ashridge even better than Nina, to whom he was distantly related. The first time he visited was just before his second birthday, when he was part of the lavish coming-of-age celebrations for the earl's elder brother, the second earl. When he died at just 25 from congenital tuberculosis, Adelbert became third and present earl.

Poor health had always plagued the Brownlow Custs, but it was a more recent death that had unexpectedly changed Harry's prospects. In the absence of children, Adelbert's heir was a first cousin – but he had suddenly died in May. Harry, next in line, became heir not to the earldom, which would die out with Adelbert, but to the barony and the estates that went with it. Given that the Brownlows' fortune was one of the biggest based on land in Britain, it was a seismic shift for Harry.

That August weekend, Harry may have looked with renewed interest at the armorial garden, where the Cust coat of arms was one of four planted in box and yew representing the families associated with Ashridge. He might have reflected on the fact that, after the earl's death, he would be the latest link in an unbroken male line of landowners since 1500. But he had more pressing matters on his mind, and his 'sunny disposition'[8] was unusually clouded.

As Balfour would afterwards tell his close friend, Lady Elcho, 'HC seemed to me rather to neglect his harem – those who were there – but was pleasant enough to the outside world.'[9] He used 'harem' without malice, for he liked Harry, as everyone seemed to. That he was 'consistently run after by women, and such was his temperament that they seldom had to run very far or very fast', mattered little, for Harry made people feel 'close to the springs of life'.[10]

For reasons appreciated by his peers, his era was often more generous to him than history has been, dismissing him lazily, even brutally, as a notorious lothario or a fornicating MP.

Two women who loved him would not have recognised such descriptions. In Harry, Nina found 'all life's stay', and she drew from him 'all life's light'.[11] The Brownlows often invited them both to Ashridge, where Nina would sit quietly with Harry's unmarried sister and watch him dazzle the wide circles the Brownlows entertained, from prime ministers and princes to playwrights.

During the last year, Nina and Harry had become closer ('And then white passion blazed in our glad eyes', she wrote in a poem),[12] although they had kept their sexual relationship from their friends. At the core of the (mostly married) Souls was the belief, originally espoused by Balfour, that platonic friendship between the sexes was possible, but often it did not remain as innocent as intended. Like other country houses the Souls frequented, Ashridge was more accustomed to concealing adulterous liaisons than embracing the passions of an unmarried couple.

Coming from an upper-class family, Nina knew that, as a single woman, sleeping with Harry could compromise her reputation, even among the unconventional Souls. But another woman had encouraged her to believe that a future with him was possible.

That woman was her friend and artistic mentor, Violet Manners, Marchioness of Granby, who attended the Ashridge party without her husband. The marquis may have been with one of his favoured actresses that weekend, but in any event, he did not share the Souls' love of intellectual pursuits, feeling more at home on the back of a horse. Violet had dutifully borne four children, including the necessary heir, although the fourth, Letty, was possibly the lovechild of Lord Rowton. Considered one of the most beautiful women of the age, the outgoing and uninhibited Violet 'floated around effectively in clinging garments', as Lady Paget observed.[13]

Violet was eleven years older than Nina and related to her through marriage: the marquis, son of the Duke of Rutland, was Nina's cousin. An acclaimed artist, Violet had drawn many of society's figures, including the Souls. Her portrait of Nina captures well the younger woman's delicate beauty: the elegant neck, the oval face with its solemn mouth and large, mournful eyes. But the hair has about it a wildness that goes beyond the decade's natural look to suggest a loss of control, and her expression is wistful. By contrast, in her self-portrait, Violet appears as the quintessential Pre-Raphaelite heroine, hair tumbling artistically, gaze direct, almost challenging, the hint of a smile around her lips.

While the difference in their demeanour may be due to their temperaments, it might also be found in a common cause. Not only did they share a love of art, but they also loved the same man. Nina had long adored Harry from afar but unbeknown to her, when Violet drew his portrait in 1892 – capturing his wide-eyed, even guileless gaze – they were lovers. More than that, she was carrying his child.

Nina had not questioned the coincidence of what Violet described as their 'chance meeting' in Venice in 1890, the year after their relationship began, telling Nina, untruthfully, that she had seen him for a 'very short time'.[14] If, when present at a social occasion with them, Nina intercepted a glance or heard them laugh at the other's wit, she could tell herself that Violet saw in Harry the same qualities she did.

When Violet gave birth to her fifth child, Diana, in August 1892, Nina assumed, as did much of society, that she was the marquis's. In an era when divorce was not a desirable option, the marquis agreed to raise Diana as his own, enabling her to retain the benefits of legitimacy.[15] But his magnanimity came with a price, for it made the continuation of Violet's affair with Harry too risky.

She thought she saw a way around it, though. If Harry married Nina, their affair could continue behind the cloak of respectability that marriage conferred.

If Nina suspected Violet of having feelings for Harry, she had nevertheless allowed herself to be persuaded that the time had come for him to settle down – with her. After all, they had much in common, sharing a deep intellect and literary appreciation; furthermore, their families were connected through blood and friendship. While his female admirers were legion, Nina believed that emotionally Harry was more than the sum of his liaisons; she felt she knew his very essence.

Like Balfour, Nina could not fail to notice Harry's distraction that afternoon. If she hoped it was consideration of their future that occupied him, she would be right, but not in the way she wished. After dinner there was 'general conversation' which, according to Balfour, was 'chiefly chaff between Matthews, HC and me',[16] and must have seemed excruciatingly long to Nina, impatient to have Harry to herself. But his intention that weekend was to break off their relationship. For probably the first time in his life, he had found a woman he really loved, and it was not Nina.

Harry's talents, like Nina's, included poetry. As well as some exquisite compositions, he was known also for his self-mocking verse. In 1892, he had written 'Marriage', which begins:

Cust, who at sundry times in manners many
Spake unto women – and is speaking still –
Eager to find if ever or any
One would obey and hearken to his will …

The poem ends:

Various vigorous virgins may have panted,
Willing widows wilted in the dust: –
To no female has the great God granted
Grace sufficient to be Mrs Cust.

That same year, Harry realised he had found her, but it was only in the last few months, since becoming Earl Brownlow's heir, that he had decided to take matters further.

Pamela Wyndham, aged 22, was the youngest sibling of two prominent Souls, Mary Elcho and politician George Wyndham. Beautiful, cultured, pleasure-seeking – 'My capacity for enjoyment is like elastic, only it has not the power of retraction – it simply gapes like the mouth of Hades'[17] – she was used to being the centre of attention. Now, as Nina and Violet each mused on the part they played in Harry's life, they could not know he was considering proposing to Pamela. By next morning, Nina realised their relationship was over.

On Monday morning, leaving the Brownlows to host a celebratory party for their tenants, their guests departed, Balfour for the House of Commons to continue the endless debating of the Home Rule Bill, Harry for his editor's desk in London to contemplate the week ahead and see what the post had brought: perhaps another emphatic letter from his acquaintance Oscar Wilde or a literary contribution from Alice Meynell or Rudyard Kipling.

For the purpose of his work, journalistic and political, he lived during the week at the Brownlows' elegant London house, 8 Carlton Terrace. He would be back at Ashridge in three weeks' time to give a party for three hundred of his *Pall Mall* staff and their families. Violet was to join the marquis and go to his father's hunting lodge in Sheffield, for the grouse shooting season had just begun.

Unless she had any social or artistic engagements in the London area, Nina would have returned to Denton Manor, her family home in Lincolnshire, in a heightened emotional state. Without a chaperone, she was considered to be in the care of the Brownlows so to sleep with Harry under their roof was an abuse not only of their hospitality but of their role, as well as a deception of them by him. Unmarried couples were, even if 'strongly incited', generally supposed to be 'restrained by virtue and the moral heinousness of yielding to desire'.[18] She knew, too, that there was a risk at a time when birth control was widely considered immoral, even for married women, and 'natural' methods were unreliable. While she fretted, Harry left London for a weekend at Clouds, the Wyndham family home in Wiltshire, to talk to Pamela of marriage.

Nina had inherited not only her mother's formidable intellect but also her fragile health. Her energy came in fits and starts, her pallor, while fashionable, indicating an underlying cause. Soon, Nina became unsettled, even frantic. Harry was not around.

Balfour had separately been to Clouds but, being less acquainted with Nina and innocent of their intimacy, he was unlikely to impart any news of significance. Presumably she had not experienced 'her monthly sickness',[19] for, at a time when no pregnancy test existed, a woman had only indications to go by. Whatever her reasons, it was surely desperation that made her contact Violet, who, alarmed on so many levels, referred her to a doctor.

Shortly afterwards, Balfour received a letter from Nina written at Denton Manor:

> I am coming to you for advice on a matter of life and death. I come to you because there is no other man in the world in whose honour & judgment I have so implicit a confidence – and because I also feel that if you did allow yourself to be biased in any direction, it would not be in my favour, who am but a recent acquaintance. I had intended to write to you fully & at length, but Violet is taking the matter out of my hands & will tell you all.[20]

The ensuing events would rock society and lead Nina and Harry to become objects of vilification and speculation. In many ways, they have been misrepresented, even misunderstood. It is fairer, perhaps, to look back at what formed them and ahead to what they became. As Oscar Wilde said, 'The truth is seldom pure and never simple.'[21]

All the Gifts

Harry Cust was surrounded by adoring women from birth. Five sisters lovingly greeted the fair-haired, blue-eyed child who arrived on 10 October 1861 as a bookend in a family with three young men at its top, the eldest of whom was already 20. Harry's father, Francis, was delighted too, for this was his first son. The other boys, along with the eldest girl, aged 10, were his stepchildren for whom he had assumed responsibility when he married the widowed Sara Jane Streatfeild in 1852. Harry was their fifth child and, at the age of 40, Sara Jane's tenth.[1]

Having a large family indicated not only fecundity but a compliance with Victorian expectations. However, according to her friend, the poet Elizabeth Barrett Browning, Harry's mother was far from conventional. The daughter of a wealthy glass and chemical manufacturer,[2] Sara Jane had met Elizabeth and her husband Robert in 1851 in Paris, where she had moved with her children after the death of her first husband. The poets were enjoying major success and, as Sara Jane knew Elizabeth's aunt, she asked to be introduced.

She immediately made a favourable impression. Elizabeth liked Sara Jane's 'face & manner' and three months later, referring to her as 'our friend', she praised her highly, 'a more graceful, winning creature, & fuller of intelligence, it would be hard to find … grace & high breeding are the great characteristics of face & person'.[3] Robert was also charmed by Sara Jane, and in those early days in Paris they both saw much of her.

The two women had much in common: they came from the north-east of England and each had endured painful emotional experiences.

As a true friend would do, Elizabeth pondered on the suitability of the man whom Sara Jane was considering taking as her second husband, Captain Henry Francis Cockayne Cust.

Francis and Sara Jane had met a decade earlier when she was in Spain with her husband, Sidney Streatfeild, already ailing. The recounting of their meeting surely appealed to Sara Jane's sense of the dramatic, a trait her son would share. Francis was a handsome young captain in the 8th Hussars, returning to England on leave from India, when he decided to break his journey. One evening by moonlight, he made his first visit to the Alhambra, and on entering a courtyard came across the Streatfeilds. The lady was tending her husband, and Francis quickly fell in love with this woman whom Elizabeth Barrett Browning found 'charming – even fascinating'.[4] From that moment, there could be no other wife for him.

Francis was from an old and wealthy landowning family of distinguished clergymen, lawyers and politicians, one of whom had risen as high as Speaker of the House of Commons. In the spring of 1852, a year after Sidney's death, Sara Jane agreed to marry Francis. Whether he would be too conventional for her was something Elizabeth pondered upon, for she had noted her friend's liberal politics and her independent nature: she 'is as wild as a bird, & won't sit upon everybody's finger'.[5] To Francis, Sara Jane's individuality was compelling; as a couple they shared 'irregular brilliance and kindliness'.[6]

Returning to England in June 1852 in preparation for the wedding, Sara Jane left her daughter, 2-year-old Barley,[7] in Paris with a close friend, and was so confident in her friendship with the Brownings that she asked them to visit the child and report on her welfare: Robert did the visiting, Elizabeth the reporting. Robert even tidied up a vexing financial matter on Sara Jane's behalf concerning a piano she had leased.

On 5 August, she and Francis were married in the church at Cockayne Hatley, the Bedfordshire estate owned by Francis's clergyman father,[8] which had been in the family since 1408. Sara Jane was 30, Francis two years older.

Just six days after the wedding, Elizabeth was concerned to receive a letter from her friend which suggested she was 'by no means in an ecstatical state'.[9] Sara Jane became inconsistent in her correspondence, with long silences that upset Elizabeth, eventually followed by warm letters that compensated for the time lapse, so that her friend forgave her.

The cause of Sara Jane's mood swings is unknown, although the timing suggests it may have been connected with her new life in Dublin, where Francis had been serving as aide-de-camp to the Lord Lieutenant of Ireland. Francis had just been promoted to private secretary and he and Sara Jane moved into Phoenix Park, the lord lieutenant's official residence.

Perhaps she was disappointed to find her husband's new role would often take him away from home, albeit often with royalty, but his appointment was short-lived. A new British Government saw a new lord lieutenant and Francis's career took a different direction.

By 1855, the Cust family, which now included Lucy, the first child of their marriage, were back in England, where Francis began a non-military role. He was to manage Ellesmere, a country estate in Shropshire, on behalf of his late cousin's son, who had not yet reached the age of majority.

At the age of 11, John William Spencer Egerton Cust had found himself with two titles, 2nd Earl and 3rd Baron Brownlow, inherited from his grandfather. After a legal battle, the young earl was allowed to succeed to his father's share of the vast estates of the Duke of Bridgewater, leading to Francis being appointed agent for Ellesmere. He and Sara Jane settled the family into Ellesmere House, a gracious fourteen-bedroom mansion.

Sara Jane 'added elements of life and music'[10] to the more serious Cust family and seemed to have everything: beauty, intelligence, charisma and, thanks mostly to her late father, wealth. But around 1860, the year she gave birth to another daughter, Annette, she also discovered she had heart problems. She began receiving specialist treatment in London, a city she was always happy to visit for its vibrancy, and her condition did not stop her falling pregnant with Harry in early 1861.

Around this time, she was saddened to learn that, after a lifetime of undiagnosed ailments, Elizabeth Barrett Browning had died. Robert replied to her condolences with a poignant letter, in which he shared with her the intimate details of his wife's last hours. 'She always loved you and never forgot you,' he told Sara Jane. Robert's relationship with the Custs would endure.

After Harry's birth in London in October, he was brought back to Ellesmere. His half-brothers missed his arrival. Sidney, by then 20, was in the Royal Navy; Herbert, 19, had joined the Bengal Army; and Ernest, 14, was away at school. But the girls were there to welcome him: Barley, aged 10; Lucy, 7; Marion, 6; Violet, 2; and Annette, 18 months. The Custs' staff was also mainly female, with a governess for the older girls and six servants; the only male presence was the footman.

Harry's christening, in December 1861, took place at Cockayne Hatley, which Francis had recently inherited. Francis was delighted, not only that he now had a son and heir to pass it to, but also that it was in a much better condition than the 'most lamentable state'[11] in which his father Henry had inherited it from his father, Sir Brownlow Cust. The baron had raised his family at Belton, his grander Lincolnshire estate,[12] and had spent little time at Cockayne Hatley.

Henry had carried out major building and restoration work, and now the christening guests could appreciate his legacy in the rich Flemish carvings he had installed in the church, illuminated by the light that streamed through the new stained-glass windows. As Harry was received at the font,[13] the sweet-faced angels in the beams above looked down on the child who was bestowed with such gifts that most children born in Victorian Britain could only dream of: aristocratic lineage, loving parents, intellect, good looks. Later that century, when those angels witnessed the baptism of Harry's illegitimate child, they may have wondered whether the gifts had been too bountiful.

The Cust household may have been predominantly female but society still celebrated men. So delighted were Ellesmere's tenants by the birth of Captain Cust's son and heir that they formed a committee (which naturally met in the local inn) to discuss what form their rejoicing should take. The birth was an opportunity to express their affection for Harry's parents and they decided that a congratulatory address would be presented to Francis, followed by a dinner at the Red Lion Hotel 'and a treat to the females, who, generally speaking, are much in the background on occasions of this description'.[14]

The premature death of Queen Victoria's husband and Prince Consort, Albert, delayed the celebrations until January 1862, but the enthusiasm was undimmed. The address paid tribute to the couple's kindness and thanked Francis warmly for everything he had done for the neighbourhood since he took up 'the difficult and important position' as Earl Brownlow's representative.

The tenants also expressed 'admiration for the acts of Christian charity that are exemplified in the daily life of Mrs Cust', whose health issues were known. At the dinner, the chairman spoke of his relief that mother and baby were doing well, for he knew Mrs Cust 'had been a little anxious about the state of her health, and when she is unwell there is nobody who knows her who is not sorry'.[15]

As for Harry, he surely had a promising start: 'May the good qualities of which he is the natural inheritor ever influence your son, and lead him onwards in the path which his parents have trod before him'.[16] Sara Jane's intellect and temperament, in all its light and shade, would manifest itself in Harry, while Francis was a model of constancy and public service.

As the subject of their celebrations approached his second birthday in 1863, Sara Jane anticipated a happy reunion with her son, Herbert, now a lieutenant, who was coming home on army leave from India. He never arrived. During the passage home, he died on board the *Simla* in the Red Sea, just before his 21st birthday.

Shortly afterwards, Earl Brownlow, Francis's young employer and cousin, reached the same milestone, although it had been a struggle. Since birth, the earl had suffered from a form of congenital tuberculosis, probably inherited from his father, and he had not been expected to reach maturity. At over 6ft tall, he had also inherited the Cust height, as Harry would.

After studying at Oxford, where he became good friends with the Prince of Wales,[17] the earl's coming of age was celebrated in great style at another of the estates to which he was now legally entitled, Ashridge in Hertfordshire. Tenants from all his estates joined the wider Cust family in celebrations that lasted for days, beginning with a grand dinner for seventy which Harry was allowed to attend. At nearly 2, he must have marvelled at the birthday cake, which was almost as tall as the earl himself and covered with frosted silver and coloured flags, while the buzz from the adults around him, drawn from the aristocracy, the arts and the highest echelons of public life, would one day be his lifeblood.

At Ellesmere, Francis and Sara Jane were known for their generosity, seldom refusing a request to allow the grounds to be used for local events. With their children, they were indulgent as far as pets and other youthful interests were concerned but firm on their education and the importance of considering others. The children saw Francis assuming wider public responsibilities, sitting as a justice of the peace in Shropshire and Bedfordshire.

Sara Jane's life, too, extended beyond the locality. Now back in England, Robert Browning accepted her invitation in 1865 to stay with her in

London. Presenting her with an inscribed copy of Elizabeth's *Last Poems*, he expressed regret that they could not meet more often. Perhaps she entertained him on the piano, a reminder of his help in Paris.

Sara Jane always enjoyed the chance to use her musical talents, sometimes joined by her daughter, Barley. During Christmas 1866, they took part in an ambitious concert in aid of a local hospital, which inspired music critics to compare it favourably with professional productions. Sara Jane, 'a full and rich soprano', sang duets with 16-year-old Barley and trios with male voices, and received several encores. 'Mrs Cust was really the guiding spirit of the orchestra, and with her carefully trained voice and good musical knowledge, kept her band of performers in excellent order.'[18] Francis was in the audience with his stepson Ernest, down from Oxford for the holidays; Harry, now aged 4, would be firmly in the charge of his sisters.

Perhaps relaxation after the hard work of the concert, together with the pleasure of Christmas, caught Sara Jane off guard because, at the age of 45, she fell pregnant for the eleventh time. Her due date was in September 1867.

That year was one of mixed emotions for the Custs. It began happily enough with the wedding of Sara Jane's eldest son, Sidney. Days later, however, the family had a shock when Earl Brownlow died in the South of France at the age of 25, having ruptured a blood vessel during a coughing fit. Dying unmarried and without heirs, his titles and estates passed to his only brother, Adelbert Wellington Brownlow Cust, an officer in the Grenadier Guards, who at 22 became 3rd Earl and 4th Baron Brownlow.

Francis continued as agent for his cousin, the new earl, and happier occasions followed in the spring. At six months pregnant, Sara Jane attended a grand London party with Barley, together with royalty, and at Ellesmere they hosted a lively celebration for the anniversary of the Ladies' Bowling Club.

As Sara Jane entered the last full month of her pregnancy, distressing news came from Allahabad of the death of Francis's sister-in-law, Emma, wife of his brother, Robert. It was the second time that Robert, until recently Home Secretary to the Government of India, had been widowed, each time losing his wife in childbirth. The Cust children, unaware of the fate of their aunt, eagerly anticipated the arrival of their new sibling, with Harry no doubt considering the pros and cons of no longer being the youngest.

On the morning of Saturday, 14 September, Sara Jane gave birth to a boy. The family rejoiced in the news of a safe delivery, and all seemed to be going well, until three o'clock that afternoon. Suddenly, Sara Jane exhibited alarming symptoms; four hours later, she was dead, the cause attributed to asphyxiation stemming from heart disease.

Six days afterwards, with the shops closed in tribute, Sara Jane's body was taken from Ellesmere House to begin its journey to Cockayne Hatley for the funeral. A procession of 200 followed the horse-drawn hearse to the station. Apart from the baby, all of Sara Jane's eight surviving children were present, from 26-year-old Sidney to Harry, aged 6 – he and Barley, walking with Francis behind the hearse, led the mourners. A special train carried the family and their household to London, from where they continued to Cockayne Hatley.

Robert Browning was in France when he learned of Sara Jane's death, 'which grieved me so much', he wrote to Francis. Browning understood his situation all too well. 'One cannot hope to be of the poorest service on such an occasion,' he said, 'but it seems natural to give some kind of witness to the existence of the feeling I have for the admirable and beloved friend that is lost, and for you who bear a blow to which mine is even light in comparison.' He felt he knew Francis well enough to say, 'Fortunately you are a brave energetic man, and will bear up, getting the good out of the consciousness of having deserved all those happy years.'[19]

The effect on Harry of the loss of his mother is incalculable. Had she lived, the course of his emotional life may well have run differently. Perhaps he derived some comfort from knowing how highly other people thought of her. Shropshire's newspapers paid warm tribute:

> Her loss will be most severely felt throughout the whole neighbourhood, where she was esteemed by persons from every rank in life. The poor will sorely miss her kindly and generous ministrations to their wants, and all who knew her will lament that one of the best of women has been taken away.[20]

On the bookshelves at Ellesmere House, her inscribed copies of the Brownings' poems not only became part of Harry's literary education but were a reminder of the affection the couple felt for her.[21]

At Ellesmere, two months after the death of Sara Jane, Harry's brother was baptised Adelbert Salusbury Cockayne Cust, his first name the same as Earl Brownlow's. Francis's immediate priority was his family. A nurse and a nursemaid were already in place for the baby and a German governess for the other children, from whom Harry quickly learned the language. He had no excuse not to, for linguistic ability ran in the family: his uncle Robert spoke eight European and eight Asian languages.[22]

Francis, meanwhile, understanding his brother's own grief and conscious of their respective children's needs, gave a temporary home to Robert's eldest child, Albinia, who had suffered the loss of both her mother and stepmother and had seen little of her father while he worked in India. Living in the Cust household with her cousins must have been cathartic. Sharing the grief of bereavement, the older girls could provide comfort to the younger children, while baby Adelbert, untroubled by the loss of the mother he had never known, provided a new focus for their love. The energy that was part of living in a large and lively family surely benefitted them all; in making his presence felt among the girls, especially with the competition of his new brother, Harry had excellent practise for the future.

Robert Cust remarried, but Francis never did. His focus remained the family, while he threw himself deeper into public life, exhibiting the energy that Browning had recognised. Determined to enter politics, a year after Sara Jane's death, Francis responded to an invitation to put himself forward as Conservative candidate for Grantham in Lincolnshire, where Belton House was situated, and which seat his family had represented many times. The opposition candidates were Liberals during a politically difficult time in Britain, in which the Conservatives opposed Gladstone's policy of Home Rule for Ireland. Francis also supported the new Reform Act, which enfranchised a wider group of men and made his particular passion, education, more important than ever. Eventually, in February 1874, Francis would be elected as one of Grantham's two MPs.

Meanwhile, with no wife to support him, he increasingly looked to the older girls to help him at home and in his social duties, particularly his stepdaughter Barley, who was 17 when Sara Jane died. It was inevitable that the younger children would look to her now, while Francis sought her company at social functions.

When Earl Brownlow invited him and other cousins to stay at Belton House in 1869 to help entertain the Bishop of Lincoln, Barley was invited too. The occasion marked the opening of Grantham church after a lengthy restoration, to which the Brownlow Custs had widely contributed as befitted their 260-year ownership of the Belton estate. The guests could also congratulate Francis on being appointed High Sheriff of Bedfordshire, and it was a good opportunity to get to know the Countess Brownlow, formerly Lady Adelaide Talbot, whom the earl had married the previous year.

As part of their marriage celebrations, the Earl and Countess Brownlow embarked upon a tour of their estates, visiting Ellesmere for the first time in November 1869 and causing immense excitement. For most people, it was the first time they had seen their new landlord, and he and his wife, both 25, tall and striking, did not disappoint. Young Harry could observe Lady Brownlow's dark beauty, a quality he would be delighted to discover later in her niece Theresa, the Marchioness of Londonderry.

Francis and the children were heavily involved in the organisation of tributes and events, including a tea party for hundreds of children from local schools and the workhouse. Barley, Lucy and Marion helped the ladies of the town to organise the young guests and assisted their father in escorting the Brownlows. At 8 years old, Harry, along with Annette, aged 9, and Violet, 10, would be expected to take their tea with the local children.

Soon Harry had to adjust to another change in his young life, for it was time for Barley to move on with hers. In February 1870, aged 19, she married Charles Donaldson Hudson, 30, a magistrate and landowner. The wedding at Ellesmere was a warm-hearted occasion, where the streets were decorated and the town had a day's holiday; Barley was held in high esteem for her charity work, as her mother had been. On an emotional day, Francis gave away his dear stepdaughter, and the children realised they would no longer have their sister in their daily lives. What Harry said to Barley as she left for the honeymoon, and what she promised her little brother can only be imagined, but they would remain close.

Now it was Lucy's turn to take charge. She was devoted to their father, and although she was said to be 'a born ruler', her task was not always easy. Francis 'for all his charm was an excitable man, with the habit of taking to his bed when unduly crossed by his family'.[23] He was upset when Lucy became engaged to a clergyman called John Storrs, despite the fact that Francis was himself the son of a clergyman. Francis relented when John was offered a living with good prospects, but the young man's experience of the Cust family was that it was 'large, abnormally united by allusion and shibboleth, and not particularly encouraging'.[24] The sharp Cust wit could be off-putting to outsiders, while the death of Sara Jane had bound them together ever more tightly.

Before Lucy's wedding, it was time for Harry himself to move on. By the time he reached the age of 10, he had begun at a preparatory school, comfortably equipped with all those gifts bestowed on him at birth but now diminished by the most valuable of them all: a mother's love.

Friends and Lovers

In 1874, aged 13, Harry burst upon Eton College, the renowned boarding school for the sons of monarchs and ministers, the influential and the wealthy. Founded for poor boys by Henry VI in 1440, the college, with its beautiful chapel, stands imposingly by the River Thames near Windsor, its pupils instantly recognisable by their distinctive uniform which has changed little over the centuries. Harry, tall and good-looking even in adolescence, would have worn it well: the black tailcoat and waistcoat, starched stiff collar, black pinstripe trousers and, as the final flourish, a top hat.

Like other non-scholarship boys whose fees were paid by their parents, Harry boarded in Eton town rather than in school and was known as an Oppidan. The boys were divided into houses, between which competitiveness in study and sport was actively encouraged, and each house was headed by a master. Harry's was Edward Compton Austen Leigh, who could boast an interesting literary connection: his great-aunt was the novelist Jane Austen.

Harry must have been a gift to teach, for not only did he exhibit literary and linguistic precociousness, but he was also a talented all-rounder. Among a coterie of adolescents destined for great things was M.R. James, later the acclaimed writer of ghost stories, who recognised his friend's qualities:

> For Harry Cust I think we did prophesy a brilliant future … An excellent Captain of the Oppidans, and of his House, a worker, the most shining of social successes, competent at games (what colours he had I

don't remember), good-looking, a most facile speaker, a delightful actor … He really was the expectancy and rose of the fair state. Any degree of intimacy with him at Eton was an honour and a delight.[1]

The games to which James referred were football and cricket but Harry also rowed, did long jump and won prizes for shooting and running. In 1880, he achieved the accolade of History Prizeman. He and his world looked perfect.

Yet, even at school, his life was marred by death. In 1879 he lost two friends. Richard Durant, 'my very greatest Eton friend whom I had worked and lived with for five years', died after a short illness, and two months later, Clarence Sinclair Collier drowned in the River Isis at Oxford. 'The loss of two real friends, almost at the same time, leaves a great blank in one's life and mind,' Harry told ex-Eton master Oscar Browning in an anguished letter.[2] He looked forward to talking about Collier at Cambridge, where Oscar Browning now taught – he had been dismissed from Eton in 1875 for his close friendship with Harry's friend, George Curzon, and now worked at King's College, where he already held a fellowship.

Meanwhile, in his last school year, Harry was entered for the prestigious Newcastle Select scholarship, Eton's highest prize. Although he confounded expectation by not winning, it put him in Eton's list of top boys, and he ended his school career effortlessly as editor of the *Eton Chronicle*. His friend A.C. Benson, later an academic and poet who knew Curzon and another future statesman, Lord Rosebery, predicted that out of the three, Harry was the most likely to become prime minister.

Harry was admitted to Trinity College Cambridge to study classics in June 1881, aged 19; without the Newcastle scholarship's prize money he had to pay his own fees, and with an active social life, he was always hard up. He met again with M.R. James, studying at King's, and together they appeared in a Greek play, *Ajax*, with Virginia Woolf's cousin, James Kenneth Stephen, in the title role.[3] Harry played Ajax's half-brother, Teucer, a great archer, and was only less memorable 'because Ajax is so dominant', said James.[4]

In 1883, he and Harry performed in the comedy *Birds* by Aristophanes, of which even the London newspapers carried reviews. M.R. James, playing the lead, observed a characteristic of Harry's which could be amusing or exasperating, depending on one's position. In addition to the delights of rehearsing and performing the play, said James:

> There were the anxieties which attended the appearances of Harry Cust (Prometheus) who had never committed any portion of his lines to memory, and had to get them from me as occasion offered, filling in the gaps with improvisation in an unknown tongue – and clad moreover in but one garment snatched up at the last moment.

Brilliance came with a price, and unpredictability could, in youth at least, be seen as endearing eccentricity. Harry's friend, Sir James Rennell Rodd, an ambassador and poet, later said, 'Impulsive, disinterested and affectionate, he could always claim indulgence and find forgiveness.'[5]

Harry needed the buzz of socialising, the thrust of witty repartee and the adrenaline of animated discussion. On Sunday evenings after a dull day of compulsory chapel and meals, he would 'summon all his wide acquaintance to what he called a Hell in his rooms at Trinity: the name indicates the miscellaneous nature of the company',[6] in which M.R. James was a willing participant. The pair were also members of the university's Pitt Club, founded in 1835 and named for the first Prime Minister of Great Britain and Ireland, William Pitt the Younger. Like most gentlemen's clubs, its purpose was to foster friendship and build contacts, assisted as desired by alcohol.

Oscar Browning, a corpulent, eccentric gay man, held noisy, cheerful music parties, also on Sunday evenings, which clashed with Harry's Hell nights, and he often had to decline Browning's other invitations, on one occasion because he was 'a devoted tho' reluctant oarsman, and have to appear at a wholly undesirable training before breakfast on Saturday'.[7] Oscar tended to make pets of those undergraduates who were handsome and attractive, but if Harry sensed he was favoured for that reason, it did not stop him keeping in touch with the Cambridge don after he graduated.[8]

Within Harry's circle was fellow Trinity student and Pitt Club member, HRH Prince Albert Victor Christian Edward, known as Eddy.[9] The son of the Prince of Wales (the future Edward VII), he had been tutored for his uncertain Cambridge admission by J.K. Stephen. Prince Eddy was two years younger than Harry and it seems unlikely they had much in common, not least because their intellects were far apart, but it would have been rude to ignore the longstanding Cust connection with the royal family. The Earl and Countess Brownlow were good friends of the Prince and Princess of Wales; another relation, Charles Cust, was a close friend of Prince Eddy's younger brother, George (later George V); and Harry's cousin, Lionel, a recent Trinity graduate, had become Eddy's confidante.[10] The elements of university life that Eddy and Harry shared meant that, in what would be the last years of the prince's unexpectedly short life, Harry would be a useful guest at family events to which His Royal Highness was invited.

One thing lacking in undergraduate life was women, for Cambridge University in the late nineteenth century was still a male stronghold. Only two women's colleges, Girton and Newnham, yet existed and strict rules regulated social contact between the sexes. Nevertheless, there were opportunities for meeting women, of which Harry would surely have availed himself. Even Prince Eddy, closely monitored as he was, attended the occasional university ball or dance at Trinity and was invited to parties by Richard and Cara Jebb at their Cambridge home.

Richard Jebb was a Fellow of Trinity, soon to be made Regius Professor of Greek, and his second wife, Cara,[11] enjoyed matchmaking and gave tennis parties for well-brought-up young men and women. Harry was likely to have been one of the Jebbs' guests, for not only was he excellent company, but he was also already known to the family. Richard knew him as a talented classicist and had enjoyed his comic performance as Prometheus, while his brother-in-law, Arthur Jebb, had given the speech that celebrated Harry's birth: he and his wife Eglantyne and their children were the Custs' neighbours in Ellesmere.[12]

In May 1883, Richard and Cara's niece, Maud,[13] arrived from her native America to stay with them. Tall and pretty, she was the same age as Harry, and before she began courting her future husband George Darwin, son of Charles, they may have shared delights of that Cambridge summer, which to her was a 'Utopia of tea parties, dinner parties, boat races, lawn tennis, antique shops, picnics, new bonnets, charming young men, delicious food'.[14]

The summer had begun with promise for Harry. Having excelled in the Classical Tripos in his first and second years, he was elected a Trinity Scholar. The bursary put him in funds and helped him repay a debt to his friend and fellow student, Henry Babington Smith, whom he had known at Eton. However, in mid-June, family circumstances curtailed the rest of his summer plans. His father, Francis, who had remained one of Grantham's MPs until a pair of Liberals triumphed in 1880, often stayed in his constituency at Belton, his cousin's estate. On a recent visit, he had fallen ill and was now worse. Harry cancelled his social calendar and settled in with him there.

Barely seven months earlier, in October 1882, Francis had proudly celebrated Harry's coming of age at Ellesmere, along with his siblings, Lord Brownlow and hundreds of local people, many of whom remembered his birth. In a series of addresses and presentations of generous gifts, they paid tribute to all the family and held a lavish banquet for Harry in the town hall, complete with choir. Whatever career he chose, they hoped it would be 'of usefulness to your fellow men [and] creditable to yourself and honourable to your family'.[15]

Harry's response was a moving tribute to the kindness the people had shown ever since he could remember. As he talked of their sympathy, 'when the first cloud of sorrow rested on our home', they knew he meant the death of his mother. But he looked to the future: 'I am told, though I hardly like to believe it, that the first chapter of my life is over. I do not know where the other chapters are to be opened.'[16]

Now, as Harry anxiously awaited his father's physician, his future seemed to be on hold. The present was 'not very exciting, nor many possibilities of work', he told Babington Smith, though 'both here & at another house 2 miles off' were 'very big, good libraries with many MSS & early printed books'.[17]

Belton may have been less thrilling than the more exotic places he had been invited to that summer, but there were worse places to spend the vacation. Often described as the perfect English country house estate, Belton had been in the Brownlow family since 1609. To Susan Grosvenor, who stayed with the Brownlows throughout her childhood, 'Belton was more compact and beautiful than Ashridge, and the house was full of lovely tapestries, pictures and fourposter beds hung with embroidered curtains'.[18]

Addy, as the 3rd Earl was known, and Adelaide were not at home, for they preferred to visit Belton in the spring and divide the rest of the year between their London house and Ashridge. As Addy was Lord Lieutenant of Lincolnshire, they used Belton for entertaining and were in the process of remodelling the house to reinstate features lost over the generations. If Harry found the refurbishment disruptive, he could find peace in the pleasure gardens, in the exquisite orangery or by the lake, while the Brownlows' magnificent collections of art and other treasures, as well as books, lifted his spirits.

But Francis deteriorated and Harry and his sisters soon found themselves in 'the saddest of positions, waiting and hoping only'.[19] Missing his friends, Harry asked Babington Smith in Cambridge if he might drive up to Belton for the day: he did not dare ask him to stay while his father was so ill, but he could talk to him about his unwise (in Harry's view) intention of giving up his subject, mathematics, in favour of classics, and he could show him Belton's glorious flowers, 'unbounded eucharis & orchids & huge flowering cactae'.[20]

Harry hoped Babington Smith would continue to write, for the situation was getting to them all: 'I am going thro' the greatest trouble of all my life here and my poor sisters are breaking up under the terrible strain'.[21] Work was a helpful distraction, and so he asked for some books to be sent, among them Plato and John Stuart Mill's *Dissertations and Discussions*.[22]

With his father's unchanging condition, there came an acceptance: 'Time is a very kind thing and facts and possibilities that once seemed monstrous and horrible now come quite gently and naturally.'[23] Released for a break in mid-August as his father seemed to be improving, Harry was invited to Sandringham, the Norfolk country home of the royal family. Life, he told Babington Smith, was 'quite enjoyable'.[24]

To the family's surprise, Francis was able to return to Ellesmere by September. Harry began the final part of his Tripos, studying law as one of his subjects, and went to Paris in preparation for being called to the French Bar, which he considered more fun than the English. He lodged in the elegant rue du Faubourg Saint-Honoré, not far from where his mother had lived thirty years earlier, telling Oscar Browning, 'I'm living in a garret … and growing thin and bearded.'[25]

But in April 1884, at the London house of Barley and her husband, Francis died. He was 'the dearest and best of fathers', Harry grieved to Babington Smith. 'I only wish you had known him to have loved him. He was our home all our lives.'[26] The day of his death coincided with the funeral of Prince Leopold, Queen Victoria's youngest son, and after the bells at Ellesmere had rung a solemn peal for royalty, they continued for Major Cust.

Dozens of family and Ellesmere friends attended his funeral at Cockayne Hatley. His coffin, carried by Lord Brownlow and other relations, bore words in Greek that Harry had selected, translating as 'the weary is at rest'. Behind it came the younger Custs, Harry walking with their brother, Adelbert, and as the coffin was lowered into the grave next to their mother's, Barley laid upon it a 4ft-long cross made of deep red roses and the other siblings laid four heart-shaped wreaths, each composed of a different flower.

The death of their father was terrible for them all, but especially for the younger ones, left parentless before they were married: Violet, aged 26; Annette, 24; Harry, 22; and Adelbert, 17. Their married sisters and brothers-in-law were of great support, but Harry, as the eldest son, felt the weight of duty upon him; although he now inherited Cockayne Hatley, Francis had appointed him guardian to Adelbert.

Death was present even as Harry returned to Cambridge for the Easter term, when his fellow Trinity student, Algernon Webb, shot himself through the head in his lodgings 'while in a state of temporary insanity', the inquest concluded. The previous term he had suffered a serious head injury when his horse threw him headfirst onto a kerb, and in the week before his death, he was stunned by a blow from a tent pole. During the summer vacation, Harry visited Webb's family at Newstead Abbey, Byron's former home, which they were restoring, and which Algernon would have inherited; his mother would remember Harry's kindness.

The death of his father and the end of his student life resulted in a roller coaster of a summer. Harry's behaviour would always be governed by his proclivity to emotional highs and lows, with a darkness that his affable persona usually concealed – travelling in northern Italy when he was 16, he had covered a self-portrait with figures of flying demons and skeletons leaning on hourglasses. During three weeks in London, 'social intercourse with a picked company [took] my moral, physical & social wellbeing to the bottom of theirs', he told Babington Smith. In a trip to Cambridge, 'the atmosphere – was it breaths from heaven or blasts from hell, I know not – made me realise I'd better go away'.[27]

He found solitude at Tresco in the Scilly Isles, owned by relations. He arrived, he told Babington Smith sardonically, 'with how light a heart & buoyant a demeanour I need not tell to one who knows my joyous nature so well'.[28] But cheered by the island's beauty and soothed by fishing and sailing, which he loved, he wandered 'lonely & half naked on the shore spouting Mat[thew] Arnold[29] & prawn catching'. He was thrilled to see *Wanderer*, one of the largest private steam yachts in existence, coming in 'fresh from a 2 year cruise around the world, the biggest afloat'. It made him yearn for a voyage but 'I ought to begin to work soon, I think'.

In those early months after Francis's death, Babington Smith's friendship was particularly important, for which Harry expressed his gratitude. Nevertheless, the disruption took its toll: instead of a first-class degree as expected, Harry took a second. In preparation for some travelling, and to augment his wardrobe now he was better off, he kitted himself out with accessories from the distinguished gentlemen's outfitters, Beal & Inman of New Bond Street, favoured by the Prince of Wales. His distinctive style of dressing would become both envied and admired. Gloves – that essential part of Victorian fashion – Harry bought by the score: stylish but hardwearing capeskin leather gloves lined with silk; alpaca gloves for warmth; white kid gloves as soft as butter, with handsome buttons, for evenings. He ordered black silk scarves and cashmere socks, and the best-quality collars and cuffs for his linen shirts, whose softness made them conducive to caresses by elegant fingers – for, after enjoying popularity in the male-dominated worlds of Eton and Cambridge, Harry was discovering that women liked him too.

With no parents left to guide him, there was little to hold him back. This dazzlingly good-looking young man, with wonderful conversation and sparkling wit, was a magnet for women, especially older, often married ones who, bored by or disenchanted with the husbands they had often been persuaded to marry for social or economic reasons, found Harry irresistible.

During that summer of 1884, even Mary Gladstone, spinsterish daughter of Britain's Liberal prime minister, and fourteen years his senior, enjoyed a 'protracted and ardent flirtation with Harry Cust, a nice boy in the cynical stage'.[30] At a time when her father's support of Home Rule for Ireland was increasingly divisive, the differing politics did not matter, for Harry was becoming part of a circle where difference in political views was no bar to friendship.

Mary Gladstone had a cousin, Alfred Lyttelton, also a Liberal, whom Harry knew from Eton and Trinity. A superb sportsman and budding barrister from a large and clever family, Alfred was courting Laura Tennant, who, with her sister Margot, would be instrumental in the formation of the Souls.

Laura and Margot were the youngest two of the six daughters (from eleven children) of Sir Charles Clow Tennant, a Glasgow chemical manufacturer and Liberal MP. The Tennants' money emanated from trade rather than from generations of inherited wealth, which differentiated them from the aristocracy but also liberated them from its hidebound customs and expectations. Although (unlike their brothers) Sir Charles's daughters received a limited education through governesses, their natural curiosity and intellectual gifts, expanded through his fine library and endless discussions among themselves, saw them develop their many talents. They formed their own ideas, while their behaviour was free of many of the restrictions of upper-class etiquette whose rules emanated from the royal court.

A list of twenty-seven 'rules of etiquette' of varying lengths printed in a schoolboy's diary of 1880 demonstrated the intricacies and pitfalls of social intercourse. 'A gentleman should be introduced to the lady, not the lady to the gentleman', instructed one. However, 'If the sexes are the same, always present the inferior in social rank to the superior.'

The Tennant sisters led the way in disregarding the rule that said, 'In conversation avoid political, commercial or religious subjects. If gifted with wit, do not make a display of it. Avoid topics you are well versed with.' The last part of the rule was 'Scandal is inexcusable'; while they did not agree with the general view of what constituted such conduct, the sisters did try to take note of it, for in scandal lay social ruin. However, not all of their friends would succeed.

After they were presented at court and officially 'came out' into society in the early 1880s, Laura and Margot's highly individual style saw them take London by storm, and on their own terms. Well-read, witty and vital, their refreshing company made them sought-after guests at leading country houses. Laura, 'an enchanting little flame-like creature', said their friend, Frances Horner,[31] 'revived half forgotten standards of conversation by treating light and banal subjects with originality and serious matters with a thistledown touch'.[32] Mary Gladstone noted admiringly that

Laura, who bewitched everyone, was incapable of being bored and could 'make the heaviest natures shine and sparkle'.[33]

The 1880s, with their mix of rigid conventions and new thinking about society, influenced by science, politics and the arts, were ripe for a group of clever, high-born friends to be brought together in 'a kind of protest against the Prince of Wales's set and the racing set of the Duchess of Manchester', said Wilfrid Scawen Blunt, poet, political radical and fringe member of 'the Gang', as they called themselves before outsiders renamed them.

The socially ambitious, German-born duchess was a hardened gambler like her close friend, the Prince of Wales, and was also part of his 'fast' set at Marlborough House, who took a relaxed view of extramarital affairs while rigorously adhering to formal etiquette. The strict rules on what topics could be discussed, the division of the sexes in leisure pursuits, the obsession with racing and gambling, together with a lack of interest in the arts demonstrated by these sets was anathema to the Gang, who would shake up the philistine complacency of their class.

Margot Tennant's directness had started young. 'Well, Johnnie, have you no conversation?' she demanded of a quiet cousin when she was seven.[34] Not everyone approved. Although captivated by the Tennant sisters generally, Mary Gladstone thought Margot 'rather pert and forward … and somewhat lacking in good manners'.[35] The girls eschewed chaperoning at a time when it was considered proper for unmarried women to have one and talked freely to men even in their bedrooms. 'We hardly knew the meaning of the word "fast",' said Margot,[36] after Laura was upset by hearing that some people said they were just that.

Unwanted male attention was dealt with briskly. Sir Charles Dilke, the Liberal politician, visited Sir Charles Tennant at the family home, the Glen estate in Peeblesshire. Bowled over by Laura, he waylaid her in a corridor and said that, if she kissed him, he would give her a signed photograph of himself. 'It's awfully good of you, Sir Charles,' replied Laura, 'but I would rather not, for what on earth should I do with the photograph?'[37]

Glen, a baronial-style mansion set amid the beautiful moors and rivers of the Borders, hosted lively parties for all political persuasions and became a symbol of liberation for the young. There, the friendships began from which the Gang evolved, and which had an unlikely source. In 1881, Margot, aged 17, had met Arthur Balfour, 33.

On the face of it, their difference in age and background gave them little in common. Balfour was a Conservative politician who had entered the House of Commons in 1874 as MP for Hertford and belonged to one of Britain's most powerful aristocratic families, the Cecils. Since the Conservatives' defeat by the Liberals in 1880, Balfour's uncle Robert, the Marquess of Salisbury, had been Conservative Leader of the House of Lords. By contrast, Margot was a Liberal and the daughter of a businessman, her confidence coming not from inherited privilege but from the knowledge that the Tennants' commercial success opened doors into the worlds of politics and culture. Margot and Laura had 'no code of behaviour, except their own good hearts', said Lady Frances Balfour, Arthur's sister-in-law.

Margot and Balfour were both sociable and popular. She was noted for her originality and directness, he for his erudition and intellect, and they found each other interesting. A philosopher as well as a politician, for whom science and religion were compatible, Balfour was charming, urbane and good-looking, at ease in female company and caring little for the conventional pastimes of his aristocratic male contemporaries. He had already suffered great personal loss: the death of his father when he was 7; in 1875, that of his sweetheart May Lyttelton, the sister of his great friend, Alfred; and more recently, the death of two brothers. Balfour's sensitivity lent him an air of aloofness that was attractive to those who knew him, although it could be intimidating to those who did not. In the opinion of 17-year-old Lady Emily Lytton, 'He is certainly very pleasant and not at all alarming in himself, except that he never tries to talk to people who do not talk to him. I am shy of him chiefly because I know I am expected to be.'[38]

Balfour was one of many politicians the Tennants invited to Glen – his own family home, Whittingehame, was also in Scotland – and he was delighted when Alfred began courting Laura. She combined 'the gaiety of a child with the tact and aplomb of a grown woman', said Adolphus 'Doll' Liddell, one of the many men who loved her,[39] but it was Alfred – brilliant, handsome, noble in demeanour and thought – whom she loved.

The Tennant sisters drew Harry into the fold, along with budding politicians, both Conservative and Liberal; the Gang 'refused to sacrifice private friendship to public politics'.[40] Among the Conservatives were George Wyndham and George Curzon, Harry's friend from Eton.

The ambitious Curzon had a curvature of the spine which gave him constant nagging pain but he found an outlet in hard work, pushing himself beyond all limits. He considered Arthur Balfour to be 'one of the most attractive men in society, and society just at the moment is passing through the phase of worshipping intellect'[41] which, together with his enjoyment of the Tennant sisters' company, saw him happily become part of the group.

The smoulderingly handsome George Wyndham was the eldest son of aristocratic yet bohemian parents. The Wyndham family home was Clouds in Wiltshire, designed by the Arts and Crafts architect Philip Webb, and would be one of the country houses to host the Gang and the writers and artists they embraced. As long as someone was interesting and good company they were welcomed by the Gang, who delighted in wit and repartee and talked morals, philosophy, literature and flirting with equal facility and enjoyment.

A common factor (although not a determining one) was money, and ideally lots of it: if not yet their own, then an expectation of it, for most of the Gang came from some of the wealthiest families in the country. Nevertheless, they shunned ostentation, considering it vulgar, and preferred reserve and refinement above exuberance and display. Their houses were more likely to be decorated either with old, good-quality pieces or in the mode of the new Arts and Crafts movement, which saw interiors shed Victorian fussiness and become simpler. Even in clothing, the naturalness of the Pre-Raphaelite paintings and emphasis on soft, flowing fabrics made visits to the couturier unnecessary for the women, at least for everyday wear. The women in the Gang were often beautiful, always striking, but most valued for their intelligence and spirit. What mattered above all was friendship, laughter and making each other think.

During that summer of 1884, Alfred Lyttelton and Laura Tennant's love developed, but not everyone in the Gang was ready to settle down. Harry embarked on an affair that would launch his reputation as a womaniser, partly because of the prominent profile of the woman concerned. Theresa Londonderry, tall, imperious, beautiful, had recently become marchioness upon her husband succeeding as 6th Marquess.

One of the era's major political hostesses, she was not part of the Gang, but Harry may have met her through the Brownlows, for she was the countess's niece. Sharing a sense of the dramatic and a love of sailing, she and Harry enjoyed a passionate liaison, although he was not her first lover since her marriage in 1875. Rumours at the time said her second son, born in 1879, was fathered by her brother-in-law, Lord Helmsley, which the family later acknowledged.[42]

At 28, Lady Londonderry was five years older than Harry and 'vibrant with vitality, living on a plane of high-pitched sensation'. Nothing pleased her more than being the centre of attention, as A.C. Benson's brother, the novelist E.F. Benson noted:

> She frankly and unmitigatedly enjoyed standing at the head of her stairs when some big party was in progress, with the 'family fender', as she called that nice diamond crown gleaming on her most comely head, and hugging the fact that this was her house, and that she was a marchioness from top to toe.[43]

Clever and influential, her favourite saying was, 'I am a Pirate. All is fair in Love and War', and she was ferocious if crossed. However, she could also be thoughtful, allocating the bedrooms at her house parties to her female friends and their lovers.

Although she possessed many desirable qualities, it seems Theresa Londonderry was not enough (or perhaps she was too much) for Harry, who also engaged in a romance with the widowed Gladys, Lady Lonsdale, two years his senior. Gladys's brother, George Herbert, the Earl of Pembroke, was a friend of Harry's.[44]

Gladys was a dark-haired, swan-necked beauty, who was 6ft tall and to whom Oscar Wilde would dedicate his play, *A Woman of No Importance*. She had been widowed in 1882, after just three years of marriage during which she had a daughter. Her husband, the Earl of Lonsdale, an alcoholic adulterer, allegedly died in the company of a mistress. In May 1885 she would marry the Earl de Grey, a Liberal politician and the best shot in England. Before then, while the press played with other names she was linked to, she occupied herself with Harry.

Margot Tennant, who knew both Gladys and Theresa Londonderry, considered Gladys to be the more intellectual but not as strong-willed.

She also thought 'there was something unsound in [Gladys's] nature … her sense of proportion was so entirely lacking that she would … throw herself into a state of mind only excusable if she had received the news of some great public disaster'.[45]

When Gladys began to suspect she was not alone in Harry's affections, her behaviour was certainly extreme. Allegedly letting herself into Harry's rooms, Gladys rifled through his belongings and found letters Theresa had sent him. Some were said to be derogatory of her husband, the Marquess of Londonderry, and Gladys took great delight in having them delivered to him. But her act of vengeance led to her being known in society as 'the letter thief', while another unhappy consequence was said to be the marquess's refusal ever to speak to his wife again in private, although in reality, he eventually forgave her, which drew them closely together.[46]

Harry's attention was diverted from his love life in September 1884 while he supported his sister Barley, whose husband was very ill with a head injury sustained while riding. Afterwards, he visited Ellesmere, which was 'lovely & refreshing, tho' rather sad from old and very dear associations',[47] and then left for Germany for several months while he considered his future. Although he had planned to travel, now was a good time to leave, allowing the dust kicked up by his love life to settle. As he turned 23, an intoxicating world of possibilities lay ahead.

From the elegance of Dresden in December 1884, Harry told Babington Smith, 'The undiscernable river of my life pursues a tolerably equal flow', adding cryptically, 'tho' I've had a number of passages of more than passing interest'. He read a lot, in German and English, and he and a fellow lodger, an American, amused themselves in the dark, snowy evenings by 'taking a sledge after the theatre and driving to any pothouse within 6 or 8 miles', where they would drink beer with the locals and 'sing and babble bad German, sometimes till 4 in the morning'.[48]

George Leveson Gower, Gladstone's private secretary, for whom Harry was the 'most brilliant and best beloved of mortals', bumped into him in Dresden and 'had a rollicking time' for several days.[49] On he went to Leipzig and Berlin, remaining in Germany until early 1885.

Returning to England briefly, he set off on a world voyage in May, which coincided with the curious wedding of his lover, Gladys, and Earl de Grey. To the surprise of the press, the union of two such well-known figures was a private and very modest affair. After the announcement of their engagement in April, the church ceremony a month later was a brief one, conducted by special licence which avoided having to call the banns. Only their closest relations attended, including the groom's father, the Marquis of Ripon, and the Earl of Pembroke, who gave his sister away. There were no bridesmaids or music, and the bride wore a brown travelling suit as though ready for a quick departure, even though the wedding breakfast took place nearby and the honeymoon was in Hertfordshire.

Earl de Grey's wealth and prospects made him a more attractive proposition than Harry at that time, even if he lacked the younger man's physical advantages and was a good head shorter than his wife. Perhaps the suddenness and secrecy were because Gladys's brother was concerned about her reputation: one newspaper described Earl de Grey as the 'latest object of Lady Lonsdale's affection',[50] while her conduct with the Londonderry letters had exposed her affair with Harry, at least within polite society. Gladys was also in the news as a witness in the sad and complex nullity suit of the Earl of Durham, whose wife had exhibited signs of insanity soon after marriage, but he was not permitted by law to divorce on that ground. Gladys gave evidence to support him, but it was whispered that Lord Durham had only brought the case because he loved her instead.

Leaving intrigue behind, Harry's voyage would start in Australia and take him away for over a year. Before he left, he was honoured and humbled to find he had been elected an Apostle, a member of the Cambridge Conversazione Society, a discreet and elite society of intellectuals which met to discuss and debate such topics as truth, God and ethics. The Apostles were drawn mostly from three university colleges, St John's, Trinity and King's, and its members included some of the most influential men in British public life. Election had to be unanimous, and a candidate did not know he was proposed until he had been accepted.[51] Harry shared his pleasure with Babington Smith, a fellow Apostle, telling him he thought the connection would be of mutual advantage.

Meanwhile, Harry grew restless waiting for his ship, which had been delayed until 20 May. He hoped to get to Cambridge before then but, as he told his friend, 'I've been rather bad again physically and drop from my perch most days'.[52] It was Harry's misfortune that all his life he would suffer from syncope syndrome, a condition often associated with heart problems, perhaps inherited from his mother. Symptoms included fainting fits which were inconvenient and embarrassing for any active young man. Harry was said to live life 'at concert pitch', and his condition might partly explain why he threw himself at each day as though it were his last.

Before leaving, Harry visited Laura Tennant, who made him a 'health sachet', as Margot called it, for his voyage. He just missed her wedding to Alfred Lyttelton on 21 May, at which the guests included Arthur Balfour and the groom's uncle, Prime Minister William Gladstone, whose toast to the couple hoped that 'their future should be a fulfilment of the bright promise of their past and their present'.

Harry's ship eventually arrived and in August 1885 docked at Victoria, New South Wales. With the curiosity of a traveller and the soul of a poet, he absorbed everything and delighted in much. After leaving Australia in early 1886, he went to Tasmania, then New Zealand, which he found 'a most beautiful country & mixes up England, Switzerland and the Tropics'.[53] In March he left for Fiji with the intention of going on to China and Japan, then America, aiming to be in San Francisco by June.

His travels were an early foray into the world in which he would always have an insatiable interest and a desire to be involved in Britain's role on the global stage.

Coming Together

On returning to England later in 1886, Harry was shocked to discover that in April, less than a year after marrying Alfred Lyttelton, Laura had died, six days after giving birth to a son. She was 23. Her sisters, Margot, Lucy Graham Smith and Charty Ribblesdale, were there at the end. Charty and her husband Thomas, Lord Ribblesdale, moved in with Alfred to look after him in the first few months of grief and to help with the baby.[1]

Laura's death devastated the wide circle of people who knew her. 'If life is measured by intensity, hers was a very long life', Gladstone wrote to his nephew Alfred, praising her 'purity and singleness of heart'.[2] Harry's experience of losing those close to him – especially his mother, also after childbirth – made him particularly empathetic. Collective grief drew the Gang closer, and at a time when a period of mourning had to be observed, curtailing their socialising, they found pleasure in each other's company.

Margot, like Laura, was one of the few among their friends who still observed the Christian practices that had been followed by their parents, at a time when Darwinism was exerting its influence. Even Harry had been 'extra religious' and used to teach in Sunday schools until an overzealous friend who had lost faith persuaded him otherwise.[3] Sunday schools had achieved their century in 1880, an occasion celebrated nationally. At Belton, the Brownlows had hosted a children's festival at which the helpers included Nina Welby-Gregory, then aged 13.

Nina and Harry were not only distantly related: their families were landowners and near neighbours. The Welbys and the Brownlow Custs had known each other for generations, sharing the Christian faith and a sense of public duty. Nina's mother, Lady Victoria Welby, worked with Lady Brownlow in charitable organisations, especially those for disadvantaged women. Lady Welby was also the founder of the School of Art Needlework (now the Royal School of Needlework), which provided employment for women who would otherwise face destitution, working closely with Lord Brownlow's mother, Lady Marian Alford. Shortly before Harry's return to England, Lady Brownlow acted as sponsor to his sister, Violet Cust, when she was presented at court.

Given their families' connections, it is inevitable that Nina and Harry met during their childhoods. Nina was considered 'a girl of great beauty and mystical charm. Her gift of silence and her green, unfathomable eyes set her apart in any society.'[4] She was 19 when Harry, now 25, returned to England.

His amorous adventures had already earned him a place in literature, or at least, romantic fiction, thanks to Rhoda Broughton, a friend of his sister, Barley. One of the Custs' friends who knew Broughton thought she had 'a quick wit and a sharp tongue and was excellent company'. She lived with her widowed sister, their tea parties 'pervaded by three turbulent pugs, named Cupid, Psyche and Sluttikins'.[5]

In 1886 Broughton's book *Doctor Cupid* was published, by which time the Welsh author was an established novelist whose work was considered 'racy'. She tended to satirise people she knew or had heard of, and she considered Harry perfect fodder, reflected in her character Freddy Ducane. Apart from 'his charming complexion, laughing eyes and his beautifully fitting clothes', it was not a flattering depiction:

> Freddy Ducane is in his glory – something fair and female on either hand. On his right Lady Betty, who, being a duke's daughter, takes precedence of the other smart woman, who was only a miss before she blossomed into a viscountess; on his left, to ensure himself against the least risk of having any dull or vacuous moments during his dinner, he has arranged Prue Lambton – 'his little friend Prue'.

A reviewer described the character of Freddy as 'a flirt, prig and egotist at once', although (fortunately for Harry) the affair with Prue was dismissed as having 'very little interest or reality'. Broughton's main gift was said to be 'a power of vulgarity which is very genial, very piquant and often extremely funny'.[6]

Harry was unlikely to be offended for, unlike Broughton's character, he seldom took himself seriously. When his hostess Lady Augusta Fane told him that a gentleman wanted to meet him, Harry said proudly, 'No doubt he has heard of my writings and speeches', only to be told it was because he was 'the only man he had ever seen who kissed a lady not once but twenty times, on the top of the Punch Bowl'. Harry was 'very angry for a few minutes but his sense of humour came to the rescue'. Years later, he reminded Lady Augusta of the episode and they 'had a good laugh over it'.[7]

Barley, on the other hand, was becoming less amused with Broughton, for she was increasingly putting her family into her books, including her husband Charles, whose head injury would cause increasing deterioration until his premature death in 1893.

For Nina, nothing about Harry could have altered her view of him. After being presented at court by her mother in 1885, she had been invited on her own account to events the Brownlows hosted. However, she increasingly found that if Harry was invited, his new friends from the Gang were there too.

With a few other exceptions, such as Arthur Balfour, Margot Tennant and George Curzon, the Gang were mostly married couples who held parties known as 'Saturday to Mondays' in their country houses. During the Season, they socialised in London, where most of them also had a residence. The single ones relied on their parents' generosity in using the family home and staff to entertain.

As Harry had no parents, it was the Brownlows who often invited the Gang to Ashridge or Belton, for although he now owned the 1,600-acre Cockayne Hatley estate, it was not particularly conducive to entertaining. Although the manor house had ten bedrooms, his father's work had required the family to live elsewhere, so it had only been used as an occasional home and needed attention. Besides, the considerable cost of hosting a Saturday to Monday was not yet within the means of the young man.

Having been drawn together during the period of mourning following Laura's death, the Gang found they enjoyed each other's company above that of many outsiders. Conversation was their lifeblood. Encouraged by

Margot and her disdain for the dull talk of much of upper-class society, they revelled in diversity of subject and depth of analysis and debated everything, 'blood sports, votes for women, monogamy, vivisection ... we questioned whether the Man made the Century or the Century made the Man, whether suicide was justifiable, Free Love to be advocated'. They discussed character and feelings:

> [and] tried to define the distinction between Genius and Talent, Happiness and Pleasure ... we asked where good manners left off and insincerity began ... And of course, over and over again, we tried to decide which six friends, six books and six pictures we would take to a desert island.[8]

Little wonder they would soon be dubbed 'the Souls', although even the origins of the term were themselves a matter of debate.

To the friends, play was as important as work, and at a time when organised sport was championed in public schools for its moral as well as its physical value, they considered play in some ways more important. Ettie Grenfell, whose acquaintance with Balfour saw her drawn into the Gang after her marriage in 1887, noted that play 'does not mingle with struggle and competition, and needs a holiday spirit of detachment and defiant idleness before it will even peep out'.[9] It was 'an escape to the great white fields, to serenity and ecstasy'.[10]

A willingness to be both silly and cerebral was vital and many games they enjoyed originated within the Tennant family. One was called Styles, where the players had to write parodies of well-known authors in prose or verse, another was Epigrams, which involved inventing new ones, and Clumps was a development of Twenty Questions but with more abstract subjects, such as 'the last straw' or 'the eleventh hour'.

Some games were not for the faint-hearted. More than one future eminent person from outside the group was reduced to a quivering wreck when faced with Character Sketches, which Margot said was 'the most dangerous of all'.[11] Someone present was described in terms of another, perhaps an animal or an inanimate object, even a colour. Everyone sat in silence as they wrote and when it was decided that time was up, their manuscripts were given to the designated umpire, who read them out loud. Voting took place as to their authorship and led to discussion about books and writing. However, as it was 'a game calculated to add to your enemies', as one reluctant player observed, some may have sat silently nursing a grievance.[12] Among the 'interesting umpires' Margot recorded were Harry, Balfour and Curzon, 'all good writers themselves'. Witty verse was also composed, at which Harry excelled.

To guests, such games could seem pretentious or too inclusive, relying on personal intimacy with others in the Gang and on a robustness in giving and taking what might be seen as offence. Many games relied on literary knowledge, and all required quickness of wit. Margot said they were 'good for our tempers and a fine training; any loose vanity, jealousy or over-competitiveness were certain to be shown up'.[13] Dressing up was always popular too, both at parties where they could throw themselves into other personas and clothe themselves in a manner more outré than was usually acceptable, and for their own, more complex version of charades, which often involved what the more conventional might see as undignified horseplay.

While the friends always protested that they were not a clique – Margot said she saw more exclusivity in the racing world – their games were designed for themselves, their nicknames remained incomprehensible to others and the language they developed set themselves apart. 'Spangle', for example, meant a romantic crush; 'relevage' was a gossipy conversation; 'spike' was an insult; a 'floater' was a gaffe; 'sitting tight' is still used; and 'Heygate' meant dull and conventional, a term which the group would certainly regard as a 'spike'. The Gang may not have considered themselves cliquey, but they could give the impression that they thought themselves rather special.

Nina had the chance to mingle with some of the Gang in December 1886, when she and Harry attended the Brownlows' magnificent ball at Ashridge. It was a celebratory occasion. The General Election in July had seen the Conservatives defeat the Liberals and Robert Cecil, Marquess of Salisbury, become prime minister for a second term. He had entered into a pact with the new Liberal Unionists who, contrary to the main Liberal Party, opposed Gladstone's First Home Rule Bill for Ireland. Earl Brownlow had previously served under Salisbury and was to be made Paymaster General;

Balfour was now Secretary for Scotland in the newly formed Scotland Office and would soon be appointed to his uncle's Cabinet.

The ball was the culmination of a week during which Lord and Lady Salisbury were the Brownlows' house guests and was said to be the grandest in the area for years. Royalty were the principal guests, in the form of Princess Mary Adelaide, Duchess of Teck, and the Duke of Teck, with their daughter, Princess Victoria May (the future Queen Mary). As 400 guests arrived for a 10 p.m. start, galvanising the police cordon and leaving the grooms with 200 horses to be stabled, they were greeted by the novel and magical sight of the mansion's façade illuminated by electric lamps, for which a London electrician had been specially employed.

Inside, the lighting enhanced the beauty of the newly refurbished drawing room, while the conservatory was garlanded with the beautiful floral arrangements for which Lady Brownlow's gardener was known. Royalty waltzed with local gentry, and elderly relations chatted and tried to eavesdrop as politicians gossiped. Lady Churchill, mother of Winston, was there alone, for her husband Lord Randolph, Chancellor of the Exchequer and Leader of the House of Commons, was embroiled in a power struggle with Salisbury and days away from resigning.

Among the Gang present that evening was George Wyndham, who had served with the Coldstream Guards on active service in Egypt. Aged 23, he was on the verge of beginning both his political career and wedded life, for he was engaged to be married in two months' time to Lady Sibell Grosvenor. Eight years older than Wyndham, she was the widow of the epileptic Earl of Grosvenor, heir to the 1st Duke of Westminster.

George Curzon was bitterly disappointed, as were many other men who had pursued her, for he loved the rich and lovely Sibell, but the poetic, exuberant Wyndham beat him to it. The liaison was possibly helped by the fact that the Duke of Westminster, whose three grandchildren Sibell had borne, was an old friend of Wyndham's mother.

Nina was chaperoned at the Brownlows' ball by her older brother, Charles, and unless Harry invited her to dance, contact with him would have been limited: so many people with whom he would socialise as he always did, laughing, talking, flirting and generally shining. By contrast, Nina was 'a presence in a room which made few demands on anyone', noted Susan Grosvenor, yet she had no reason to feel inferior.

Nina came from a line of talented women with royal connections. Her late grandmother, Lady Emmeline Stuart-Wortley, was a daughter of the 5th Duke of Rutland and a close friend of Queen Victoria's mother, the Duchess of Kent. Widowed young, Lady Emmeline became a fearless explorer and respected writer and poet. She died suddenly in the Syrian desert in 1855 aged 49, while her 18-year-old daughter and travelling companion, Victoria, had to be rescued. She was taken under her grandfather's wing at Belvoir Castle and, after his death in 1857, went to live with the elderly Duchess of Kent at Frogmore, becoming part of her court. When the duchess died in 1861, Victoria was appointed a maid of honour to her godmother, Queen Victoria, remaining in her service until her marriage to Sir William Welby, two years later.[14]

Nina, the younger of the Welbys' two surviving children, was born in 1867. Her reserved nature was perhaps shaped by the death of her 11-year-old brother when she was 8, and by familial expectations. Her academic and linguistic ability made her a fine intellectual assistant to her brilliant mother, who, since leaving the royal court, was developing the theory of significs, which looked at the psychology and philosophy of meaning. Lady Welby relied on Nina to translate correspondence she received from German academics.

Nina possessed the talents of her mother and grandmother but, instead of their lavish communicativeness, 'her gift was silence. She was the scholar, the editor, the translator.'[15] In her art, she was the quiet observer such work demanded, and she had long observed Harry. She knew 'the fire of his mind', and, compared to him, she considered herself 'less than nought'.[16]

But unfortunately for Nina, romance, refined and poetic, was part of the Gang's essence. Balfour believed that platonic friendship between the sexes was possible, forged in shared pursuits where everyone's contribution was valued. When one was married, a form of courtly flirtation was acceptable, the code defined by fringe member Henry Chaplin as, 'Every woman shall have her man but no man shall have his woman'. But when a husband was absent too often, or a wife, after delivering the necessary heir and a 'spare', wanted a sexless marriage, or when temptation was simply too much at a time when divorce was not a positive option, the code might be pushed beyond stolen glances and extravagant letters. The Souls liked to think they were different from the Prince of Wales's set, but when it came to adultery, they rarely were. It was just that their foreplay was more intellectual.

When the Brownlows' ball ended, Nina was no closer to Harry than she had been before. At 25, he was still enjoying his bachelor status and always needed to explore romantic possibilities with new women he met. For him, their love was as vital as breathing, even though his intellectual life was rich and he valued the friendship of men.

Within the Souls, as well as beyond, he would usually find himself the object of interest and often of love, lust disguised by the elegance of prose in correspondence with women who had the time to elevate letter writing to an art form. When no physical relationship resulted, the parties might tell themselves that no spouse was betrayed, yet emotional dependency itself was surely a kind of infidelity.

The courtly ritual, often self-indulgent, even self-deluding, was not something Balfour himself indulged in. As a philosopher, he understood the vital link between language and truth, particularly when it came to human feelings. His love poetry had been reserved for May Lyttelton, whose early death, and that of others close to him, had made him emotionally wary: the writer H.G. Wells, who would come to know the Souls through Harry, observed that Balfour had 'no hot passions but only fine affections and indolences'.[17] His letters to his women friends were informative, discursive and never sentimental. Yet, while remaining a bachelor all his life, Balfour would maintain an intriguingly close relationship with George Wyndham's married sister, Mary.

Balfour had done little to win Mary from her future husband, Hugo Charteris, even though he cared for her. Balfour was 31 and Mary 17 when they met in 1879 at the studio of artist Sir Frederic Leighton, whom Mary was visiting with her mother and brother. The following year, Balfour invited her and her parents to his Scottish hunting lodge, but Mary's youthful awkwardness did not help and subsequent invitations from her family did not lead where she wanted. 'Mama wanted you to marry me,' she rebuked him later '[but] you got some silly notion in your head because circumstances threw Hugo and me together and accidents kept us apart – you were the only man I wanted for my husband … but you wouldn't give me a chance of showing you nicely … and you were afraid, afraid, afraid!'[18]

For all their privilege, upper-class women were not free of the expectation to marry, usually someone favoured by their parents. Margot Tennant considered herself and her sisters fortunate because, although their father said they should make 'worldly marriages', in the end, he let them choose the men they loved and gave them the money to enable them to do it. Most parents, she said, 'sacrifice their children to loveless marriages as long as they know there is enough money for no demand ever to be made upon themselves'.[19]

In 1883, at the age of 21, Mary Wyndham married the man her mother had introduced her to, having long known his family. Hugo, 26, was MP for Haddingtonshire and had just taken the title Lord Elcho on, becoming heir to his father, the Earl of Wemyss and March. The family estates included Gosford in East Lothian and Stanway in Gloucestershire. With her younger sisters, Madeline (known as Mananai) and Pamela, Mary would be immortalised in John Singer Sargent's portrait *The Wyndham Sisters.* George, the eldest son, was the second of the five Wyndham siblings, followed by Guy. Their upbringing, aristocratic by birth and bohemian by inclination, made them the quintessential Souls.

Their beautiful dark-haired mother, also Madeline, was proud to descend from aristocratic French and Irish rebels with all the romance that came with it. Raised near Dublin in a large but not particularly wealthy family whose father died when she was 12, she was encouraged to read freely and educate herself. She became a follower of the Pre-Raphaelites and a friend of artists and was said to be the first woman in England to smoke, enjoying a cigarette after each meal. She also liked to write with a flock of tame doves circling her head.

Her husband Percy, youngest son and unexpected heir of the exceedingly rich Lord Leconfield, was determined his children should enjoy a less rigid upbringing than he had received. He and Madeline gave their children intellectual and physical freedom, encouraging them to roam and ride in the wilds around their country home and appreciate the natural world. Mary was a tomboy and, being big for her age, was affectionately nicknamed 'Chang' by her parents, after a Chinese giant who had once come to London.

With a passion for culture, Percy and Madeline took pride in being 'the first members of Society to bring the people of their own set into friendly contact with the distinguished folk of art and literature',[20] with whom their children mingled. Discipline was used sparingly, the result being clever, creative but uncontrollable youngsters, who got through a string of governesses and whose neighbours in their London house thought them wild. When George was in his teens, said Mary, 'no matter how many men of note and learning were seated at the table, my father would put up his hand and say: "Hush, George is going to speak!"'[21]

As was the prevailing attitude, their daughters' intellect was not always well received by those unaccustomed to brains in women. A suitor of Mary's was heard to say, 'A very nice filly but she's read too many books for me!', reflecting the philistinism which was anathema to the Souls. Mary had a warm and natural manner, together with an air of vagueness that suggested her mind was in several places at once; often it was, for she was interested in everything and everyone and unselfconsciously struck up conversations with total strangers, whether shop assistants or train passengers. She resisted almost anything that smacked of organisation, although she loved planning outings and parties. Impulsive and kind, she attracted confidences and inspired love.

Hugo was very different. Although sharp and witty and noted for his brilliantly amusing speeches in Parliament, he was also moody and unpredictable. Being heir to the earldom played to his weaknesses. Although gambling filled his father with horror, Mary noted that 'as if by a malicious irony, fate developed in his sons a serious tendency to harass him in this respect'.[22] Laura Tennant had found Hugo amusing but completely unscrupulous. Mary was aware of his faults before they married, including his flirting, and initially tried to break off their engagement after he ran up a large gambling debt, but bowed to parental pressure.

Hugo's upbringing was much more formal and socially rigid than Mary's. The novelist and campaigner Mrs Humphry Ward stayed with his parents at Gosford, her experience highlighting a difference between the Souls and other aristocratic sets:

> The pleasure was mixed. Lady Wemyss [Hugo's mother] I love more than ever, but the party in the house was large and very smart … it is difficult for plain literary folk who don't belong to it to get much entertainment out of a circle where everybody is cousin of everybody else … and where the women at any rate, though pleasant enough, are taken up with 'places', jewels and Society with a big S … Most of them are good and kindly … but naturally the paraphernalia

> of their position plays a large part in their lives, and makes a sort of hedge round them through which it is hard to get at the genuine human being.

Her next country house visit was very different:

> Perhaps our most delightful visit was a Saturday to Monday with Mr. Balfour, at Whittingehame. There life is lived, intellectually, on the widest and freest of all possible planes, and the master of it all is one to whom nature has given a peculiar charm and magnetism, in addition to all that he has made for himself by toil and trouble.[23]

Hugo was not predisposed to be the ideal husband. From 1886, Mary's friendship with Balfour grew deeper, initially helped by proximity. In May, just before she gave birth to their second child, she and Hugo moved into a new house in Cadogan Square, Belgravia, a gift from his father. They spent the summers there while Hugo was in Parliament, as was Balfour, whose London home at 4 Carlton Gardens was nearby.

During the recess, Balfour would invite the Elchos to Whittingehame, where he and Hugo went shooting and they all played golf, Balfour's passion, at North Berwick. As Mary was married and (theoretically, at least) unavailable, Balfour felt safe in resuming the bond he had enjoyed with her, with an increasing familiarity that she did not discourage.

Like other women in the Gang, Mary refused to follow fashion slavishly, but sometimes she took her indifference to extremes. When Balfour heard she was ordering a gown from Paris for Queen Victoria's Drawing Room, a formal occasion at which ladies were presented at court, he remarked, 'I cannot imagine you dressed according to the taste of Worth, instead of your own. I don't much like Parisian millinery on any shoulders: on yours it will seem to me absurd.'[24]

❧

Harry Cust met Hugo and Mary Elcho around late 1886 at a party at Wilton, the grand Wiltshire seat of the Earl of Pembroke, which had been in the family since the sixteenth century. The political world was reeling from Lord Randolph Churchill's recent resignation as Chancellor of the Exchequer over the rejection of his budget proposals, a decision about which Margot Tennant, on meeting him for the first time, got away with saying audaciously, 'I am afraid you resigned more out of temper than conviction, Lord Randolph',[25] and which Pembroke publicly condemned as 'the reckless selfishness of a spoiled child'.[26]

But while their guests doubtless discussed the situation, Pembroke and his wife, Gertrude ('Gity'), made sure they were entertained too. Gregarious and hospitable, the earl was a man of deep intellect and wide interests. With Russian blood from his grandmother, he was 6ft 4in tall with a face whose beauty could never be forgotten, according to Margot, who considered him one of the finest-looking men she had ever seen. Gity was ten years older, less good-looking than her sister, Adelaide Brownlow, but with the same magnificent stature and masses of red-gold hair. She also had an eccentric, even unstable streak and a keenness for abstract utterances that could be hard to follow.

The Pembrokes 'made Wilton a house of delight … shooting parties in winter, theatricals, expeditions … every sort of interesting man and woman was made welcome there', enthused another guest, Lady Horner, who attended with her husband, Jack.[27] The Tennant sisters looked on Frances Horner as a sibling. Like them, she came from trade, but her impressive intelligence and aesthetic awareness made her a good fit for the Gang. Her merchant father was an art collector and patron of Dante Gabriel Rossetti and Edward Burne-Jones, who had first painted Frances when she was around 15. She was not conventionally beautiful but had a striking profile and sensitive expression, and what a child once called 'ghost eyes'. Despite being twenty years older and married, Burne-Jones fell helplessly in love with her. Frances remained his muse, and they maintained a close relationship until his death; he was very different from Jack, who was quiet and moralistic and, while he looked on his wife's dinners with her friends benevolently, he was not part of the group.

Frances was joyful and fun-loving but, on moving to the Horners' family seat, Mells in Somerset, she found she had married into a 'feudal' family at a time when 'no one had begun to doubt the power of the landlord or the divine right of the gentry'. Her brother-in-law, the rector of Mells, 'was celibate, vegetarian, teetotal, anti-sport, anti-smoking, anti-all amusements'. When she took up bicycling, her sisters-in-law were horrified by her vulgarity. Frances loved the freedom of sailing on the Earl of Pembroke's yacht, *Black Pearl*, but Jack hated the sea. Little wonder she felt at home in the Gang and appreciated those who made her laugh, like Burne-Jones, 'one of the wittiest and jolliest of talkers ... a great laughter lover', and Harry Cust.

Frances and Harry would get to know each other well, sometimes finding themselves together on *Black Pearl*. She liked his ability not to take himself too seriously, whether it was running around in a farmyard pretending to be a duck just as the Russian Ambassador appeared or writing his self-mocking poems. He became 'a very gay companion and present at most of our feasts ... a very well-read and cultivated man, with a great deal of personal charm and a sunny disposition'.[28]

Mary Elcho liked Harry too. In January 1887, shortly after they met, she wrote to him in Paris, where he was staying again in rue du Faubourg; it was the first of many letters between them. In his extravagant style, he replied that he welcomed her letter, for not only were her artistic flourishes 'a masterpiece for their unconsciousness' which occupied his attention and kept him from the Louvre, but her letter was to his loneliness 'like water in a thirsty land'.[29] It was, he said, 'humanity's loss that people like you and Addy Brownlow shouldn't have had to work for your living: perhaps you aim to, with all those faculties running to lettuce seed'.

For Harry, the need to exchange socialising for a period of solitude was, in those days at least, quite common. After Wilton, he told Mary, 'my body and mind began to break up so rapidly that I fled my country and my kind in mere terror'. Now he was living the life of 'a rather well-to-do hermit', reading a lot, seeing no one, going nowhere, except to one play and one concert a week, and he suggested a play she may be interested to read.

Mary immediately wanted to invite Harry to a party she and Hugo were giving at Stanway, their beautiful Jacobean house in Gloucestershire which was a wedding present from Lord Wemyss. She mused on it in a letter to Hugo, who was away, and when he did not refer to it, was more direct the next time: 'Don't you think I'd better make an effort to get Cust, although I know it will be a vain one – tell me by telegram.'[30]

Parties at Stanway were always popular and became a model for the idyllic country house weekend. Mary held her first party when Laura Tennant was still alive and had enthused about all the laughing and talking and quarrelling, and how they played the piano and enjoyed games: '[We] scribble & scrawl & invent words and reasonless rhymes'.[31] On another occasion, Mary watched amused as Margot chased one of the men along the church wall with a large sponge, and Hugo, accustomed to the dull formalities of his parents' parties, was astounded by Margot's habit of talking in her friends' bedrooms until the early hours.

But Harry's presence at gatherings was intermittent during 1887, for he was back and forth to Paris, where he was completing his studies for the French Bar. In February, he came home to give away his sister Annette at her London wedding, a joyous affair with nine bridesmaids and a multitude of guests, many from their large family, who did their best to fill the gap left by the Cust parents.

The groom, William Wheatley, was Earl Brownlow's manager at Ashridge,[32] and Lady Marian Alford, the earl's mother, hosted the reception at her London house, where guests could admire the beautiful Fountain of the Siren she had commissioned from a 'close friend' – for Lady Marian, widowed for thirty-six years since she was 34, had her own romantic attachment.

In Rome, the year before Harry's birth, she had met Harriet 'Hatty' Hosmer, the American sculptor and a lesbian. They were part of a creative crowd that included Harry's parents' friends, Robert and Elizabeth Barrett Browning. Lady Marian was well known for her patronage of the arts, and the two women were drawn to each other. Elizabeth, noting that Hatty called Lady Marian 'divine', was present when Lady Marian knelt down before her 'and gave her – placed on her finger – the most splendid ring you can imagine, a large ruby in the form of a heart, surrounded and crowned with diamonds. Hatty is delighted, and says so, with all sorts of fantastical exaggerations.'[33] When in England, Hatty stayed with her, and they remained close friends until Lady Marian's death in 1888.

Lady Marian knew some of young Harry's friends through their parents, particularly Mary Elcho's mother, Madeline Wyndham, who shared her passion for needlework as art and installed it at Clouds. According to Mary, it was while she and Hugo were entertaining during 1887 that Lord Charles Beresford, a Royal Navy commander, coined the nickname 'the Souls'.

They were in the middle of one of their deep discussions, which could be disconcerting to outsiders unaccustomed to emotions being analysed or taboo subjects discussed, when 'he said chaffingly, "Oh, I can't talk to you people, you are all Soul"'.[34] Although Mary thought the term fitting in some ways – the Souls were witty, which translates to *l'esprit*, then into spirit, and thus into soul – they did not use it themselves, for they resisted labels or anything that suggested they might be a clique. Balfour disliked it, saying it suggested 'organisation and purpose' rather than friendship.

Nevertheless, those who were not part of the group often looked with envy upon those who were. Lord Haldane said, 'They cared for literature and art, and their social gifts were so high that people sought to be admitted in their circle. … One or two outside men were welcomed and were frequently guests on these occasions. We were not "Souls" but they liked our company and we liked theirs because of its brilliance.'[35]

When James Rennell Rodd visited England that summer from Berlin, he discovered his friends had a new moniker and were 'engrossed in a study of ethics with a young girl-graduate from Newnham lecturing to them. They were discussing the most comprehensive problems of philosophy with pleasant irresponsibility, although some of them seemed very much in earnest.'[36]

Intellectual playfulness, though, was only part of their essence. A vital element was love.

4

FLIRTATIONS

For the men in the Souls, friendship became increasingly entwined with their professional lives. In March 1887, Lord Salisbury made Arthur Balfour his Chief Secretary for Ireland, an important appointment but also a dangerous one. Balfour asked George Wyndham to be his private secretary. He was interested in people and had the qualities needed in a politically volatile climate.

Wyndham, who had married Sibell just the month before, greatly admired Balfour and cut short his prolonged honeymoon in Italy to take up the post in Dublin. It was just as well that Wyndham did not hear the cynical prophecy of his cousin, Wilfrid Blunt, that 'these marriages with widows are a mistake for young men who are made slaves of & only regain their freedom when it is too late'.[1] Sibell, who at the insistence of her former father-in-law the Duke of Westminster retained her title of Lady Grosvenor, was considered by many to be sweet-natured but also, regrettably for a group of friends so full of vitality and fun, increasingly rather a bore.

One of the Souls women to whom such a description could never apply was Ettie Grenfell. In February 1887, the same month as Wyndham's wedding, 19-year-old Ettie Fane married William Grenfell at a ceremony attended by Prince Eddy and a large swathe of society. Balfour had only met Ettie a few times before her marriage but told Mary Elcho he thought her 'a nice girl, and clever'.[2]

Ettie was tall and elegant, with dark hair and heavy-lidded blue eyes, and she possessed a deep, slow, drawling voice. Vibrant and socially accomplished from a young age, she had enjoyed the attention of many admirers before she met Willie, a gentle giant of a man. He was a gifted and versatile athlete from a Liberal family, but not aristocratic like his wife, nor was he as rich.

Ettie was heiress to far greater wealth, a compensation of sorts for an emotionally turbulent childhood in which her parents died when she was 2 and her brother when she was 8. She had lived for much of the year at glorious Wrest Park in Bedfordshire with her grandmother, who died when Ettie was 13.

Her adored aunt and uncle, the Earl and Countess Cowper, took over her care and, being childless, made Ettie their heir – their Hertfordshire estate, Panshanger, would become hers. After their wedding, she settled into the magnificent house Willie had inherited when he was 11, Taplow Court in Buckinghamshire, said to be one of the finest residences on the River Thames.

Ettie's immense charm and skill in entertaining would see the young wife become one of the great hostesses of the period. While the intellectual qualities of female Souls were valued as much as the men's, upper-class society generally set great store by the social skills women possessed and the ways in which they could influence people, which was particularly advantageous for the men. Unusually, Ettie did not appreciate culture as the others did – she disliked music and was uninterested in the visual arts – but she was sharp and observant, and well informed on current affairs.

Having lost those close to her in her young life, she was determined to garner affection, especially that of men. Unlike the spontaneous Mary, with whom she became good friends (save for their vying for Balfour's attention), every gesture of Ettie's was calculated for effect. Flirting was second nature to her, 'She had a way of lowering her eyelids, when she was really attending to what was said, that was entirely seductive,' said her friend, Violet Cecil.[3] Yet, while she was self-aware, she liked to find the best in others, drawing out their talents, however simple, and joining them to the social orchestra she liked to conduct, for which her parties would become known.

Margot said she was the first person she would go to if she was unhappy, although not if she were guilty, 'because her genius lay in a penetrating understanding of the human heart and a determination to redress the balance of life's unhappiness'.[4] Cynthia Asquith said Ettie had 'an enthralled interest in human beings combined with both the power and the desire to dominate them'.[5]

As friendships developed among the Souls, Harry was expanding his relationship with Margot Tennant and her married sisters, Charty Ribblesdale and Lucy Graham Smith, to whom he wrote fondly of his visits to their family home, Glen, and sent presents of books and bonbons. Margot was not only appreciative of her gifts but the fact that Harry did the same for all of them: 'We 3 little fellers all compared notes & were thrilled to think you had sent us all something. This is what I love best, people who care for all of us & see all the beauties of Glen.'[6]

Laura was never far from their thoughts, and illness was again blighting the Tennants. Their elder sister Pauline Gordon-Duff, known as Posie, who had two young children, 'has been & still is so ill – if you have a little time you might write to her, it wd. delight her tout bonnement', Margot implored Harry, ending with a reminder of the humour they shared. If they were together, 'I'm sure we would scream with laughter in a moment or say something to delight each other'. Harry did write several times to Posie, who was suffering from that pernicious malady tuberculosis, from which three Tennant children had died, and sent her books. She was delighted and asked him to recommend others.

There was clearly a spark between Harry and Margot. She was not beautiful, but her looks were arresting. She wrote of herself, 'I do not say I was ever what I would call "plain", but I have the sort of face that bores me when I see it on other people'.[7] She was, however, slim and trim from her horse riding and her presence was electrifying. Like Harry, she was a great flirt.

In the beginning they danced around each other, trying to determine what they wanted their relationship to be. He frequently pleased her. 'You perfect dear & clever person,' she wrote from a hotel, 'I was enchanted with your poem … mama and I were delighted – you are a nice friend Mr Harry … thank you for your letters that have come between me & much Harrogate ugliness.'[8]

He could annoy her too. When he criticised her response to a book that he had sent her, she retorted crossly, 'I daresay I am not literary but you mustn't say I'm not fond of books – no, because this is not so, nor must you insinuate I express more or less than the truth.' He did not know her fully, she said, but some day they would understand each other, because 'I am ever so fond of you & feel absolute confidence in you & a sort of delight too'.[9]

She sent him a striped hanky and commanded him to wear it, and praised his poetry with the sort of original, if odd phrase for which she became known, 'Your verse deserves cataracts of congratulation, it really is first-rate.' Harry mused on romance between them, but Margot, wiser, put him straight in a way that would settle the course of their relationship:

> You say you wish you were quite in love with me & to make me so with you. First be thankful you are not & then let me tell you it is not a question of will: if I fall in love with you, I fall in love. If I don't, neither your will, nor mine, nor legions of angels can effect this … Let us be dear friends, playing at nothing, loyal & affectionate & real.

She added, with prescience, 'I am not the least sort of woman you would ever be in love with. She will be prettier & more dependent.'[10]

Mischievously, he asked her to go to Paris with him. Margot's response highlighted the difference between the liberal attitude of her family and his, the Brownlows, cultured but traditional nobility, 'It wouldn't do – we aren't able to chaperone ourselves & your relations aren't like mine.' However, she would be in Paris for a night on her way to Hyères in the south: 'It would be rather fun shopping together, wouldn't it, only I don't want to be any way remarked on by your relatives, & if they thought it odd standing on Lord Charles' shoulders, they'd think it much weirder being in Paris with you.'[11]

Shortly afterwards, Harry was at a party at her parents' house in Grosvenor Square. After strolling through the garden, where he kissed Margot's hair and told her that not all his kisses were the same, she decided to test the opinion of the other guests and announced, 'I don't think it at all proper that I should travel alone with Mr Cust', only to be met with agreement that she should not. 'Harry is a great flirt,' said one titled lady, 'and likes breaking down conventionalities.' Margot was infuriated at their 'dull sort of understanding' and that they thought him a flirt, worrying that Harry might think she was one too, and decided not to go.[12]

She was also concerned for him, knowing about his health and foreseeing pitfalls ahead. 'Dear Mr Harry, I wonder if you will be well enough to do much with your life. You are too intelligent to be idle & I can imagine your life a very full & successful one with any amount of interests in it.'[13] Harry replied with one of his amusing poems, expressing his pleasure at receiving her letter:

And I found that the life I was thinking so leavable
Had still something in it made living conceivable
And that, spite of the sores and the bores and the flaws in
My own, life's the better for small bits of yours in it.

He had also seen her sisters when he was deep in study:

But today Lady Charty and sweet Mrs Lucy em-
Broidered the dusk of the British Museum,
And made me so happy by talking and laughing on
That I loved them more than the frieze of the Parthenon.[14]

Presented with such an expression of affection, laced with unmistakable poignancy, it was little wonder that Margot would remain a faithful friend. In later life, she would reflect that he was 'the most brilliant young man I have ever known'.[15]

Rather than travelling with him, she met him in Paris, then joined Posie at Hyères, a winter resort favoured since the eighteenth century by the wealthy ('Old Miss Alice Rothschild is here,' Margot observed) with a mild climate recommended for TB sufferers. 'You were <u>very</u> dear to me, Mr Harry, in Paris,' she told him later, 'much, much nicer than I deserve. You quite spoilt me & yr violets slept on my pillow & mixed with my hair all night, so delicious!'[16]

She also saw in him, as did Nina, his spiritual self. Few did, for it was not on show to those who sought him for entertainment, and those who failed to be charmed by him saw only what they wanted. He had sent Margot a book of his own, 'a little sad coloured book', she thought, with an embroidered cover and his name inside, and she wondered for how long it had nourished him, and:

> … whether fashionable discussions under trees with your legs stretched & a cigarette between your lips and a heedless smiling audience delighting in what they would call your unconventionality & applauding your well-turned blasphemies made up to you for the quiet solitary communions you have had with your inner self & the unaccountable reverence that made you bend your knees & bow your head acknowledging a mystery higher than yourself.[17]

She told him, 'Don't ever say you are ashamed of your old prayers or orthodox days … I have never met the man who could afford to be ashamed of any good impulse even if it were mistaken & if your only mistakes are prayers, God is with you.'[18]

That he had revealed his inner self, and she had understood it, indicated true friendship, although Harry's definition of mistakes was unlikely to coincide with God's.

That year, Britain celebrated Queen Victoria's Golden Jubilee, in which the upper classes led the way in celebrations all around the country. In July at Ashridge, where, in 1826, Princess Victoria had planted an oak tree, the Brownlows held a huge party and gave presents to their estate workers and suppliers. Local aristocracy were there – the Earl and Countess of Lytton, the prime minister's daughter, Lady Gwendolen Cecil, as well as some Souls – giving Harry the chance to catch up with newlyweds George Wyndham and Sibell, and Henry Chaplin who, although he mixed mainly with the Marlborough House set of the Prince of Wales, was an 'occasional Soul', as Burne-Jones called those like himself on the perimeter.

Chaplin was of the Brownlows' generation, another Lincolnshire landowner and MP, who had suffered a traumatic romantic life. Jilted in a publicly humiliating way by his fiancée, he later married, but his wife died in childbirth. He never remarried, and it was perhaps fitting that he should have articulated the Souls' courtly code.

Rhoda Broughton was there too, as was Rennell Rodd, who noted that Harry 'seemed to bear her no ill-will on account of a recent volume, the much courted but not impeccable hero of which was regarded by a number of friends as having a not wholly accidental resemblance to himself'.[19]

Unusually for an event hosted by the Brownlows, Nina was not there, but she had other demands on her. At 20, her life was more restricted than many of the Souls women, largely because she was single and living at home at Denton Manor. Although she was putting her talents to use in a real way, including assisting her mother in her work, she was also expected to be involved in community activities and set an example. As the daughter of the lord of the manor that the Welbys had held since the sixteenth century, she understood their sense of duty. For the jubilee, her parents had funded the complete restoration of the parish church, while in a neighbouring village, her clergyman uncle conducted meetings of the Church of England Temperance Society, where he spoke sternly of the demon drink and the need to observe the virtues of temperance, purity and godliness.

Of interest to Nina and other young women was the Primrose League, a newly formed political organisation. Named for the favourite flower of the late Conservative Prime Minister Benjamin Disraeli, its aim was to spread Conservative principles by holding social activities, bringing politics to men and women who did not have a vote.[20] Nina's father, until recently a Conservative MP, was a member and the Brownlows were major figures. The countess was a League Ruling Councillor and in 1886 had founded the Brownlow Habitation, with its first meeting held at Belton and attended by 2,000 people.

Nina helped serve teas at such a meeting where local MP Malcolm Low was speaking.[21] He expressed the well-received view that it was time the Conservative Party made room in its agenda for the cause of rate-paying women being admitted to the franchise. While the league's formal position was disengagement from the debate on suffrage, some members did actively support or oppose the issue. Ultimately, the league was said to have furthered the suffrage cause, undoubtedly helped by female political influence in the higher echelons of society, such as Lady Brownlow. In 1887, neither she nor Nina imagined that they would come to have a hostile brush with the cause.

Nina had been to London earlier that jubilee year when she was commanded to attend the Queen's Drawing Room. Her mother and grandmother's close association with the royal family gave her a direct connection; as a child, she had been mentioned in the Queen's diary. Other attendees were familiar, including relations of Harry's and Mrs Henry

Manners, as Violet then was. The following year, she and her husband would become the Marquis and Marchioness of Granby upon the death of his uncle (Nina's great-uncle), the 6th Duke of Rutland. As Henry and Nina were related, she may have met Violet through him at the ancestral home, Belvoir Castle, situated not far from Denton and Belton.

Violet had married Henry Manners in 1882. A granddaughter of the Earl of Crawford, she was considered very beautiful, her auburn hair and deep-set eyes captured by many artists. When she was Miss Lindsay, G.F. Watts painted her as a Virgin of the Rocks in a Prussian blue gown. Violet's strongly developed sense of the aesthetic and her unique dress sense, often dramatic, always imaginative, made her a distinctive figure, while her own artistic talent was recognised early on by Burne-Jones.

By 1887, she had three children, and Henry had become Lord Salisbury's principal private secretary. Good-looking, affable and dull, Henry did not share the cultural interests of the Souls, preferring shooting and fishing, and, of all the husbands, he was the least connected to the group. Although he and Violet shared an interest in theatre, where she became familiar with backstage life and acquired an outré set of friends, he discovered his real interest lay in the actresses themselves. His favourite was Violet Vanbrugh, tall, imposing and graceful, who gave her first West End theatrical performance in 1886. Although she married in 1894, at some stage she had Henry's child, and when (as Duke of Rutland) Henry died in 1925, he left her money in his will.

After the Queen's Drawing Room, Violet Manners was involved in a huge jubilee party for 30,000 schoolchildren held in Hyde Park, attended by the Queen and the Prince and Princess of Wales, where, from ten specially built marquees, aristocratic ladies and gentlemen distributed refreshments to the mass of children and their teachers. Among Violet's co-workers was Gladys de Grey, who would soon be credited with saving the Royal Italian Opera at Covent Garden, and Mary Elcho and Charty Ribblesdale, all of whom Violet would draw; she was gaining renown for her soft pencil portraits of society's best-known figures, for which her friendship with Queen Victoria's daughters helped. Violet had sat for the youngest, Princess Louise, a talented artist herself, who made a terracotta statue of her, and later Violet would draw Princess Beatrice.

Violet was seen as a suitable artistic mentor for the younger Nina. It has been said that Nina was in thrall of this beautiful, uninhibited woman and while there is undoubtedly some truth in that, the dearth of letters or diaries of Nina's means that much remains speculative. Violet may have seemed like the sophisticated, older sister who Nina never had, and at a time when it was hard even for aristocratic women to be recognised for their professional talent, her artistic contacts were useful. Violet's cousin, the watercolourist Sir Coutts Lindsay, had opened the Grosvenor Gallery in London, which was devoted to exhibiting the works of the Pre-Raphaelites as an alternative to the Royal Academy, which considered them too stylised. Burne-Jones and G.F. Watts were among the artists the Grosvenor displayed.

Another creative Soul who was also present at the Queen's Drawing Room was Lady Windsor. Christened Alberta, she was known always as Gay. Tall and slim, with large, sad eyes and copper lights in her dark hair, her handsome appearance that day – her hair threaded with diamonds, her blue and gold satin gown harmonising perfectly with her corsage – drew admiring comments in the press. Gay was a vegetarian and anti-vivisectionist, her progressive views influenced by her mother, Lady Paget, who by birth was a German countess, Walburga von Hohenthal – as a close friend of Queen Victoria, she had helped arrange the marriage of Edward, Prince of Wales to Princess Alexandra of Denmark. Gay's father, Sir Augustus Berkeley Paget, was an eminent diplomat who, from 1884, was British Ambassador at Vienna.

Unlike most of the Souls women, Gay was solemn and enigmatic, with an air of sorrow that some believed was caused by a thwarted love affair before she married. It was captured in Burne-Jones's portrait of her, famed not only for its muted beauty but for its distinction in being his only full-length painting.

Like Ettie, Gay married young. In 1880, aged 17, she was introduced to Robert Windsor-Clive in Rome, where her father was then British Ambassador. Lord Windsor was a talented draughtsman and very knowledgeable about art and architecture, endearing him to Lady Paget who had also received art training. He was en route to Greece to draw the illustrations for a travel book.

They married in London in 1883 when he was 26 and Gay was 20. Within a year he was designing their home, Hewell Grange, a neo-Jacobean mansion in Worcestershire on the site of an earlier family house.

After having a son, Gay gave birth to a daughter in December 1886 and was back in the social loop in time for the Golden Jubilee, which also saw the couple among the favoured few invited to the queen's evening party at Buckingham Palace.

❧

The Souls may have considered themselves culturally superior to the Marlborough House set, but there was an inevitable overlap between the groups, and while the royal court remained at the pinnacle of society, the Souls could not entirely ignore etiquette. In December, Harry was among a favoured group invited to stay at Ashridge as part of a shooting party at which the Brownlows' main guests were the Prince and Princess of Wales.

Nina was not there, but she would see Harry again in early 1888 at the Grantham Hospital Ball, a major charitable event that was to be honoured with the presence of Prince Eddy. He stayed for several nights at Belton and, given Harry's acquaintance with him, he was invited too. While Harry found royal occasions dulled by the sort of formality the Souls eschewed, it would be considered rude to decline an invitation.

Prince Eddy's presence caused great excitement in Grantham. The ball was necessarily an even grander affair than usual, at which the patron, Lady Thorold, looked after the prince with Lady Brownlow, both decked in more diamonds than usual, for what was a demanding night.

Nina was with familiar faces. Harry's unmarried sister, Violet Cust, was there, while local gentry included Henry and Violet Manners and most of the extended Welby family, including Nina's new sister-in-law, Mollie, a granddaughter of the Marquis of Bristol.

It was a busy week for the town, for on the day before the ball, Lord Salisbury, travelling by train to Liverpool, would be stopping at the station for three minutes. Lady Brownlow was there to greet him and formed the official reception party with Harry and the Mayor and Corporation. Behind them gathered hundreds of local people hoping for a glimpse of their leader.

In a comedic scene, as the train stopped, the only indication anyone was on board was an engaged sign on one carriage, to which the door remained closed. Henry Manners, as Salisbury's private secretary, opened it, only to reveal a sorry-looking prime minister with wrappings around his head for relief from a bad cold, which he regretted would prevent him getting out and into the fog in case he got worse. He stayed there while the Chairman of the Conservative Association delivered an address. The disappointed crowds had to make do with an apology delivered by proxy, and off went the train to Liverpool.

Harry's presence was not merely to support the Brownlows or because he had friends in Salisbury's government but because, at 27, he had decided to follow the Cust path into politics. He had not yet completed his legal qualifications, but he needed to get the ball rolling. After all, most of his contemporaries had started on their career paths while he was travelling, and although he gained valuable experience, some viewed that period unfavourably as an example of his restless nature.

That his father had been Conservative MP for Grantham and well-liked would, he hoped, give him some advantage, as might the fact that his cousin Earl Brownlow was a prominent county figure, as well as Paymaster General. A century later, speculation would arise as to whether Harry was the biological grandfather of Prime Minister Margaret Thatcher, whose mother (like Thatcher herself) was born in Grantham.*

While Harry considered the practicalities of getting selected as a candidate, Mary Elcho invited him to Stanway, having had her third child, Cynthia, a few months earlier. Afterwards, he visited Sandringham, telling Mary that being with royalty was like being 'in a great smart party where I can't quite find myself, as they talk a language of their own'. He had enjoyed being at Stanway: 'I always enjoy seeing you more than I think and imagine beyond that I feel the better for it'.[22]

His letters to Mary during 1888 were courtly but with an increasingly erotic undertone that she did not discourage. He told her he was working hard and had been musing on a theory of alternative sexual mores, based on the idea that if the apple had been allowed in Eden:

> … and all the rest forbidden, we shouldn't have been now where we are. Imagine polygamy advanced by God and man, and at this moment all the upper classes would have been dwelling in the joys of illicit constancy and despising the cowardly unenterprising middle classes who were forced to content themselves with profligacy.[23]

---

* See Appendix 1.

He wrote her a flirtatious ditty:

Let me be acolyte, pelican anything
Serving or feeding you after my measure
And if I should buy you a two-or three-penny thing
Why should you thank me for what gives me pleasure.[24]

And he made it clear he wanted to see her soon.

In the summer he went to Germany, writing to her from Munich in August and Berlin in September, his letters combining lightness and literature, and eager to tell her about 'a Norwegian called Ibsen who writes the most reckless psychological plays'.[25]

Whatever the content of her replies, Mary told Hugo it did not matter what she wrote to her admirers, whom she called 'conks'. Referring to herself in the third person, using her pet name, she told Hugo, 'Migs thinks it doesn't matter *what* she says in her letters to men conks, provided she only *implies* it ... for if brought to book she can say that they have misunderstood her – and nice men conks never take one to task.' It was a tricky ruse, but it might fill an emotional gap in a fond but less-than-perfect marriage.[26]

Meanwhile, Mary and Balfour had become closer, indicated in their frequent correspondence and in her diary with entries decorated by flowers and hearts with angels' wings. Cynthia's birth would give rise to speculation that she was his. Certainly, there was a physical element to their relationship, and Balfour's paternity was something Cynthia herself pondered as she grew up – he was very much a part of her life from babyhood.

Mary would always be a source of comfort to him. In 1888, his brother Gerald fell seriously ill and having already lost two brothers, Balfour told her, 'I have a shrinking horror of separation caused by the death of those I love.'[27]

Separation by death was not something from which the Souls' privilege could protect them. In November, Posie died. Harry learned the news from Lucy Graham Smith and immediately wrote to the family. Feeling 'tired and lifeless', Margot shared with him her sister's last moments, when:

> [the] air vibrated so much with Posie's moans I prayed that God would take her at once … She looked intensely beautiful, such a power in the little dead face as I had never seen in life … I wish you could have seen her, I do.

After the 'almost murderous rapidity' of Laura's death, she had known 'how the end would come about & how soon'.[28] Now no grief would find Margot unprepared. As always, Harry knew exactly what to say.

AMBITIONS

If Harry saw Margot less often than he would have liked during 1888, it was because he was preparing to stand as candidate for Stamford, a major Lincolnshire town. Stamford already had a Conservative MP, the popular John Compton Lawrance QC, but they wanted a candidate ready should they lose him; he was likely to be made a judge and would have to quit politics.

Harry's presence in Germany had been for a serious purpose, to study social trends and, in particular, a new law requiring workers and employers to protect themselves in respect of sickness and old age. In his view, every MP should acquaint himself with the politics, opinions and customs of all countries that 'may at any moment be either the warm allies or the bitter enemies of England', and he had done the same when studying in France. Far more useful, he said, than playing cricket.[1]

Harry had given his first major speech in support of his selection at a large public meeting chaired by Nina's father, Sir William Welby-Gregory. Thanks to recent reforms, around 60 per cent of men in Britain now had the vote. Although the Custs had served Lincolnshire for generations and he had influential friends, Harry did not seek Stamford's support on personal grounds, 'unless you are convinced that my political opinions are in substantial agreement with your own'.

In a rural community, he understood the importance of agriculture. He believed in the abilities of Salisbury's government, and he was against Gladstone's Home Rule Policy for Ireland because it was 'unwise and unjust, impracticable and ill-considered'. While he regretted 'the wrongs and cruelties from which Ireland has suffered in the past', the way to contentment and prosperity was not through anarchy but through establishing the rule of law and removing the causes of discontent. Cheers came at encouraging intervals, as when he declared himself a member of the Established Church with its 'civilising and humanising effect'.[2] The question of trade was always a thorny one, and Harry reassured his audience that he would support measures to reduce the advantages of foreign against English trade.

Harry was accepted as a prospective candidate and during the rest of 1888 he continued to speak all around the division. While he was usually well received – his charm and humour always came across – he also learned to deal with hecklers, often by sitting on the table, calmly rolling a cigarette and waiting for them to stop shouting. His ability to speak easily to all classes endeared him to many. Evening meetings often ended with refreshments and dancing, especially those organised by the Primrose League. On one occasion, when he spoke in place of the incumbent MP, a ditty was composed, 'Then for a member let us trust/ If not a Lawrance, then a Cust'. In his inimitable style, Harry assured them that he would not talk for long 'for he saw so many ladies he would like to dance with'.[3]

Among the local grandees who supported him was Henry Manners, who, upon the recent death of his uncle, the Duke of Rutland, was now the Marquis of Granby and heir to his father, the 7th Duke. Violet was therefore marchioness, but her title was not the only addition to her life that year. She gave birth to a fourth child, Violet, known as Letty, allegedly the daughter of her lover, the philanthropist Montagu Corry, 1st Baron Rowton – eighteen years her senior and unmarried, he had been Benjamin Disraeli's private secretary and was a family friend. Whatever the marquis's knowledge of Letty's paternity, she was raised as his daughter, but it was not the last time such an issue would arise.

The *Stamford Mercury* said of Harry, 'He is a vivacious and good-looking youth, blessed with the highest possible opinion of himself', adding mischievously that he was thought to be Broughton's model for Freddy du Cane.[4] Whether that made him more or less attractive to women and caused them to influence their husbands' voting decisions was not something Harry could do anything about. He just hoped that when it came to it, they would think he was up to the job.

The following year, 1889, was a significant one for the Souls, with careers advanced and relationships formed. While Harry continued to woo his would-be constituents, Balfour was busy in Ireland aided by George Wyndham. 'Arthur is very kind and pleasant to me', Wyndham told his wife Sibell, shortly after starting the post. 'We have been talking about poetry … and playing an extraordinary game of politics.'[5] In the fashion of the Souls, he and Balfour talked about 'Shakespeare, Shelley, the story of Hero and Leander, the difference of accent, quantity and numbering of syllables in English, Latin and French territory, politics, principles, warfare etc.'. They often visited Abbeyleix, the beautiful Dublin home of Hugo Elcho's married sister, Evelyn, who enjoyed entertaining the Souls with her husband, Viscount de Vesci, and often stayed at Stanway.

Harry met Evelyn at a party at Wilton and told Mary he would like to get to know her sister-in-law but could not see his way. Ironically, Charty Ribblesdale managed it, enjoying a 'delicious little party' at Stanway and became besotted with her. 'It has been a baptism into beauty morally & physically getting to know Lady de Vesci', she enthused to Harry, 'I have been longing to for years', and although she was 'paralysed with fright' at first, 'it is one of the few things that has not disappointed me in life. She is a glorious being. I can't take my eyes off her … she is so inspiring.'[6]

Mary was expecting her fourth child in May 1889 and, in the early months, was feeling under the weather. She and Hugo had promised to go to Abbeyleix to shoot with the de Vescis, so in January Hugo went alone. After seventeen years of marriage, his sister was expecting her first (and only) child. In April, Hugo visited once more, again without Mary, who was shortly to give birth herself. Unfortunately for her, it was during one of these visits that Hugo met his sister's close friend, Hermione, Duchess of Leinster.

When she 'came out' in 1881, the 'divinely tall and vivacious' Lady Hermione Duncombe, as she was then, a daughter of the Earl of Feversham, was feted. Men ran 'like hares down Rotten Row to see her ride' and Ettie Grenfell thought her the most beautiful woman she had ever seen.

Her marriage in 1884, when she was 20, to Lord Gerald Fitzgerald, the squat and ponderous heir to the Leinster dukedom and twelve years her senior, was probably her father's design. Their marriage had begun happily enough at the Leinsters' family home, Carton House, a Georgian mansion near Dublin, and after a daughter died, she bore Gerald, by then Duke of Leinster, two sons, Maurice and Desmond.

But she was prone to depression, made worse by the docility Gerald expected of her and his lack of support for anything she wanted to do for herself or the children, while his constant focus on their finances in a troubled Ireland was wearing her down. 'I cannot live like this any longer', she confided to Evelyn. 'I worship [Gerald], yet to go on like this would kill everything in me.'[7] Hidebound by aristocratic conventions, she found the Souls refreshing.

Hermione was immune to the handsome looks and poets' romanticism of George Wyndham in whom she detected 'a superciliousness of manner',[8] but she was touched by the reckless Hugo's 'patience and courage'.[9] After their first meeting, she told Evelyn she thought about her 'poor brother' often and gave her a note to pass to him. Hugo's head could not fail to be turned.

According to the Elchos' great-grandson, the 13th Earl of Wemyss, it was Mary's fault Hugo strayed during their marriage. 'She didn't love him.'[10] That is perhaps unduly harsh, and given Hugo's predilections and Mary's feelings for Balfour, their union should never have happened.

Hermione's interest in Hugo coincided with a time when, after less than six years of marriage, he was in the throes of an intense infatuation with Ettie Grenfell. A few months earlier, they had been to Ettie's Christmas party at Panshanger, where Mary's pregnancy was making her feel 'very seedy'.[11] By contrast, the sparkling Ettie presided over a wildly amusing party, and while Hugo rarely enjoyed the Souls' games, despite their being more fun than polite parlour games, he could at least admire the view, as Doll Lidell did, 'gazing at such a circle of striking females'. That evening, they enjoyed Dumb Crambo (similar to charades), in which Frances Horner 'clothed herself in breeches & boots & appeared as Napoleon crossing the Alps, the horse being Ettie Grenfell, & the Alps chairs covered with table cloths'.[12]

After the party, Hugo was invited to Ettie's house but found her not at home. The more difficult it was to see her, the more desirable she became. In May, the month Mary was due to give birth, he wrote to Ettie, 'When shall I see you? I feel quite low at my repeatedly unsuccessful endeavours to accomplish this object of my desire. I hear such a lot of you too, that I feel I am singularly unfortunate in never being thrown across your path.'[13] Even after Ettie fell pregnant with her second child in June,[14] he continued his pursuit, writing to her from Achnashellach in Scotland, where she too would soon be going, 'It is almost maddening to think that in a fortnight you will be living in the same house, perhaps sleeping in the same bed I now am … Every word I speak, every line I write, remind me of our feelings for each other.'[15]

Hugo's letters would continue, and while Ettie did not discourage them, enjoying his attention and her power, she did not allow it to become anything more. She would later explain her philosophy to the Elchos' daughter Cynthia, who recalled:

> We discussed 'lovers' and their compatibility with happy marriages. [Ettie] said she was not monogamous in the strict sense of the word, and had never been in love in the way which excluded other personal relations. To be at her best with one man she must see a great many others.[16]

Mary gave birth to a boy, Colin. It was said among her friends that when Hugo was asked the sex of the child, he said he did not know. 'The usual hardy annual', he presumed.[17] Mary was considerably weakened by the birth and a month later her doctor ordered her back to bed, warning that having any more children would endanger her life. According to Mary, it was around this time that sexual relations between her and Hugo stopped for six years.

Deprived of marital relations, and without the contact he craved from Ettie, he turned to Hermione Leinster. A description of her in the Irish press on 1 June 1889 – coincidentally, the day Mary gave birth – extolled her appearance:

> The Duchess of Leinster looked lovely in pale mauve satin, draped with soft diaphanous muslin of the same colour. She has exquisite arms and shoulders and the muslin appeared to be folded around these … Her small head, with its lovely poise upon the graceful neck, was *coiffe* very high under its diamond ornaments.[18]

Evelyn de Vesci knew her younger brother well. Hugo's weakness for women and gambling were no secret, while his mood swings were perhaps the sign of something darker. Their eldest brother, Francis, had shot himself when Hugo was 13, and three years later their next brother, Arthur, died at sea on his way home on army leave. Above all, Evelyn disapproved of the affair. Although many of her letters do not seem to have survived, Hermione's replies make this clear: 'You have not realised the one wide essential difference between us – that what to you seems "revolting", "miserable", "hideous" and "squalid" – to me in my love seems <u>none</u> of these things.'[19]

Her disapproval hurt Hermione, who had often wondered what Evelyn saw in her to love or care about, 'and now you know the extent of my moral blindness'. Hugo's love was 'the one happiness' of her 'unhappy life', and yet their affair caused her guilt. 'My soul has consented to earthly darkness and my punishment is to see and love the light and to know that I have failed.' Earthly love could bring no peace or happiness, and any delight was 'nearer torture. But I chose it. I loved with all my heart and strength and blindly and selfishly I gave everything up to it.'[20]

As Hermione battled with her conscience and her 'black dogs', as she referred to her depression, Mary received several letters from Hugo sent from the Leinster home, Carton House. He was affectionate as always, calling her 'My Darling Migs', and the content was inconsequential, making no reference to why he was there. Perhaps he had given Mary a reason before he went – a courtesy visit to the Leinsters, perhaps, for the duke was Ireland's premier peer – or perhaps she suspected an affair but chose to ignore it as long as it remained discreet.

In the days when divorce was not a socially acceptable option for either sex, but particularly damaging for women, discretion was vital for extramarital affairs. A gentleman never publicly humiliated his wife or rubbed his rival's nose in it. At least Harry was single, even if his lovers were not, and some of his flirtations within the Souls stayed faithful to their courtly code. Others remain ambiguous, although the extravagance of the claim made by one writer, with which others have readily run – that many babies in many nurseries were Harry's – remains to be substantiated.

One such relationship was with Margot Tennant's sister, Charty, four years his senior, who had also been engaged at some point in a dalliance with Hugo and with whom Harry had cultivated his relationship while in Germany. Charty and Thomas Ribblesdale were both tall and good-looking. Tommy's patrician looks and breeding would cause Edward VII to dub him 'the Ancestor', his aristocratic hauteur captured in John Singer Sargent's full-length portrait. Margot liked her brother-in-law, with his fine manners, sense of humour and original viewpoint, and for the fact that he was respectful to their father, while Charty had 'wonderful grace and less vanity than anyone that ever lived and her social courage was a perpetual joy'.[21]

Like her sisters, Charty enjoyed Harry's friendship. She loved the cheerfulness of his letters, and she trusted him to critique portraits she had drawn under the tutorship of Burne-Jones (whom she thought 'most fascinating').[22] She was delighted when Harry made a donation to a babies' charity she supported, and when Posie died, she shared with him her sense of loss. Harry began sending her gifts beyond the books and bonbons he had sent to her sisters, particularly gloves, an item which, when sent to a married woman, was charged with eroticism. Charty wrote to him from Gisburne in Lancashire, the marital home:

> I was never too proud to be the privileged one, it may show a want of self-respect but I can't help this. I revel in this form of humiliation, and yet, when the 5th pair of gloves arrived last night, I felt rather … you are <u>so</u> naughty, you deserve such a scolding, you must really mend your ways & not send me anything more, no never again. But thank you all the same, they are quite the most delicious gloves I have ever felt.[23]

Her life was overshadowed by Tommy's illness, the precise nature of which is unclear, but the agonising pain of rheumatic gout was part of it. Sometimes he spent a month in bed under doctor's orders, followed by recovery somewhere warm. His father had committed suicide, and Tommy suffered from depression, with a temper that would become increasingly foul. Although Charty loved him, she found it hard to deal with him and felt guilty. 'I am very low & so troubled about him,' she told Harry. 'It is so disappointing that it fills me with despair & I don't feel even brave, a quality never supposed to desert me. My heart dies within me.'[24]

By contrast, the joy Harry brought made her want him in her life. 'We will hobble about together & I will love your children & you will be kind to mine. I am not at all a happy woman either & life seems to me too difficult & hard to fight through it.'[25] Harry calmed her fears, and yet Charty felt that he too needed help. She wrote:

> I was very touched by your dear letter, from which I am red hot. It is very dear of you to say all you do. How I wish I were more worthy of it & I hate feeling that all I can do in return is to long to help you & to love you very much as I do.

Sometimes she was more direct. 'I hear you're looking thin and handsome', she purred, when she had not seen him for a while, 'you know I like you thin'.[26]

While Lord Ribblesdale knew of their friendship, Charty's letters suggest it was more than that, which he may also have been aware of. When Harry joined them in sailing to Dieppe, he and Charty spent so much of the evening together that the next day, Tommy told her 'from what he knew of us both, he half expected that I mightn't come back till next morning'.[27]

The temptation to cross boundaries was great. Life was fenced in with 'inch-high spiked railings', she said, over which one was not supposed to climb. 'I would willingly risk being impaled on the top for your sake, for as you know, we are not rigid conventionites.' And yet something held her back, for 'beyond the personal satisfaction it might be to me to suffer for anything I loved, it would be a barren effort as far as you were concerned, I fear'. All she could do for him was to 'keep the candles lit before the little shrine you have in my heart which is all your very own, & to hope for you & trust in you. Now don't tear down this altar of trust, I pray you.' She longed for him 'to help the world', but it was important that he help himself first:

> Don't disappoint me, Mr Harry, & don't delude yourself with thinking that brains (of which you have perhaps more than your share) are enough to carry you through triumphant. Character is so much more important, and do, I entreat of you on my knees, cultivate self-discipline & reservation; deceive your best friend rather than yourself. I would

> rather you sacrificed me. Do you hate this lecture? You must forgive it, for my whole being is full of longing for you.[28]

When Charty heard from Lucy that he had passed his law exams 'with flying colours', she was delighted and proud to have 'such a clever creature for a friend' and Tommy also congratulated him. Charty was certain Harry would love the law intensely, as did Alfred Lyttelton, who was now a barrister, but she reminded him that as he would be making a 'new start' in life in London, he would have to 'form habits and not only make resolutions'. She wished his character were 'as dependable' as his brain.[29] But Harry had already decided that any new start would not be in law but in Parliament.

That it was Lucy who first knew about Harry's success pointed to an increased intimacy between them. Her sisters were amused that, on a day out with Charty in London, Lucy, 'from a sense of duty' to Harry, had left early to have her photograph taken for him.[30]

For the petite and pretty Lucy, Harry was the man she should have met years earlier. She was just 19 when she married 28-year-old 'fatuous horse-breaking' Thomas Graham Smith,[31] who was 'silly, ineffectual but very kind', said Margot.[32]

Although her family thought her too young to marry, she obstinately went ahead and settled with Thomas at his family home, Easton Grey, in Wiltshire. There they rode, at which they both excelled, and Lucy played the violin and painted watercolours, for which she had received training and was very accomplished – Margot considered her the most talented of the family. But they felt she had spoiled her early life, and Thomas proved to have an uncertain temper: a sister had died, then his mother, followed by his father, who shot himself.

Mired in an unhappy marriage, the childless and sweet-natured Lucy, now 28, became obsessed with Harry. It was not long before they began an affair, which would become common knowledge within the Souls.

Harry always enjoyed pushing boundaries. One day, after he visited Charty and Lucy together, Charty told him she had lunched with Gladys (probably de Grey) and George Curzon: 'They pretended to be shocked & disgusted at Lucy & I having bathed with you! I scoffed, & did not let on about your second visit to us'.[33]

Curzon's reaction may not have been a pretence. In 1889, he was nearly 30 and single, having lost Sibell Grosvenor to George Wyndham.

Although he was heir to Kedleston in Derbyshire, his father, Lord Scarsdale, was known for his austere temperament and was described as 'a despot from the thirteenth century'.[34]

Unlike other Souls, Curzon was not allowed to invite his friends to his magnificent home. A brutal childhood at the hands of a cruel nanny affected him, as did his spinal problem, but it all made him fiercely determined. Hard-working and intelligent, his expression of 'enamelled self-assurance', as Margot called it, unfortunately gave him an arrogant air. It was captured in the ditty allegedly composed by J.K. Stephen, which would haunt Curzon all his life:

My name is George Nathanial Curzon
And I'm a very superior purzon
My cheek is pink, my hair is sleek
I dine at Blenheim once a week.

While he did not suffer fools gladly, beneath the surface lay a great sense of humour and a need for affection. The Tennant sisters adored him, especially Charty.

Curzon was then Conservative MP for Southport, but he had a deep interest in foreign affairs. He had already travelled extensively through Russia and Central Asia and written expertly on the political situation, while his passion for India saw the birth of his ambition to be viceroy. Although he usually preferred not to socialise with those with opposing political views, the Souls' friendships were above party politics.

His affection for them manifested itself in the summer of 1889 before he left on a journey for his health, followed by a major Persian expedition that would launch his foreign career. On 10 July, he gave a grand dinner for over thirty Souls at the Bachelors' Club in London, an elegant establishment that, unusually for the time, admitted women as guests.

On their chairs they found a long and amusing poem he had written in which each person had lines dedicated to them. Of Harry, Curzon said, 'Harry Cust could display/ Scalps as many, I lay/ From Paris as in Piccadilly.' His rhymes about everyone were apt. Balfour was 'the High Priest' of the Souls; the lines about the Elchos made sly reference to Hugo's infidelities (Mary was absent, still confined to bed) and his verse about the Tennant sisters captured them well:

To Lucy he gave
The wiles that enslave
Heart and tongue of an angel to Charty
To Margot the wit
And the wielding of it
That make her the joy of the party.

Even absent friends were mentioned. George Wyndham 'can't sit/ At our banquet of wit/ Because he is standing at Dover', where he had just been elected MP in a by-election.

Some Souls were forced to miss Curzon's hospitality because their attendance was required at events given in honour of the Shah of Persia. Amid much fanfare, His Imperial Majesty was making a formal tour of Europe, the first shah to do so, and spending eighteen days in Britain. Lord and Lady Windsor were hosting him at Hewell Grange, and her absence was regretted:

We have lost Lady Gay
'Tis a price hard to pay
For that Shah and his appetite greedy;

Harry had met the shah a couple of days earlier, when he and Nina were invited by the Brownlows to help entertain him and his entourage at Ashridge, together with Prince Eddy. The shah had been staying with the prime minister at his home, Hatfield House, and now it was the Brownlows' turn, in a visit that had required months of organisation.

Two troops of Hertfordshire Yeomanry, one of which had Lord Brownlow as its colonel, provided an escort for him and the shah on the 4-mile drive from the station to Ashridge, where they were greeted by the countess and joined by a swathe of nobility and local grandees. A lavish dinner, at which the band of the Life Guards played on the lawn, was followed by a glittering party where the shah commented on 'the galaxy of tall and handsome English women',[35] to whom he paid compliments in French and was seen spending a long time talking to Hermione, Duchess of Leinster. She was there with the duke, who was unaware that his beautiful young wife was in the throes of a passionate affair with Lord Elcho.

The evening was not merely for entertainment but to observe formalities: exchanging gifts and presenting honours, while indulging royal whims and deploying diplomacy. It was fortunate the shah's visit fell when it did, for just two days later, a scandal threatened when Prince Eddy was implicated in a police investigation into a male brothel.

Harry and Nina were among the overnight guests and joined the shah for breakfast, after which he strolled through the countess's conservatory, where a tent made of coloured silks that once belonged to his great-grandfather had been erected amid a forest of palms and ferns. Harry and Nina appeared in photos taken in the gardens with the shah and Prince Eddy and their hosts, but, strangely, in one picture Nina's mouth seems to have been scored out as though, on seeing the photograph, someone tried to remove it from her face, perhaps impatient with the memory of her quietness amid the throng of conversation and laughter.

Her life had recently been occupied, as it often was, with the good causes her parents were involved with. She had helped them host a jamboree for the Young Men's Christian Association (YMCA), of which her father was local patron. In the spirit of the organisation, which was based on the principles of 'muscular Christianity' designed to develop a healthy body, mind and spirit, they invited the men to use Denton's grounds for fishing and rowing, cricket and quoits, followed by a tour of the manor house given by Sir William. It was Lady Welby's interest in theology and the interpretation of the Christian scriptures that had led to her work in significs, on which her first book had been published in 1881.[36]

A healthy body, though, was not something Nina enjoyed, for like her mother, she was plagued by ill health which caused her pain that came and went. The effect was like a cloud that suddenly obscured the sun on a bright day and gave no indication of when it might reappear. She would eventually be under the care of an obstetrician. One possibility is that she suffered from endometriosis, which would have caused her frequent pain and help explain her pallor and quietness.

Lucy Graham Smith was blighted, too. In October 1889, she suddenly fell gravely ill at Glen when, as Margot told Ettie, 'a blood vessel burst in her womb – this is entre nous, dear – she has to be quite still for 7 or 8 weeks' and they thought she was likely to be ill for three months.[37] Such trauma is usually associated with pregnancy; if that were the case, the child would probably be Harry's. However, Lucy never would become a mother. Their liaison was naturally paused while Lucy recovered, but, meanwhile, circumstances were pushing him increasingly towards Violet, Marchioness of Granby.

6

A Kind of Fame

Lady Granby's attractions had been acknowledged by George Curzon in his poem for the Souls:

> Is there one of the Gang
> Has not wept at the pang
> That he never can Violet's man be?

Violet remained occupied with her lover, Lord Rowton, until at least 1888, the year she drew his portrait and gave birth to Letty, by which time she was 32 and he 50. Although she and Harry were part of the Souls, it was not until he began campaigning for Stamford and was spending more time at Belton that their paths crossed more often.

Lord Rowton may have been fine-looking and clever, but with his age and position came a sense of worthiness. By contrast, young Harry, with his exuberant presence tempered by poetic sensibility and the impression that behind his cool, blue-eyed gaze, the devil lay waiting, was a different beast altogether. As 1890 dawned, he and Violet were on the verge of becoming lovers; not for them the Souls' creed that each woman might have a special friend who would remain only a friend.

Harry's early letters to her maintain a formality, and although written with a frantic energy, often as he dashed between towns to give talks, and never overtly sexual, their message is clear. 'I feel inclined to begin a most unnecessary letter in a most 16th century manner by "most beautiful lady" & other words to the same effect: and they wouldn't be the least overdrawn or unreal.'[1] This he wrote on 19 January, a couple of days after going to Belvoir, 'thinking no evil, resolve & all in perfect working order'. He sent her a poem he had written at school and published in the *Eton Chronicle*:

In this mad maze of heat and sound
My old resolve is mine no more:
A darkness covers all around,
A black veil hangs on all before.

Yet thy clear image shines to me
As o'er some whirling streets a star,
Till dreaming what may never be
I gentlier find the things that are.

Ah dids't thou dearest even now
A single moment near me stand,
And lean upon my aching brow
The coolness of thy gracious hand.

And, bending nearer silently,
Lean down & pity all my pain,
And light those dear grey eyes for me,
I think I should be well again.[2]

His words must have had an effect, for his next letter asked, 'Haven't I reason to be ashamed, you mighty magician.'[3]

Harry sought opportunities to see her. It would not be proper for them to be alone together in public, so their meetings were largely dependent on invitations from others or on attending events, all the time maintaining discretion. He became a patron of the Grantham Industrial and Fine Art Exhibition, an annual event of cultural and social importance, along with prominent local figures including Violet's in-laws, the Duke and Duchess of Rutland, the Brownlows and Nina's parents. While it was in Harry's interests to be seen to be associated with such a good cause, the fact that the Marchioness of Granby would be opening it was a strong incentive.

He suggested convoluted ways of seeing her at Belton or Belvoir, at hunts at nearby Harlaxton. Having lunched with the Rutlands at Belvoir Castle, he tried to get himself invited back; although the Granbys lived there too, the invitation should come from the duchess. He sent Violet an 'audacious' request to sleep at Belvoir after he spoke at Woolsthorpe, which would save him the 10 miles back home to Belton. 'I could let it be known that I was going to ask the Duke to take the chair, tho' of course he won't, & then perhaps the Duchess would ask me: don't think me too rude or bold, only very, very …', he trailed off tantalisingly. He had also made a suggestion to Adelaide Brownlow, 'in a way that she might believe she's thought of it herself, to invite Lady Granby to Belton … If she hasn't, I shall hate her and never come back to please her'.[4]

But his hopes of seeing Violet at Belton were dashed, thanks to Adelaide's change of plans. 'There are two things, my friend,' he lamented to Violet, 'that God himself cannot recapture: time and opportunity. Hours that might have been spent one way in full happiness and were not, & occasions whose skirts weren't caught and held tightly as she passed'.

Violet's letters have not come to light, but it is clear she wrote less often than Harry wanted. He considered letters a poor substitute with their limitations. 'Pen and ink are not flesh & blood … I can't write what I want to and I'm afraid you'll grow to regard my envelopes as I do political posters.' Concerned that she was battling with herself, he urged her to 'retract nothing … Mad moments are the only ones I've never regretted at all: sanity is so endlessly common & commonplace.'[5] He still hoped she could arrange for him to stay at Belvoir, 'I want to see you: my god, how I want to see you.'

Harry was a tangle of contradictions. Politics were important to him, and yet, during one successful speech, 'I kept thinking all the time where I might have been but for the infernal "career" one's supposed to want to make'. His diverse talents meant he could have done many things, but the expectations of his class and upbringing were that he should choose a specific path. Despite his assured persona, he told Violet he loathed public speaking, yet he was very good at it and was pleased, even surprised, when his audience laughed at a quip or praised him.

For a young man noted not only for his libido but for his intellect, for his confidence and his company, the shards of doubt, even depression, that pierced the paper on which he threw his thoughts were surprising, the lows where others might have found highs resembling self-pity. Perhaps it was weariness of the endless meetings and speeches that made him talk of life being 'dull and damned' when he wanted to taste again 'the angel's fellowship'. Maybe, too, it was lover's anguish, for Violet had broken his resolve 'into so many thousand little bits as I never thought it could be shattered: I'm not now sure if I like it, but the fact again remains'.[6]

Quite what his 'resolve' was is unclear – perhaps to stop getting involved with married women or at least not more than one at a time – but he was not happy when she spoke of her own doubts. How his heart had bloomed on seeing her letter, then shrivelled when he saw it 'contained indications and bad threats of a "resolve" too … you know one's only alive once and I hate waste worse than the devil'.[7]

He hoped he would see her at a hunt the next day and apologised for 'being an ass' the previous week, but the 'visions and electric memories it wakes won't let go of me'.[8] In case she could not make the hunt, he drew a plan of where they could meet, at the edge of a park.

Meanwhile, he was writing poetry in German. He felt he could have been a great poet if he had been German, for it was 'such a handsome language for rhyming in but my nationality has made me strictly commonplace', and Harry loathed ordinariness.

Sometimes there was no chance of seeing Violet because he had to be in London; at others, his frustration was worsened by being near Belvoir as he travelled around the county, and he railed against the stupidity of being alone. Violet sent him a telegram telling him she was ill (although he did not believe her), which he read at the Belvoir Inn 'not 400 yards from where you my influenzic sweet were lying in all your whitest fragrantest loveliness'. He was unrepentant, 'My friend, I regret nothing and would change still less.'[9]

In February 1890, Lawrance's appointment as a high court judge was confirmed and he resigned as Stamford's MP, triggering a by-election for March. Harry's opponent, the Liberal candidate Arthur Priestley, was equally young and lacking in political experience. Harry's days got busier still, with ten meetings in three days, which continued for another week, and he suffered from headaches. His heavy smoking would not have helped, but his condition was never far away.

Although the campaign seemed to be going well, Lawrance had been 'a far stronger candidate than I & his opponent equally weaker than mine, so there's a levelling down & up each way', he told Violet. At Belton, the buzz of electoral preparation was palpable, with 'an amazing insurgence in the house of MPs, agents & helpers, all strange to one another & to us … Please send me a little line.'[10]

As election week began, Violet attended a meeting called in support of his candidature and chaired by her husband. Among the half a dozen supporters sharing the platform with Harry and the Granbys was Nina. No doubt Violet chatted to her friend as always, trying not to give anything away. Harry's sister, Barley, came to Belton to support him and he urged Violet to visit her while he was away at meetings. His previous day had started at 8.30 a.m. and finished at 2 a.m. the following day, with another five meetings that night, and yet 'triumph ain't a bit certain … you help me more than you think'.[11]

If Harry was not confident about success, Balfour was. He told Mary Elcho that his political friends were talking of nothing but the recent St Pancras by-election in London, which the Conservatives had lost 'but not discreditably … and of the Lincolnshire election, which will I suppose end in sending us our Harry Cust (with a greatly reduced majority) to add a psychological charm to the H of Commons'.[12] Balfour's prediction of Harry's limited victory was a pragmatic one, based on the increasing popularity of the Liberal Party.

On 8 March, election day, Harry's sisters, Lucy Storrs and Violet Cust, loyally accompanied him to the polling station at Bourne, near Stamford. With nearly 52 per cent of the votes, he beat Priestley in a result that proved Balfour right and aroused national interest. While his small majority caused the Liberals to crow that it did not bode well for the Conservatives in a general election, Harry was pleased because it reversed the St Pancras result.

His success was celebrated with great fanfare – literally – as a brass band led a procession that carried their new MP around the town. Thanking his voters, Harry told them, 'I have made one friend at least during the last fortnight and that is Mr Priestley, and I do not think that in the course of the contest any man in the division has gained an enemy or lost a friend.'[13]

Harry and Priestley dined together at the Angel Hotel at Grantham, causing the press to congratulate them on:

> … that significant little act of mutual good fellowship. If Parliamentary candidates – on both sides – would learn to accept victory or defeat in a similar spirit, public life would be all the better for it. An occasional dinner at the Angel – the Angel of Concord – would do much to improve the tone of contemporary controversy.[14]

In maintaining a civilised relationship with his political opponent, Harry was putting into practice the spirit of the Souls.

On Monday morning, 10 March, 27-year-old Harry entered the House of Commons, as had his forebears, and was formally introduced as the new member for Stamford. Taking his seat proudly, if a little nervously, he listened to the questions being put to ministers and sat through a lengthy debate, during which one MP spoke for nearly three hours. Harry knew that eventually he would have to give his maiden speech, the idea of which he did not relish, but the important thing was that his political career had begun.

Continuing to divide his time between London and Lincolnshire, he found himself apologising to Violet for getting his timings wrong, more out of stupidity, he said, than naughtiness. Now he was MP, his time was seldom his own. In April, he was lauded for contributing to and organising with the Brownlows a feast for the hungry families of ironworkers at Spittlegate who had ended a seven-week strike. With help from Harry's agent and local people, they fed over 2,000, many of them children, with food bought from local businesses who had suffered financially during the strike. It was done, said Harry, 'to show good feeling after the settlement & to remove the popular reproach that though I'd tried to mediate, I had subscribed nothing'.[15]

While the Welby-Gregorys were pleased for Harry's success, Nina was not around in the aftermath, having gone abroad to a place her mother referred to as the 'Enchanted City'. In a letter that made clear the reliance she placed on her daughter, Lady Welby told her that although she longed to hear her news, she could not envy her travels, because:

> … all my energy has to run at present in this one channel of my message to the world … For my own child, it is clear that a message there is which you must help in delivering … The living truth itself is now becoming accessible to us in a way never before possible [referring to her work in significs].

Academics were praising her papers and lectures, and she was delighted that the eminent biologist and sociologist Professor Geddes wanted her to write a book, but she felt her energy failing. 'I no longer have the strength to carry out a great work. For I can't, darling. I have realised lately ... how inevitably this wave of mental energy must decline before long.'[16] Yet, while she may have been physically weak, her mental energy would continue and, with Nina's help, her reputation flourish.

Meanwhile, Harry was regretting he could not always see Violet between engagements, even in London where she had a residence in Bruton Street. While his constituents in rural Lincolnshire looked to him for support on agricultural issues, Harry also kept his eye firmly on Britain's position on the world stage. He was particularly concerned about defence, which was threatened by a call for lower expenditure. '*Si vis pacem, parva bellum*,' he told his supporters ('If you wish for peace, prepare for war'). Whenever possible, he cultivated his contacts with foreign representatives and others in positions of influence.

In May, he attended a reception for the Austrian Ambassador, Count Franz Deym, an occasion with a potent combination of the Ambassadors of France, Germany and Russia, a smattering of European royalty and a complement of British Army generals. The evening was made lighter by the presence of beautiful and interesting women and opportunities for gossip. The Leinsters were there, Hermione keeping up public appearances with the duke in between lovers' meetings with Hugo, while Harry's eye was bound to be drawn to her elder sister, Lady Helen Duncombe, another great beauty, who would shortly marry diplomat Sir Edgar Vincent; together the couple would entertain the Souls at their house, Esher Place.

For Harry, the evening was perfected by the presence of Violet, there without the marquis, who was obliged to attend Lady Salisbury's reception at the same time. By late May, though, Harry was becoming concerned that he had not heard from her. 'Won't you please send me one short line to tell me how & where you are and why you are so very sternly silent. It's deadly enough here [at Belton] to make one want much comfort and I get just none at all. Please make a small subscription.' He was fulfilling a 'daily function' and making speeches twice a day, 'till body and soul are sickened & I feel that if politics were certain to produce a quick millennium, the end wouldn't justify the means. No reading done & no pleasure, no party and no playmates.'[17]

But Violet had been busy too, with invitations to her and the marquis that were impossible to refuse, such as a luncheon party for the queen on her visit to Waddesdon Manor, home of Baron Ferdinand de Rothschild, a friend of the Souls. George Wyndham and Sibell were there, too, and the Brownlows. Violet was also a sponsor, together with the queen, at the christening of the daughter of their friends, the Duke and Duchess of Portland, having facilitated their marriage. Harry referred to them as the 'Welbecks' after their home, Welbeck Abbey, and had dined with them recently at Belton.

Opportunity seemed to escape them. Harry hoped Violet would be going to Ettie Grenfell's Saturday to Monday party at Taplow Court 'and shall you speak to me there?' He was restless, 'The laburnums are squandering their gold and the hawthorn are like moonlit ivory and the hedges are drifted snow & the chestnuts foaming over and it's very very dull. I'm off to Bourne to speak speak speak – I shake hot hands and never finish.'[18]

Still Violet remained 'fatally silent'. Harry found himself with free time and thought of going to London but 'had no certain motive', and now had a garden party to attend. Could he come to lunch with her on Saturday? They need not go to Taplow until the evening, although, 'I think not by the same train'. He was hurt. He could not remember anything as 'sterile' as her last note to him, which was just 'anonymous interrogation'. As excitement, he said, he would read Elizabethan plays to Adelaide Brownlow's sister, Lady Lothian, at Belton. 'Their impropriety is almost epileptic and I watch the results with interest.'[19]

Violet did go to Taplow, but she and Harry would have to be careful. Ettie was still at the stage of treating admirers such as Hugo in the courtly manner of the unattainable woman, as was the Souls' way, and would not knowingly facilitate adulterous liaisons under her roof.

In July, a potential situation arose that would make their meetings easier. The marquis was considering taking a lease on Harry's Bedfordshire estate, Cockayne Hatley, to use as a country residence. The house was lying empty for much of the time because Harry was elsewhere, all of his sisters except Violet were married and his brother was in the army.

Without a salaried job, money was tight – MPs would remain unpaid until the Parliament Act of 1911, which enabled ordinary men without an independent income to enter politics. The estate was a financial burden, not only the maintenance of the house but Harry's responsibilities as lord of the manor. Even the upkeep of the village school, small as it was, fell to him, and while he benefitted from tenants' rents, his duties to them were considerable. Periodically, he had been selling off his trees for timber, partly for land management and partly to fill the coffers, but it was a temporary solution.

The idea of the Granbys leasing the house may have been discussed a few weeks earlier at the Brownlows' soirée at Carlton Terrace, given for the Prince and Princess of Wales. A large reception was preceded by a smaller dinner at which the select guests included the ducal Portlands and Pembrokes, Hermione Leinster, without the duke but with her sister Lady Helen, the Grenfells, the Granbys, Harry and Nina. While the Souls among them may have preferred less formality, talking to whomever they wished about whatever they wanted, such occasions demanded formal etiquette. Harry would be desperate to talk to Violet, and Nina would be longing to catch up with Harry, but they would have to wait.

Clearly progress was made, for shortly afterwards Harry wrote anxiously to Violet:

> I've been very nervous all day thinking of the results of your visit to Hatley and how it seemed to you: it would be very pleasant thinking if you were settled there ... May I come tomorrow to hear the outcome directly after lunch before 3.30. You must put it off if it's inconvenient but later I think I must be at the House, as Ireland is roused and the air electric.[20]

They had the chance to meet in the company of other Souls in July when Curzon, who had returned from his Persian expedition and was writing a book, *Persia and the Persian Question*, held another dinner at the Bachelor's Club for forty-nine Souls and associated friends. This time, the guests presented their host with a handsomely bound book of photographs of themselves, prefaced with an amusing inscription in Latin. The evening, which became increasingly lively, continued at the Tennant parents' house in Grosvenor Square, where 'people were dancing or thought-reading or making music as it pleased them'.[21] The next morning, Harry stumbled into the Brownlows' house to find Adelaide hosting guests after dancing through Covent Garden in the early hours.

Overnight, the Souls achieved a kind of fame, the press abuzz in extolling the qualities of the 'select circle known as the Souls'. 'This highest and most aristocratic cult comprises only the youngest, most beautiful and most exclusive of married women in London,' said one paper, not entirely accurately.[22]

> Its high priest is Mr A.J. Balfour and its Egeria Lady Granby. Ladies Brownlow and Pembroke exercise a sort of motherly chaperonage over a society as liberal in its views as it is exclusive in its composition. Very few have been initiated into its mysteries but it receives and welcomes distinguished foreigners into its ranks.

Such hyperbole reinforced the cliquey image the friends objected to, while Violet Granby may have scoffed at her depiction as a goddess from Roman mythology who was counsellor to a king. Among their intellectual qualities was 'a limited acquaintance with Greek philosophy', although the Souls were 'not indifferent to the amusements and delights of the flesh', which, while referring to Miss Tennant's dancing, trod dangerously near to other pleasures they enjoyed.

Not everyone was in favour. Queen Victoria, who disapproved of country-house-style antics, said, 'They really should be told not to be so silly!'[23]

After seeing Violet at Curzon's dinner, Harry received a letter that upset him because 'there's so much that's not true'. She had decided not to accept an invitation, sent also to him, to Wollaton Hall in Nottinghamshire, where, he pointed out:

> … we might have walked and talked & for hours lay there among people who knew neither of us. I wish, <u>I wish</u> you would still come & I will promise to try so hard to be the person you once said you liked. Think again my friend and don't blame me if I don't see you enough in the cream of life if you throw away all the little calm places & green islands.[24]

Perhaps Violet was having second thoughts about their relationship. She cannot have fooled herself that she would be his only lover, but perhaps she feared she could not cope with that – or did not wish to. Meeting him was difficult when he and her husband were both at the House of

Commons, although when Parliament was in recess in August and the marquis went shooting, she relaxed a little and dined with Balfour at the House. He told Mary Elcho that he had never known Lady Granby more forthcoming. Violet sent Harry a letter that Balfour had written to her, in which he was mentioned positively both by Balfour, which always pleased him, and George Wyndham.

His own summer plans were fluid, but they began at Castle Menzies in Perthshire, where the Marquis of Granby had just stayed. Harry was part of a shooting party where he particularly enjoyed the company of Curzon and Lord and Lady Windsor, finding Gay 'very delicious'. She invited Harry to her family's home, St Fagans, although he declined.

Back in London, he told Violet he planned to go to Austria next, taking plenty of reading material with him – 'Mill, Stephen, Bagehot, Tocqueville' – for his soul was 'in trouble', and he thought he would try to discover 'its aims & methods & above all its ends: so I'm going to consider it philosophically & see if I can come to any conclusion'.[25]

He could not see her in Lincolnshire, for he had no reason to be there, but there was an invitation they might both accept from a mutual friend. Harry suggested she take Mrs Tree,[26] one of her theatrical friends, and he hoped to see her around 20 September. Importantly, he had heard that the marquis would take the lease on his house. 'I'm so very delighted & happy about Hatley & can hardly believe it.'

While arrangements were made to move the Granbys into Cockayne Hatley, Violet and Harry were making plans of their own on a scale more daring than before. In October, they escaped, separately, to meet in Venice, a city favoured by Europe's wealthiest, who were enticed by its elegance and its romantically melancholy aura. 'You desire to embrace it', wrote a captivated Henry James less than a decade earlier, 'to caress it, to possess it; and finally a soft sense of possession grows up and your visit becomes a perpetual love-affair'.[27]

Its romantic effect on Harry, however, seems to have been less potent. According to Violet, on their return he realised the risk they had run and thought the story would come out sooner or later, so he had written home, saying only that he had 'spent two days in the south' and that she should not mention the trip or say anything unnecessary.

Anxiously, Violet turned to Ettie Grenfell, who had also been travelling and met Harry en route. Violet told Ettie that she did not intend to tell anyone who did not ask 'anything about "my abroad"'. Violet said she had only spoken to two people about it, one of whom was Nina, and she had lied to both of them, saying her meeting with Harry was by accident. 'I only talked about it as one afternoon & that I had no idea that he was going to be there!' she told Ettie. 'Nobody knows the truth save you!'[28]

She was also worried that Hilda Brodrick, Hugo's married sister, who was known for her sharpness, might find out, 'but I hope to keep out of her vile tongue's way!' She thought Harry was particularly worried that Adelaide Brownlow might find out – and Lucy Graham Smith. For, ungallant as it was, he was still seeing Lucy.

Violet told Ettie that she was particularly cross because Margot had invited her to Glen for the first time, but Harry told her he hoped she would not be there. He did not want Violet to think him rude but 'if when he got to Edinburgh he found I was at Glen, he thought he wouldn't come … So I like an unselfish idiot have given up a visit I much looked forward to just to please him & let him see his Lucy, without prying eyes of mine!' Violet excused her absence to Margot by saying she had a cold.

Ettie was not Harry's greatest fan, finding him ingratiating, but if she had any sympathy with Violet up to that point, she lost it with her next letter when she asked Ettie to lie for them:

> I ask you not to mention that you met him travelling but only that you saw him in Venice. But you might say that you met me on your way to Venice, at a junction, me coming from Switzerland on our way to Venice, & that we travelled together. Don't you think?[30]

She followed with examples of what else Ettie might say, particularly that Harry was going on elsewhere and about to leave, which had an element of truth to it. 'I hear he was on his way to some other shooting when he went to Venice.' When Violet and Nina met later at the Belvoir Hunt on a chilly winter's day, and were among the few women riding, no doubt Violet steered their conversation towards safer subjects than the summer holidays.

Violet had made a mistake in compromising Ettie. Margot always said she would not go to her if she was guilty of anything. Ettie took the moral high ground and challenged Harry.

In a letter to Ettie written while he was spending Christmas with the Horners at Mells Park, he apologised for the delay in replying but 'even now I hardly know what to say. I believe very strongly in working out one's salvation in these things.'[31]

While it has been said the episode turned Ettie against him and Violet, it did not stop her inviting Harry to parties or asking his opinion of books or how to approach a poem, all of which he took seriously and answered elegantly and patiently across copious pages. As Margot observed, Harry was 'more faithful in friendship than in love'.[32]

Ettie may have taken a stance on their affair, but she was still allowing Hugo to pursue his obsession with her, despite her growing friendship with Mary. She and Willie were the Elchos' guests at Stanway in November with other Souls including Balfour, Harry and the de Greys. Seeing Ettie reminded Hugo of what he was missing. 'If from the excess of my bountiful affection for you,' he wrote afterwards, 'I could fill up the void in your feelings for me, we should meet on equal terms … I should like to be a great deal to you.'[33]

As Mary prepared for their Christmas at Stanway, Hugo wrote to Ettie about an event he had missed:

> I heard from Alfred [Lyttelton], through Charty from Arthur B through May that you had made an otherwise dull party delightful to them, so you see you scatter comfort wherever you go – May dragged me down here – domestic life in the country in winter is delightful if you like it long enough but for a few days it is odious & I never get beyond that stage, or stay long enough to feel its charms & the house is bitterly cold.[34]

At the same time, Hugo's affair with Hermione was continuing, he being oblivious to the emotional torment she suffered and shared with his sister. Hermione feared her love for him might affect her sons. 'Will it matter to the children?' she asked Evelyn. 'Will it make any difference? … I would cut myself in pieces to save them trouble and suffering'.[35]

At least Harry was not guilty of adultery within a marriage of his own, and Ettie's opinion of his affair with Violet did not particularly bother him. However, he did care what Adelaide Brownlow thought. He relied on her hospitality at Belton, and he worked closely with her in the

Primrose League. He knew she was fond of him (perhaps too much, as he had noted) and, if she was disappointed in him, she would no doubt convey her displeasure to the earl.

That Harry was sleeping with the wife of a political friend, who was the next Duke of Rutland and the Brownlows' neighbour, at a time when his political career was just starting, might be seen to be foolish, even distasteful. But he could not have imagined that it was not his affair with Violet but with another Soul that would cause a scandal.

Temptations

As 1891 began, so did a whirlwind of events, both political and social, which Harry, as an MP, was obliged to attend. The Grantham Hospital Ball on New Year's Day was a glamorous affair attended by local aristocracy and their friends from further afield. Dancing until 3 a.m. in the beautifully decorated Guildhall, the guests looked splendid, most of the men wearing the scarlet dress coats of their hunts, with some introducing a new fashion of adding black silk stockings and knee breeches.

Among the gorgeous and glittering women was the Countess Brownlow, in rich grey satin with a magnificent tiara and diamond necklace, but the one who commanded the most attention was Violet Granby, in 'an exquisite costume of white satin so well suited to her delicate beauty. She wore armlets of diamonds of snake pattern, which were exceedingly effective and pretty.'[1]

Nina was there too, without her parents: Lady Welby was patron this year but was absent because Sir William was ill, but Nina brought a large house party from Denton. While her appearance went unremarked in the press (titled women took priority), at another ball a week later, she was noted for her lovely outfit of white embroidered chiffon. She was always stylish, if less dramatic than Violet.

Harry's time would scarcely have been his own that evening, but perhaps he asked Nina to dance. Violet, who was there without the marquis, would have diverted his attention, at least for a short time, for they should not be seen together too much. However, there was someone else at the ball who would come to interest him even more.

Pamela, the youngest sister of George Wyndham and Mary Elcho, was there with her father, Percy. He was proud that she did 'not allow her [dancing] partners much time for talking or nonsense but kept them going'.[2]

Pamela and her mother were also part of the Brownlows' house party at Belton that week, along with Harry, his brother, Adelbert, and sister, Barley. Considered the most beautiful of the Wyndham sisters, Pamela was 19 and lived with her parents at the family home, Clouds. She had come out in 1889 but her days were still dictated by study: '9 o'clock piano scales; breakfast till 10.30 … read German with Fraulein … If wet, French or German translation … golf or riding, tea at 5.'[3]

Clever and well-read, Pamela adored literary romances and stories of her family's past. She collected folk stories and local dialect, and she had an affinity with nature, particularly birds. Her desire for attention was indulged at an early age; she loved an audience and liked singing folk ballads while accompanying herself on her guitar.

While Harry could not have failed to notice her since she had come out, opportunities to get to know her better had been limited, and in any case, his romantic life was already keeping him occupied. For the time being, at least, neither featured with any significance in the other's life.

After the ball, Harry was busy giving talks and attending meetings around his constituency, interspersed with attendances in Parliament, but he kept up with his friends as best he could. If Ettie Grenfell held a grudge against him for his Venice escapade, she was hiding it well.

In March, responding to a letter she had sent him, Harry discussed Rudyard Kipling and hoped she was not in London, because 'a great sleet storm is scattering curses & consumption through men & women & being alive is even less justifiable than ever'.[4] That month he made his maiden speech in the House of Commons. It was in support of the Small Holdings Bill, a significant piece of legislation designed to give agricultural labourers the ability to buy their own plots of land. Although he said it made him 'wet with the sweat of terror', it was widely praised, as were his skills as a speaker. 'It is curious indeed to notice how powerful is the effect of good delivery and good manner upon the House of Commons and how rare are the speakers who take the trouble to cultivate either', commented one newspaper.[5]

Given the amount of travelling involved between London and Lincolnshire, by train and by carriage, it was surprising Harry had time for much else. Opportunities to see Violet alone remained limited and he also had to fit in with her own professional engagements. While he was occupied with his speech, she was busy sketching Kipling; her drawings of Lord Salisbury and the Duchess of Portland were already on display at the Grosvenor Gallery.

Some invitations gave Harry the chance to see her with the marquis. As a guest of the Duke of Rutland in April, Harry joined them at a race meeting at Croxton Park, another of the duke's estates, along with Nina, his sister Violet and Margot Tennant.

Harry took advantage of the Easter recess to do what he loved best and joined the Pembrokes on *Black Pearl*, manned by twenty-four crew. They were spending two months in the Mediterranean and Harry travelled with them to Gibraltar, with interesting company that included Henry Kingsley, a doctor, traveller and writer, and brother of the social reformer, Charles.

At least Violet's presence at Cockayne Hatley gave Harry an excuse to visit. The Granbys' occupation carried with it an unspoken expectation that they would dispense largesse within the community, and in June, Violet was patron of two musical concerts in aid of the church choir, using her contacts to bring in some distinguished musicians who performed alongside local talent.

An event which occupied the Souls and society generally that year was the state visit in July of the Emperor and Empress of Germany. Kaiser Wilhelm II was the eldest grandchild of Queen Victoria, and London and its environs buzzed with events held in their honour. At Hatfield, Lord Salisbury gave 'such a party as you never saw', Balfour told Mary:

> Royalties in such numbers that everyone of a less exalted rank had to be billeted out in the Town. We sat down seventy-eight to dinner on Sunday; the private secretaries turned grey with anxiety as to how we were all to be seated (we were arranged at small round tables), but so far as I could learn only one German officer was mortally offended by the place assigned to him.

Balfour had 'no serious conversation' with the emperor, just 'feeble chaff about Golf', so could not form an opinion, although he thought he had great energy and self-confidence, 'while the fact that he firmly believes he has a mission from Heaven, though this will very possibly send him and his country ultimately to Hell, may in the meanwhile make him do considerable deeds on the way there'.[6]

Few could imagine what the future held. For now, *The Times* took an optimistic view of the Kaiser's reception, seeing it as 'a fresh and most important symptom of the close friendship and political intimacy of the two countries'. A German newspaper said that so many important people in the English political world greeted him that the visit might be seen as more than mere courtesy and that, in contrast with Russia, England showed a 'sincerity of intercourse that seemed to spring from the heart'.[7]

Celebrations were also held for George Curzon, whom Salisbury had appointed Under-Secretary of State for India, a step towards his ambition to be viceroy. James Rennell Rodd was there to appreciate the Souls' company: 'I was entertained at a dinner remarkable for brilliant sallies of unconventional oratory by my friends Curzon, George Wyndham, Harry Cust … The flow of wit was brilliant and unrestrained.' Wyndham was 'at his best and a very good best it was on such occasions. Cust was quick as lightning in quip and repartee', while those who knew Curzon only in an official capacity could not have imagined the 'Rabelaisian humour and inventive spirit of mischief' he was capable of.[8]

Updating Mary on the Kaiser's visit, Balfour told her about a supper party at a Rothschild's house, which had 'degenerated into a dance' which led to an invitation by the Duchess of Leinster to go and see the progress of her sculpture. Hermione had created 'a little nude nymph, about two feet high', looking down with a mixture of malice and triumph 'on a discomfited Cupid; the latter not yet modelled'. He pronounced it 'very clever and spirited, and if she has had as little training as I gather she has the work is really remarkable'.[9]

Balfour was unaware that Hermione found sculpture helped with her depression. He surely could not have known of her affair with Hugo, because to mention her in such an admiring way to Mary would have been tactless, even cruel, although he was not above being waspish. Soon, though, Mary would have greater cause to be upset about the affair.

Meanwhile, the seeds of scandal were being sown elsewhere. Oscar Wilde was enjoying fame that year after the publication of his novel

The Portrait of Dorian Gray, and he and his wife Constance were feted everywhere. In July, they were guests at two dinner parties hosted by the Brownlows at Carlton Terrace, with combinations of Souls and others. Harry attended both occasions and Nina the first. At Wilton, the Wildes were guests of the Pembrokes in a week-long house party that included Margot Tennant, who impressed Wilde sufficiently to dedicate his story, *The Star Child* to her.

Also present was the composer Sir Hubert Parry[10] with his wife Maude, the Earl of Pembroke's sister. Parry took a strong dislike to Wilde, considering him occasionally brilliant and amusing but too often fatuous and ignorant.

Balfour was introduced to Wilde by Harry and the Tennant sisters at 'an amusing dinner at Lady Charty's', reported Harry. 'The result was good and before the entrées Oscar proved very conclusively that martyrdom carried the unfailing stigma of a weak and selfish mind and character.'[11] Balfour knew what to expect when he met Wilde again at a Saturday to Monday at Wrest Park, home of Ettie's uncle and aunt, the Cowpers. With its 'delicious yew thickets, ponds, summer houses and gardens', it was 'perfect for all conversational purposes. Every taste, every "systeme" is suited', Balfour told Mary, and he imparted gossip on the guests.[12]

Curzon did not approve of the inclusion of Wilde in the Souls' circle, partly because he was not part of the landowning classes, neither was Herbert Henry Asquith, an MP and barrister whom Ettie had recently met. She invited both men and their wives to Taplow, upsetting Curzon, who saw their inclusion as heralding 'the decadence of our circle … the dissolution of the fairest and strongest band of friends ever yet allied by ties of affection'.[13] Curzon dubbed the pair, and outsiders like them, 'the Osquiths'.

Ettie was unrepentant and charmed Wilde so much that he dedicated a fairy story to her, as he had done for Margot. But Wilde had already met Lord Alfred 'Bosie' Douglas, a young poet and journalist, and they were enjoying the relationship that would seal the older man's fate.

Ettie's kindness at Taplow would not be repeated, although she must have been aware, as were most Souls, of Wilde's proclivities. The American diplomat Harry White, a fringe member, sympathising with Curzon over the author's inclusion in the group, said, 'I'm inclined to draw the line at Oscar Wilde, about whom everyone has known for years.'[14]

Although illegal, homosexuality tended to go unpunished even when transgressions were well known because the publicity would contaminate third parties and cause scandal. Reticence was the paramount principle of the public sphere; it was unfortunate that Wilde would find himself in it.

For Nina, the chance to see Harry at the Brownlows' that summer, without Violet's presence, was surely a welcome change; like others who knew them well, she must have had some inkling of their affair. In November, she found herself at Ashridge with both Granbys and Violet Cust, although Harry was absent because, at the invitation of the Italian Parliament, he was in Rome, taking part in the third Peace Congress. Two years earlier, peace activists had formed the Inter-Parliamentary Union (IPU) – the forerunner of the League of Nations – with the aim of encouraging governments to solve disputes by peaceful means, and annual conferences were held to refine the process.[15] Harry welcomed the opportunity to take part with the representatives of seventeen countries.

In December, while Violet was involved in a flurry of royal visits to Belvoir and Welbeck Abbey, Nina had another opportunity to feel as though she had Harry to herself when they were part of a house party at Ashridge with Lord Salisbury and assorted Souls. But what no one yet knew was that Violet had fallen pregnant by Harry.

By the time she opened Grantham's art exhibition in January 1892 amid 'a distinguished company … among them Mr Harry Cust MP',[16] Violet must have realised her condition. No reliable method yet existed of determining exactly how advanced the pregnancy was, so the birth date could only be estimated, and the time of conception surmised. In Violet's case, a calculation back from the actual birth date shows conception must have occurred around mid to late November 1891. Such lack of precision could be advantageous where couples were still having marital relations, for the child might be assumed to be of the marriage, but in the Granbys' case, they had already ceased; their public appearances were for formality only. The conference in Rome had concluded on 16 November, so even assuming Harry stayed until the end, he would have been home by around the 19th.

Violet had to hope the marquis would treat the child as his own. By now, her affair with Harry was known among the Souls, who might guess the child was his. Violet must have realised that, for all their sakes, if she was to continue to see her lover, it would have to be on different terms. She knew Nina loved Harry, and if they were to marry, Violet could continue to see him discreetly.

During 1892, it seems she encouraged Nina to get closer to him, to believe a future may be possible. On the face of it, Nina and Harry were well suited: they were intellectual and literary, and they were related by blood and family connections. It was a supremely selfish tactic on Violet's part and one that could have foundered. But Harry liked Nina. If she encouraged more intimacy, it would have seemed unkind to refuse her; after all, she knew he was not a saint and therein lay the poignancy. She knew him and could forgive him anything. Perhaps she could save him from himself.

Such was the secrecy of their liaison that no one would discover it for well over a year. Nina was still at home and working on her art portfolio. Sitters for portraits included her cousin Katherine, wife of (later Sir) Neville Lyttelton, Alfred's brother, who was enjoying a stellar army career while she held the fort at home. Even when people did find out, few details would emerge, although Violet's part became clearer. Wilfrid Blunt, who had met Nina, 'a quiet, dark-haired girl', more than once at Violet's house, surmised that Violet encouraged the attachment because she considered Nina to be 'of too little personal importance to interfere with her own permanent hold over [Harry]'.[17] It could not end happily.

Unusually for one so popular with women, Harry inspired deep friendship and loyalty in men, who sought his company in the drawing room and the clubroom. Although some disliked him – Alfred Lyttelton found him the most excessive person he had ever met – to many, he was 'a debonair, witty, friendly fellow whom one could not help liking'.[18]

In January 1892, the country was shocked by the death of Prince Eddy, the Duke of Clarence, at the age of just 28. Harry received a special invitation from Queen Victoria to attend his funeral at St George's Chapel, Windsor, where he was seated in the choir area, an inner sanctum reserved for the prince's personal or most distinguished friends. Of the 100 or so in that area, Harry was one of only three friends from the prince's Cambridge days.[19]

Male friendship was important to Harry. He liked the companionship it offered without the distraction of sex. In 1889, the all-male Crabbet Club had been revived by Blunt, whose Sussex home gave the club its name. Unlike the Souls, the only women in evidence were Blunt's wife, Lady Anne and daughter, Judith.

It had closed for a time while Blunt, a Home Rule supporter, was imprisoned in Ireland for chairing an anti-eviction meeting in support of Irish tenants which had been banned by the Chief Secretary Arthur Balfour. His cousin George Wyndham,[20] another Crabbet Club member, was part of the administration and effectively responsible for his incarceration – not that Blunt held any grudge against him. Blunt was an activist, campaigning against the wrongs of the British Empire, and an advocate of Egyptian nationalism. Wyndham was a politician and imperialist who was in a position to bring about change as well as speak of it. The cousins, both handsome and literary, had great affection and respect for each other, despite their differences in politics and age; Blunt was twenty years older.

Frivolity was the purpose of the club's meetings. Its motto was 'In Youth and Crabbed Age'. In 1892, Blunt asked Wyndham to bring in fresh blood. Harry joined in July and found familiar faces, including Hugo Elcho and George Curzon, and Liberal MPs Lewis 'Loulou' Harcourt and Eddy Tennant, Margot's brother. Bosie Douglas was a member too, and Oscar Wilde attended one meeting. New candidates had to be proposed by one member and opposed by another, and, unfortunately for Wilde, he had Curzon against him. He attacked Wilde in a 'brilliant, humorous, witty but deadly speech', said Bosie, 'in such a very scathing way that he never could be induced to go to another meeting of the Club'.[21]

Blunt bred Arab horses, loved entertaining and had a sense of the dramatic: he presided over meetings dressed in gorgeous silks like an Arab sheik, with an enormous turban. Every year, the club held a lawn tennis competition for a silver mug (which Bosie won in 1894, the club's last year) and a poetry competition for the post of the club's Poet Laureate. They enjoyed 'really brilliant meetings', said Blunt, 'with post-prandial oratory of the most amusing kind [which] were productive of verse of a quite high order'.[22] They swam, played tennis, occasionally naked, as Wilde witnessed – 'just as they were, stark naked, the future rulers of England, I shall never forget the scene'[23] – and took great care over their literary contributions. Wyndham composed a long, complicated poem 'in hardly more than an hour, between sets of lawn tennis'.[24]

Harry's offerings included:

O Harry Cust the golden
With youth and beauty blest,
Beneath thy contemplation
Sink heart and voice opprest

And his poem on marriage, a self-mocking view of his bachelor state, was 'so full of wit that we nearly gave him the prize'.[25]

Blunt considered Harry to be 'interesting, full of wit, of great abilities but given up, so his friends say, to the vice of women'. At least he had the grace to add, 'But it is not for me to speak', for Blunt himself was a notorious lothario whose wife accepted that his life was devoted to art, poetry and other women.

That summer of 1892 was a significant one for Harry in several ways. The erudition that impressed Blunt and many others brought about a change in his life that would give him great satisfaction. At a lunch, Harry met William Waldorf Astor, the richest man in America, who soon discovered what others knew – that Harry was 'the best talker of his day … a reader deep and wide … he knew the modern literature of many tongues'.[26]

Astor had moved to Britain with his family and had just bought the *Pall Mall Gazette*, an evening newspaper (and forerunner of the *London Evening Standard*) which had been published since 1865. Astor was so taken with Harry's conversation that he instantly offered him the editorship, even though the only experience he had had was at school as editor of the *Eton Chronicle*. Neither man knew anything about newspaper work; those who did gave the paper two years.

How wrong they would be. Their misgivings, though, were understandable. As the outgoing editor, Edward Cook, remarked, Harry would be 'attempting to do two incompatible things at once, sit in the House and edit the *Pall Mall* … Mr Cust will have to choose. If he has any journalistic instinct in him, he will not hesitate a moment as to which course to choose.'[27]

Harry would also be following in the recent steps of the *Gazette*'s great editor and social campaigner, W.T. Stead, who had shown how the press could be used to influence public opinion and government policy. In the first example of investigative journalism, Stead's exposure of child prostitution had led to the age of consent being raised from 13 to 16, and while his methods saw him briefly imprisoned, the campaign also raised the profile of the *Gazette.*

Harry had no intention of choosing between politics and paper, even though Stead also thought he should. 'It is only a question of whether you have the strength for both, and I hope I have', Harry confidently responded. 'The connection between the two is often so advantageous as to outweigh other considerations.'[28]

As its fifth editor, he had many hopes and ideas. Above all, he wanted 'to see good in both [political] parties, to maintain an independence which may criticise legislation from the point of view of "the man in the street"'. Wisely, he ran his approach past Lord Salisbury and Balfour, telling them that while adhering to the main principles of Conservatism, he would seek to retain the right of independent criticism and speak his mind even when it was adverse to them and their conduct of affairs.

Salisbury's only concern was that it would be hard both to represent Stamford and edit an evening paper, and Balfour would get annoyed when the *Gazette*'s independence meant supporting the Progressives in a critical London County Council election and hitting the Conservative Party, although he tried to stop any complaints going to Astor.

Harry also wanted to give literary matters prominence and would encourage and attract many gifted writers. Aware of his lack of experience and never too proud to admit it, he hired as his sub-editor Ernest Iwan-Müller, former editor of the *Manchester Courier*, and sought the advice of W.E. Henley, a lauded poet and editor of the *National Observer*; despite their very different backgrounds – Henley's father was a bookseller and stationer – he and Harry would become close friends.

One who witnessed Harry's debut at the *Gazette* quickly assessed his qualities: 'After three years of Cook's lymphatic handshake, it was like old times to get from Cust a grip as cordial as Stead gave.'[29] Unlike Stead, who cared little about his appearance, Harry 'was almost a dandy', whose cartoon in *Vanity Fair* was an affectionate representation. He moved into the *Gazette's* rather shabby offices in Northumberland Street off the Strand, put a notice on the door saying, 'The Editor is invisible until after twelve o'clock', and installed in the corner his beloved dog, Lo Ben, named for Lobengula, a Matabele chieftain.

Meanwhile, he also faced his first General Election in July and, in the middle of campaigning, had to deal with political muckraking. Eli Crabtree, a local Radical and uncle of his opponent, Arthur Priestley, accused Harry of refusing applications from his tenants for allotments at Cockayne Hatley and alleged other instances of estate mismanagement. On the grounds that there was no truth in the allegations – a fact supported by Harry's biggest tenant farmer, who declared him the best master anyone could hope for – Harry issued libel proceedings against Crabtree and a newspaper.

In persuading his electorate to vote for him again, he had to address questions arising from the allegations. Harry thought the Liberal Party 'must be very short of political argument [to descend] to personal abuse in order to damage an opponent'.[30] Had Crabtree taken his concerns to him, he would have been pleased to assist, but 'to spy in the backyard of a man's property to find all the possible dirt he could, and then come back home to scatter it about …', and he set out his position.

Supported by his uncle Robert Cust and Nina's brother, Charles Welby, Harry gained the sympathy of his voters. One chairman spoke of the 'noble way' in which he was fighting the contest and of the shame the Liberal Party should feel at stooping to such tactics. The importance of Harry's personal qualities and the trust they had in him was clear. That he was accompanied by his sister added to the picture, for it all showed that 'not only was he a good landlord and a good member, but also a good brother, otherwise his sister would not take any part in the political battle he was fighting'. Pamphlets shouted, 'Electors! Vote for Cust and let Truth prevail.'[31] Balfour supported Harry in his campaign and libel suit, saying the 'falsehood is hardly worth the trouble of refutation', while regretting the tactics of his opponents – their desperation was a 'happy augury of the approaching triumph of your cause and ours in the Stamford division'.[32]

Harry did win, amid extraordinary jubilation, despite his majority being less than at the by-election. The overall result saw the Conservatives (with the Liberal Unionists) win the most seats but it was insufficient to give them a majority, following a raft of social reforms proposed by Gladstone. Salisbury refused to resign but was forced to a month later upon a vote of no confidence. In his fourth term as prime minister, Gladstone formed a minority Liberal government, with the Irish Nationalists holding the balance of power.[33] Margot's friend, H.H. Asquith (Henry, as she called him), whose wife had died of typhoid less than a year earlier, was appointed Home Secretary. Balfour was now Leader of the Opposition, his party determined to resume power in the next election.

When Harry's libel case was heard the following year, it was held that the libel had contributed to his reduced majority, and he was awarded damages against both Crabtree and the newspaper involved. He could not imagine that in the not-too-distant future he would be involved in another libellous matter, on which he would seek Balfour's guidance.

While Harry's estate was the focus of controversy, it was also the place of new life. During her pregnancy, Violet enjoyed being at Cockayne Hatley. 'It is very lovely and peaceful here', she told Ettie, 'and the sun seems always to shine. You must come some day to see me & it.'[34] The country air may have helped her, but only briefly, for when George Leveson Gower saw her in London in May, he thought she was 'looking more ill than ever'.[35] On 29 August, she gave birth to Harry's daughter, Lady Diana Manners, her fifth child.

Diana would spend the first six years of her life at Harry's estate. The opening words of her memoir, written after she became on marriage Lady Diana Cooper, were, 'The celestial light shone most brightly at Cockayne Hatley'. The Marquis of Granby failed to register her birth, reportedly saying that he did not think girls counted,[36] which was unconvincing since their other daughters had been registered and their births announced in the newspapers. Perhaps it took him longer than Violet had anticipated to come to terms with the issue of paternity.

However, the marquis was named as her father at her christening, which took place on 21 October 1892 at St John the Baptist, Harry's family church where generations of Cockayne Custs had been christened. With Balfour as a godfather, she was named Diana Olivia Winifred Maud: Winifred for her godmother, the Duchess of Portland, and Maud for Mrs Beerbohm Tree.

Harry's involvement would necessarily be limited. While the raising of a lover's child by a husband meant the child retained the benefits of legitimacy, it made meaningful contact with the biological father undesirable and the continuation of the affair risky.

In the public eye, meanwhile, the Souls were elevated to a plane of higher beings. The press teasingly described Balfour as 'a fixed Sun around which the lesser luminaries revolve', who believed in 'the harmless and platonic association of men and women' whose relationships were 'purely spiritual'. No hint was given of the passions and predicaments that raged behind their civilised façade.

Lady Granby was mentioned, both as a beautiful dancer (with Margot Tennant) and for being the most delicate and artistic of all the Souls. 'That slender and ethereal figure, those dark, sad beautiful eyes, that graceful and refined mien mark at once the artist and the lady.'[37] They would not see those dark eyes, or those of her husband, reflected in her new daughter. And those who were pleased to see Lord Elcho returned as MP for Ipswich in the General Election[38] would not know that in May that year his mistress, the Duchess of Leinster, had given birth to his love child.

SUFFER THE LITTLE CHILDREN

Hermione's child by Hugo was her third son, and she named him Edward. Before his birth, at a house in Chelsea, she decided to leave Carton and move to London, telling Evelyn de Vesci, 'I love Hugo and as long as it is his happiness to keep me I cannot go back.' Evelyn had warned her friend about her brother's insincerity, but she did not listen:

> I will not change – the worst is now over – it is done. And he is already beginning to prove I did not put my faith in him in vain ... I have proof that there are great possibilities in him. And there will be a return to ours in his life. I feel it and know it.[1]

But although Hugo acknowledged the child as his, he would not join Hermione. He could not leave Mary, and he could not face the disapprobation or the inevitable scandal that would stain him and his family. Broken, Hermione blamed herself. 'I am not eloquent enough or clever enough to make him see things as I see them,' she told Evelyn. 'I only succeeded in further convincing myself of my own utter selfishness & cruelty in having made him care for me.' Her self-loathing knew no bounds, 'He has a right to feel bitter – for I made him love me.'

Whatever his feelings about Hermione and her child, her husband Gerald, as Duke of Leinster, did not wish to be involved in scandal either. Britain was still reeling from a scandal that had erupted in late 1890 and brought down the leader of the Irish Parliamentary Party, Charles Stewart Parnell. He had been cited as co-respondent in a divorce case between Captain O'Shea and his wife, Katherine – referred to by anti-Parnellites as Kitty, slang for prostitute – which exposed Parnell's affair with her and his paternity of three of her children. Parnell chose not to be represented in the case, thinking it would be disposed of quickly, and refused to step down as leader. However, the Liberal Party and the Irish clergy declared against his leadership. Gladstone said if he continued to stand, it would mean the end of relations between the Liberal and Irish parties. With Gladstone's threat to abandon support for Home Rule, the Irish Party split, with the majority of Parnell's party opposing him. He fought fiercely to regain his leadership but failed. After the divorce, he married Katherine but died four months later, in October 1891.

Parnell's fall had been riddled with lies and hypocrisies. The O'Sheas' marriage had broken down before the affair began. Katherine gave evidence that O'Shea himself was a serial adulterer and cruel to her and had exploited her association with Parnell for personal gain. But the Church was against him: the archbishops regarded him 'as a man convicted of one of the greatest offences known to religion and society', their views formally endorsed by nineteen bishops.[2] Whatever the nuances of the case, one message was clear: anything involving sex and politics that risked public exposure was potential suicide, professionally and socially, for all parties.

The fact that the Duchess of Leinster had given birth could not in itself be concealed, and it would have been foolish to try. Days after Edward's arrival on 6 May 1892, the newspapers carried the announcement that she was delivered of a son and that both were doing well. The public would infer the child was the duke's. Later that month, however, another announcement said she was 'not gaining health and strength. She is suffering from a bad cough and is causing anxiety to all her friends.'[3] It was the start of TB.

For the first few months at least, neither her cough nor her situation prevented Hermione attending social events, alone or with her sister, Lady Helen, who was worried about her mental state. As Hugo would not be sharing her life after all, Hermione knew that for the sake of all her children, she would have to return to Ireland. She gave Gerald five conditions which were necessary 'for the probability of the continuance of our life together and for the happiness of the children and the peace of their home'.[4] For a while, matters remained in abeyance, perhaps because

Gerald was busy fighting Gladstone's introduction of the Second Home Rule Bill, and Hermione became increasingly depressed.

Eventually, Helen wrote to him. '[T]he circumstances of your married life have been peculiar to the highest degree,' she said, pointing out that it would only be fair to give Hermione a similar amount of freedom as he enjoyed.[5] It would help if she did not have to spend eight months of the year at Carton. Helen hoped an agreement could be reached without any need for publicity but by 'justice and commonsense'. After all, Gerald already had two sons by Hermione, so the Fitzgerald line of inheritance was safe and to treat Edward as his own was not asking too much.

Clearly Helen's intervention had some effect, and during 1893 Hermione returned with Edward to Carton. The duke agreed that, for all legal purposes, he would be treated as his son.

When Mary learned of Hermione's pregnancy, for the first time she considered leaving Hugo, but she stayed, knowing that, despite his many faults, too much lay at stake. Besides, affection still bound them, as did their children. 'No woman, wife or mother, can be quite her own master', she would say sadly, a sentiment surely felt by many women of the time.[6]

Soon, Mary experienced greater sorrow. On 21 December, she and Hugo arrived at Clouds for Christmas. It was the first time Mary had seen the children for a month, for she had been busy with social engagements. On Boxing Day, the children and Hugo fell ill with scarlet fever but Colin, aged 3, was particularly poorly and two days later he died. Mary's sister Pamela, replying to Ettie's condolences, wrote, 'I think there must be <u>no</u> heartache like that of losing a child – for lovers' love, children's love, husband's love, are none of them so deep and high as Mother's love ... for it has more of God in it'.[7]

Colin's death was a particularly cruel blow because Hugo's son by Hermione lived. Mary's grief was made worse by guilt, for lately she had not spent much time with her son. As always, she turned to Balfour, himself no stranger to death, who urged her not to torment herself, 'And after all it is not the last farewell, the last look, the last word that <u>ever</u> matters ... What matters is the life that preceded departure; the endless trifles of which everything really important consists.'[8]

Balfour's position as Leader of the Opposition, while still demanding, relieved the pressure a little and he and Mary found themselves together more often. Everyone knew what a womaniser Hugo was, in contrast with the virtuous Balfour. Ettie, for one, could not understand why Mary never saw Balfour alone, and put it down to her prudence and courage. Mary referred to 'our position of unstable equilibrium!'[9] Despite his own womanising, Hugo wanted to know where his wife and Balfour stood. On one occasion, when all three were at the same event, Hugo interrogated Mary as to whether Balfour had ever openly expressed affection for her. It made her so nervous, she told Balfour later, that she was unable to talk to him properly all evening.

At least Mary had the social advantages conferred by marriage, however imperfect the union. In 1892, only two Souls women other than Nina remained single. At 21, Pamela Wyndham was still fairly young in marriageable terms, but Margot Tennant was 28. For all their wealth, intellect and confidence, being single was not a desirable state.

When Charty Ribblesdale gave birth to a daughter, Laura, in January, it cannot have helped that the papers talked of how Margot was the only unmarried Tennant sister and the 'constant companion of her handsome father'.[10] Now, however, she had two suitors: Hugo's brother, the artistically minded Evan Charteris, and Asquith.

While she considered them, she was happy for her friend Wilfrid Blunt to relieve her of her tiresome virginity, an event he recorded sweetly in his diary on 20 August, '[At Glen] she made me come with her to her bedroom to make love to her there … Her bed is a little one, plainly virginal.' Days later, he wrote of her 'sweet little body' and her soul which was 'unique in all the world', but realised, sadly, that she had probably slept with him 'through weariness of her virginity'.[11] Later, she would seek his advice on which man to marry.

Meanwhile, Pamela had become the object of Harry's ardent attention. A burgeoning romance is suggested by Balfour's letter to Mary in February that year: 'By the way, I do not think Mason [a friend] nearly good enough for Miss Pamela: though I admit he will make a much better husband than poor dear H.C.'.[12]

In July, shortly before Violet gave birth to Diana, and while he and Nina were getting closer, he joined Pamela and Mary at the opera. Knowing Harry as she did, Mary was concerned at his flirting with her younger sister. To ascertain his intentions, she invited him to Stanway, which he declined, and she warned their parents, who forbade the pair to see each other.

But on 15 August, Harry arrived unannounced at the Wyndhams' house in Belgrave Square, to Pamela's delight. He and her mother Madeline had a long conversation in which, as Pamela told Mary later, he explained that he had not gone to Stanway because it would give the impression 'that he wanted to make love to me (only less crudely expressed by him!)'. Instead, he asked 'to be allowed to be on the list of other men & not treated to a column by himself (all these my words, his meaning)'.[13]

Importantly, 'His whole point is that he is not in love with me except in theory, so don't let him think that we imagine him to be'. Harry's flirting at the opera was misunderstood, she explained, for his manner misleads people. 'He says, "How do you do" as if it was, "You are the Soul of my life" but he is unaware of this.' She could only get to know him properly by seeing him 'in the light of common day'. She had already tried *not* seeing him, but 'it only proved to place the whole thing at an uncomfortable tension whereas before it was calm & undisturbed & I think can return there the better for this explanation'. Pamela did not want to spoil her life by any decision she took, 'and it is my conviction that it will not be spoiled by anything he may do or say'.

Pamela's protestation that he had not been flirting, and his promise to Madeline not to do so, saw him invited to Clouds. There, he found another suitor, Arthur Paget, of whom Pamela thought more highly than any man before, 'delightfully clever, original & nice – good & kind & honest'.[14] When Harry arrived, he was 'as charming as usual & as kind & nice', but Paget's presence made him 'jealous and miserable'. Harry ended up telling her, 'in a long, quiet conversation' in the hall, everything he had not meant to say: that he loved her 'very much & very truly' and asked her whether, 'if in two years or so he could make himself able to come freely & ask me to be his wife, did I think I ever could say yes!'

For probably the first time in his life, Harry was in love, or believed he was. This time it was not with a married woman but one with whom he might have a future. Unfortunately for Nina, she and Pamela were very different people.

Pamela's excitement in telling Mary reflected her surprise at the turn of events, but she surprised herself still further by her answer. 'Oh

Mary! – what do you think I said – what do you think I felt? That I couldn't; and I felt my own voice saying it.' Pamela told Harry she feared that, in the summer, she had let him think she was prepared to do more than she actually was and that she had changed. She outlined their conversation:

> He looked very miserable and said, 'Perhaps you are right'.
>
> I said, 'But I cannot believe it – it seems so odd if you could, would you ask me to be your wife?'
>
> 'I would'.
>
> 'And if in this next year I was to marry somebody, would you mind?'
>
> 'I would mind *awfully*'
>
> & then we were quiet for a long time.

Harry got angry with himself for having broken his promise to her mother, blaming his jealousy and his feeling that to lose Pamela would be to miss 'a most perfect good'. She kept asking if he really loved her, or merely thought he did. He replied, 'I love you, & you only, & you always.' Surely, she asked Mary, not even the worst flirt would say that? And yet she still felt negative. Crucially, 'If the two stood side by side together & I must choose, I feel I should go to Mr A.P.!'

Her change of feelings puzzled her. Was it a kind of numbness, from surprise or perhaps from happiness? They seemed to have changed positions. 'He formerly (I know) was not in love with me but only wanted to be; now, after staying in the house with me, he has grown to care for the material "me" instead of the ideal of me.' She, on the other hand, still liked 'the ideal of him'.

Pamela believed he was sincere, despite his wish to wait. '[He] would like to explain & tell me the things about why he could not (as well as money matters, I imagine) but he wished to have nothing to tell me for which he would have to ask my forgiveness.' He wanted 'to get as right as he could & in the meantime no words of his were to tie me in the very *least*'. If she tired of him meanwhile, she should discard him '& marry the best man I could'. Then he added, 'I shall be *furious* if you do – but that will be nothing to you.'[15]

Unexpectedly, Harry's words made her feel 'as free as air – a reprieved being, & not a bit inclined to marry him! Perhaps I only wanted him to say all he did?' Meanwhile, they would wait to see whether his assertion was 'only the fruit of an impulsive nature never destined to ripen, or the fruit of a true part of a nature that we know is weak & may get strong'.

Pamela was undoubtedly right when she guessed his wish to wait was at least partly due to money. He was conscious of the Wyndhams' great wealth and his relatively modest inheritance, although his editorship at the *Pall Mall Gazette* was starting and its salary would help compensate for a lack of pay as MP.

There too, his political life looked promising in challenging times. On his own account, and as one of the Souls, he was often in the press. Their moniker may not have been of their making, but the *Glasgow Herald* used it to satirise the Souls in a way that emphasised their influence. It imagined a drawing by Lady Granby depicting Balfour (whose portrait she had recently drawn) 'surrounded by devotees, with Mr Harry Cust and Mr George Curzon kneeling on one side and Mr Asquith on the other, looking up adoringly into his eyes', which would help Anglo-Irish relations more than anything else.

The 'Association of Souls' was surely a force 'of moral regeneration', said the paper, seeing Curzon and Asquith 'attack each other as opposing statesmen but embrace as brother Souls and as planets that revolve around Mr Balfour'. It noted that Balfour believed 'in the Platonic and harmless association of men and women … As yet no serpent has entered this Eden.' But even Plato divided the soul into 'the rational, the irascible and the appetitive elements'. And so, it asked, 'Is it always – and entirely – afternoon tea and talk?'[16] Alas, it was not, as Balfour would discover.

The Souls developed plans to launch a literary paper of their own called *Tomorrow*, but it did not happen. It is hard to see where Harry would have found the time. In November, he began his editorship of the *Gazette*, causing the press to speculate, sometimes sneeringly, upon his appointment. His lack of journalistic experience meant he was 'a risky experiment', although 'he dances well and sings a comic song'.

He updated Nina on how things were going in London, although possibly without mentioning that he had spent Christmas in the company of Lucy Graham Smith. Understanding the social good the *Gazette* could do, he provided a 50ft Christmas tree for 4,000 children from London's East End, contributed to 'Penny Dinners', and gave '800 a day' from funds supplied by *Gazette* readers.

On New Year's Eve, he was busy with the paper's move into new premises in Charing Cross Road. 'I've no time or energy for any dash', he told Nina, 'till the new presses, premises and staff are settled. It means never less than 12 hours a day and I'm rather run down. I shall try for a week's holiday before Parliament. I've seen nobody and read nothing, merely grubbed'.

His politics were causing concern. 'I grieve that your father should grieve over my politics; but I think they're consistent with themselves, tho' not with those of either Party, and I believe other people will think more in accord with them before two years are over.'[17] Sir William Welby-Gregory toed the staunch Conservative Party line, but Harry was increasingly in favour of a new 'central' party, a point the press was picking up on, for it was becoming clear that Mr Cust MP preferred doing things his own way. Like his mother, he refused to 'sit on everybody's finger', although it would not do him any favours.

When interviewed about his first year at the *Gazette*, he cheerfully admitted that it had been 'like taking command of a ship when you don't know the ropes'. It was 'a very hard life but I hope to stick to it. I often don't get home from the House till past midnight and at 7.45 here I am at the office.'[18]

His staff liked his 'sunny, amused smile, wonderful laugh, companionable air'.[19] Sometimes he took his chief staff for weekends to a former inn called the Sussex Belle, converted into a private house run by a cook and her handyman husband. Harry enjoyed the fact that their surname was Yeoman and called them 'the Yeomanry'. He always insisted the cook came out after a meal to be complimented and the two developed an easy banter, for he 'drew out the horse-sense and rustic wit of Mrs Yeoman whose personality delighted him [and was] more than equal to every encounter'.[20] One journalist said admiringly of their new editor, 'We never knew what he might not do.'

One of Harry's strengths was sniffing out a potential story, for which he paid top money. In early 1894, he would predict the resignation of Gladstone and was abused in the press for his presumption. When, a month later, Gladstone did resign, the doubters were forced to apologise. He introduced a satirical style of headlining. When Turkey was causing problems, the story was headed 'The Voice of the Turkey'. When the possible execution of the Chinese statesman Li Hung Chang was in the news, the headline was 'Li Chang – Hung?'[21]

On the literary side, Harry published poems under a column called 'Occasional Verses' and was keen to find the best talent, both new and established. Soon, a procession of distinguished writers began to arrive in the office, in person and by post. Letters arrived by the bagful from writers and statesmen, actors and artists, sportsmen and dukes, many of whom he knew personally, full of gossip and ego, grievance and gusto.

Rudyard Kipling wanted reassurance that a poem he had submitted of thirteen stanzas would be published in full and not cut to save space. The artist James Whistler sought 'a pretty place in the paper' for a letter about the author George du Maurier, whose novel *Trilby* contained a character who was a thinly veiled and unflattering portrait of him.

George Meredith wanted help for a woman who wished to establish county council scholarships for cooks. Oscar Wilde desired to 'contradict in the most emphatic manner, the suggestion that I am the author of the *Green Carnation*', a scandalous novel whose characters were based on him and Bosie, published anonymously by someone who knew them both.[22]

Harry was also busy with the pleasurable but time-consuming task of wining and dining contacts, although such conviviality, combined with long hours in the office and in Parliament, would take their toll.

Harry welcomed women contributors including Alice Meynell, who in 1893 began a weekly column called 'Wares of Autolycus', named after the Shakespearean 'snapper-up of unconsidered trifles'.[23] It allowed her to write on whatever topics took her fancy and was intended to attract female readers with its commentary on food, fashion and women's place in English society. In one column, Meynell mused on whether platonic friendship between the sexes was possible. In another, she asked, 'Why is it that though every separate curl of a woman's fringe will bristle with indignation if she be called strong-minded or plodding, only the mildest of simulated anger ruffles her brow if she be called a flirt?'[24] and led on to her critical consideration of the nature of the heroine in novels. She also developed a strain of nature writing that emerged from her earlier work as a nature poet. She and Harry would meet for the first time in January 1894 at his Christmas tree party in the East End.

One of the writers Harry published was W.E. Henley, described by H.G. Wells as 'a magnificent torso set upon shrunken withered legs'.[25] Henley was already a noted poet[26] and critic and, as an editor himself, provided Harry with advice and friendship. 'Henley can never be repaid or forgotten', he would say. 'I came to him a perfect stranger and I found in an hour a friend for life, a master of difficulty and emergency, a wise, if somewhat strenuous, master and counsellor.'[27]

George Wyndham also knew Henley well, for he was a critic at the *National Observer* under Henley's editorship. After the General Election of 1892, Wyndham had more time for his literary pursuits because although he was returned as MP for Dover, he was no longer in office.

Wilfrid Blunt said his cousin missed 'the excitement of great affairs' and wanted 'a *grande passion*'.[28] Since giving him a son, Percy, in 1887, Sibell had preferred an increasingly sexless marriage. Wyndham may not have been to Hermione Leinster's taste, but many women found him extremely attractive. His persona alone thrilled. The Irish poet and novelist Katharine Tynan Hinkson worked under Henley at the same time as Wyndham, and although they never met, they corresponded on literary matters. For her, Wyndham 'stood for so much romance; who was half Lord Edward [Fitzgerald] and half his gracious, charming self to me … He belonged to a more romantic age.' She wrote of his 'charming personality, his gifts of imagination and poetry, his courtesy, his graciousness, his beautiful presence'.[29] Soon they corresponded on more personal matters, a relationship that lasted for years.

Wyndham's literary devotion was such that in Africa, he crossed the Limpopo with a copy of Virgil in his haversack. Bored at meetings, he translated medieval French into English. Like his sister Pamela, he sought sensation and loved the dramatic, seeing himself as 'the reincarnation of a Provencal troubadour'.[30]

Sometimes his romantic nature nearly got the better of him. In 1892, he became infatuated with Ettie Grenfell and began corresponding with her. They exchanged photographs and he sent her his poems, full of references to chivalry and ladies with fair faces. But by April 1893, he was verging on the obsessive, no doubt exacerbated by seeing her at Lady Londonderry's, even though contact was limited, as he was with Sibell and his 'Dearest Primavera', as he called Ettie, was with Willie. 'Lying awake last night I could think of nothing but the ghastly waste of life', Wyndham wrote to her from the House of Commons. 'I have tried to see you every day. I am telegraphing a humble request that you will write to me.'[31]

He started stalking Ettie at Taplow, hiding near the church to catch a glimpse of her, then engaging in near-farcical behaviour by rowing up and down past the Grenfells' jetty and involving the waterman in his connivances – all of which he shared with the object of his desires, thinking she would be charmed by his efforts.

He was mistaken. When he told her that at Margot's dinner, Lady Randolph Churchill had alluded to their 'involvement', it must have been the last straw for Ettie, who had a horror of indiscretion. Soon, she was welcoming the attention of John Baring (later Lord Revelstoke), who would remain an admirer for life. But Ettie and Wyndham would be in touch again a few months later over a matter that was set in motion in May.

That month, just as the Brownlows returned from a six-month visit to India, Harry's unmarried cousin Ernest, heir presumptive to the childless earl, died suddenly at the age of 43. The effect (of complex inheritance provisions) was to make Harry the earl's heir presumptive to all the settled estates, which included Belton, and although the earldom would become extinct, the baronetcy would survive and pass to Harry. Although the succession was a presumption rather than a certainty – if the earl had a son, he would supersede Harry – it was likely to come to pass, for the Brownlows were both 49, and Adelaide, like her sister Gity, had never managed to conceive.

Overnight, Harry's prospects changed in a way he could scarcely have imagined. Although a date could not be predicted, suddenly what had seemed impossible took on a new reality. It is highly likely that Harry's newfound status determined his next actions.

At the Brownlows' Saturday to Monday party at Ashridge in August, his mind was elsewhere, as Balfour observed. While there was much for the politicians in the group to be thinking about – after three months, debate on the Home Rule Bill was still dragging on for eight hours a day – Balfour was able to switch off and found time to write a little of his next book, *The Foundations of Belief.* For Harry, however, the presence of Violet and Nina must have served as a reminder of what, or whom, he really wanted.

Only a year had passed since he told Pamela he loved her, rather than the two he had envisaged. Nevertheless, he knew he had to take the opportunity now of talking properly to her about marriage and no longer pretend to himself or to Nina that their affair was sustainable. He intended to break it off that weekend, but in doing so, they slept together, doubtless not for the first time. The difference was that on this occasion, the ramifications would be long-lived.

Three months earlier, Harry had been at a dinner with duchesses, ambassadors and Margot Tennant, at which Wilfrid Blunt noted, he 'defended the cause of his sex and explained the lack of virtue among us'.[32] With his inimitable style, he was amusing and charming. But whatever arguments he had offered on behalf of men, it would not stop his own conduct coming under scrutiny.

After the Ashridge party, on 16 August, he went to a meeting in Lincolnshire, where he was greeted by a band playing 'See the Conquering Hero Comes'. After speaking vehemently against a government bill whose purpose was to stop the licensed sale of alcohol, which he said would be a 'stupid injustice'[33] to the working classes and publicans, he left to appreciative laughter. His arrival at Clouds around 17 August may not have elicited quite the same fanfare, at least from Pamela's parents.[34]

Pamela wrote to Mary, who was away in Sweden, to update her on the situation: 'The whole thing is like an extremely delicate weather glass or some scientific weight machine, the slightest shade of movement of importance to be registered!'[35]

After Harry's visit, she and her sister Mananai had been left to host a Saturday to Monday, at which the mostly male guests included Balfour, Asquith and Richard Haldane, all there without their 'satellites' ('We called it the Rape of the Sabine Men', said Pamela, in a gender reversal of the mass abduction in Roman mythology). Having worried that they would not be able to keep their guests intellectually satisfied, Pamela was pleased that Asquith and Haldane 'troubled themselves to get to know me', with the latter discreetly advising her on Harry and suggesting she postpone a decision. During a walk with Balfour, she hoped to talk about Harry, but could not, because Balfour was 'on a pedestal of perfection as always', so instead they returned home 'having discussed civilisation!'

Pamela could not make up her mind. 'I have moored my little boat of indecision up against an island for the moment', and she did not want any guidance for now. But she was grateful to have learnt one thing so young, 'that to look for peace & happiness in perfect entirety is a wild goose chase in this world … the chances of happiness are more equally balanced than one thinks, what may seem "wreckage" viewed one way – may not be more "wreckage" than lives outwardly perfectly matched'.

She realised marrying Harry would not be a smooth journey and wished it did not feel as if she were 'going out alone to meet an army', but another part of her said it would be better than to 'just live and be passive'. However, her response to Harry must have been more definite than her letter to Mary suggests. As Wilfrid Blunt learned later, 'All was settled for a marriage but it was not announced, apparently because they thought Lucy [Graham] Smith might make trouble in the matter. They knew nothing of Miss Welby.' But no one except Violet did know of their 'intrigue', as Blunt called it.[36]

While their arrangement may have fallen short of a formal engagement, Harry seemed to be closer to making Pamela his wife. As for the mention of Lucy, it is more likely her name came up as the lover who should be told first because no one knew about Nina. What happened next was muddled by panic, hearsay and fear of the story becoming public.

From information given to Blunt by Loulou Harcourt, some Souls became aware of a crisis while they were guests of the Duke of Norfolk at Derwent Hall (between 16–24 August), among them Curzon and Wyndham. Curzon received a series of anonymous telegrams 'apparently from a lady, saying what trouble she was in, and how unhappy, and these he very foolishly showed around, making people think it was a crisis in Lady Granby's affairs with her husband'.[37] Then a telegram came signed 'H', which Harcourt deduced was from Harry, proposing a meeting with Curzon in Sheffield (where Violet happened to be staying). Curzon hurried there and came straight back, then left the party with Wyndham without saying where they were going.

The situation eventually became clear. The woman in trouble was Nina, and she was pregnant.

Panic

Even as Blunt recorded his first entry of the furore, there was doubt: 'She had become or thought herself with child'.[1] The truth remains elusive, the situation described largely by others. When Nina heard about Pamela, wrote Blunt, she 'was very angry', for Harry had 'always refused to marry her … and after writing a number of letters to Harry which he answered with great brutality, she got Lady Granby to take up her cause … and finding herself with child they procured a medical certificate which they sent to Harry', but without result. Desperate, Nina appealed to Balfour – she knew Harry admired him and hoped he might intervene. She left it to Violet to give him the full story.

Unless Nina thought she was pregnant before the Ashridge party of 12–14 August, she could not have had realistic grounds to believe she had become so in the mere week or so between the party and the telegrams sent to Curzon. Her health was always fragile. If all that was necessary to procure a medical certificate was a late or missed period and some gynaecological detail provided by Violet, who had carried five children, then a doctor might well have been persuaded that she was pregnant.

Although Violet had hoped Nina and Harry would marry, she surely could not have wished it to happen under such scandalous circumstances. Later would come whispers that Nina had deliberately set out to ensnare society's favourite bachelor, and it is not hard to imagine her disappointment, even fury, when she discovered he wanted to marry Pamela. However, given the opprobrium she knew would fall on her as a single woman, that theory is unlikely. That the married Lady Granby had borne Harry's love child was one thing; for Nina to do so as an unmarried woman was a different matter altogether.

Yet while Nina's situation was seen by many as shameful, and at the very least regrettable, it was Harry's initial refusal to marry her that caused the biggest shockwaves. There was a reason that the letters among Balfour's papers marked, 'Re. Harry Cust' bore the note, 'Mr Balfour says burn eventually'.[2]

For the Souls, to seduce an unmarried woman outside one's class was bad enough; to do so with a lady of the same class was unforgivable. Nina must have hoped, even believed (with encouragement from Violet), that her intimacy with Harry would lead to marriage. It has often been said that she was only a recent acquaintance of his, but as they had known each other for years, it is far from the truth.

Shock and disappointment made Harry cruel, but if he continued to refuse to marry Nina, Violet feared it would lead to 'worldly disgrace' from which she had to save him. From Denton Manor, where she was comforting Nina, Violet told Balfour she had written to Adelaide Brownlow and George Curzon and had, without their knowledge, consulted Asquith too. She felt 'more fiendish than anyone can ever have felt before', and was anxious that Harry should never know her 'falsity'. Balfour's reply concerning Nina must have been gentle, for Violet told him she was 'so glad to be taking back a bit of kindness to poor Nina from you – she will grasp so eagerly at it'.[3]

Harry did not want to be forced to conform to societal expectations; neither of them should have had to. In reality, though, society was not ready to deal with unconventional, or what it considered immoral, behaviour among the unmarried. Never mind that children were born within the Souls who might never know their true fathers: the essential thing was to sort the problem out and keep it within themselves, away from the public eye and the inevitable scandal that would ensue.

The Souls were known for their cultivated sensibilities; they understood the language of love. To have Harry behaving like a cad was beneath them and, frankly, him too. No one seemed to have the full facts, and gossip flew. George Wyndham wrote melodramatically to Ettie about 'dark things' and saw himself as a crusader: 'I am fighting for truth, individual liberty of judgement, and essential verities, as against sheer & mere worldliness so ruined & corrupted by intrigue & lying that for its very rottenness it gives no purchase to an honest hand … Believe nothing that you hear.'[4] Days later, he told her that he and Lord Brownlow 'know the facts which no one else knows, except those who pervert them or not see them as they are', but he did not share them for they were 'private and confidential'.[5]

Balfour, for whom Harry had great respect, warned him of the consequences if he did not marry Nina, for they would be social outcasts, but if he did, he would ensure their marital path was made smoother. Harry's first step was giving up Pamela, at a miserable meeting on 3 October.

On 14 October, he and Nina were married in a hastily arranged ceremony at a London registry office. The following day, a brief announcement in the 'Court Circular' of *The Times* told the world they had 'recently married' and left for the Continent. For an aristocratic bride marrying for the first time, the terse notice resoundingly suggested that something was amiss. As for Harry, 'For a man so much in Society as Mr Cust', said one newspaper, 'it has excited surprise that he should have kept his wedding so much a secret that only a few of his intimate friends knew of its imminence and most folks were left to hear of it from the marriage column of the *Times*'.[6] It speculated that perhaps Rhoda Broughton's depiction of him meant he 'did not want to revive general interest in his matrimonial affairs'. If only it were that simple.

The Custs went to Paris, from where Harry told Balfour:

> I have followed your judgment and trust with all my heart it may be the right one, for it has cost a great many people a very great deal. Of course the weeks of this knowledge may have wrecked the kindly tolerance you had of me before, but I cannot think myself that my subsequent conduct has been wrong, and I shall always be grateful for your counsel & sympathy … Pamela has been a little heroine throughout, a little saint as well.[7]

George Wyndham was in the house when his sister had her last meeting with Harry and, when their mother had a breakdown as a result, arranged for Pamela to go to India to escape the fallout. She miserably clutched Harry's letters on the train.

For a while, they continued to write to each other and send gifts, until her father found out. 'In my judgement, the things seem very far indeed from over with the chains, rings, and copies of Browning's poems! I feel they are all so sunk in fatuity that no words can save them.'[8] Percy Wyndham intended to tell his daughter 'that letters from him after his marriage which would have been so harmless under ordinary circumstances ceased to be so after what has passed between them'. If Pamela gave any thought to Nina's predicament, her reaction has gone unrecorded.

Shortly after the wedding, Lady Welby thanked Balfour warmly for his 'kindness and true help in this overwhelming and bitter trouble' and regretted he had to be brought 'into this circle of wrong, shame and misery'. It was a situation that, even within a few hours of the ceremony, had 'seemed all but hopeless'. Although she had had 'a terrible interview with HC in his editor's office', one thing that gave her hope was that the only portrait on his wall was Balfour's; another was that Harry's face and voice changed when he mentioned his name.[9]

In an interesting adjunct, Lady Welby enclosed with her letter notes she had received from a woman she did not know well but who was grateful to her for helping her through a painful time. The writer told Lady Welby that, on 1 October, she had had a vivid dream about her, in which she felt Lady Welby was experiencing 'a great, unapproachable sorrow' which she could not reach, and gave her a feeling of 'entire desolation'. When she woke, she longed to comfort her. 'It was as if you were sitting in the shadow of death,' said the writer, 'and I could not understand why God should have allowed this to come upon you.'

That the woman felt, without being told, the pain she was feeling at that time, and spoke of the redeeming love of God, helped Lady Welby. She wanted to share the woman's experience with Balfour, who at that time was President of the Society for Psychical Research (SPR), set up to scientifically investigate alleged psychical phenomena. Lady Welby thought Balfour's sister, Eleanor Sidgwick, a major figure in the SPR and married to the head of Newnham College, might be interested 'with the object of doing good'.[10]

The Custs continued to Fontainebleau, from where George Leveson Gower got a letter from Harry and seemed unaware of the underlying drama. 'He does not say when he is coming back', he told Lady Wenlock, who had enjoyed Harry's company when the three were in Bayreuth, for he had made her laugh so much. 'Now that he is married, I shall never again believe in anybody remaining a bachelor.'[11] The Earl of Pembroke, who as yet was also ignorant of the background, even wrote a mischievous poem:

Nina Welby
You may well be
rash to marry
wicked Harry;
Still I trust,
if you must,
you will break him,
mold him, make him,
till the Devil wouldn't take him,
and with virtue so endow him,
that his friends will hardly know him,
and he grow for all to see,
very near as good as me.[12]

Unaware of such folly while he and Nina struggled, Harry was grateful to Balfour for being 'as just and generous and patient and pardoning a friend a peccant ass could have'. He would do all he could 'to make things & life possible' for Nina. Crucially, 'Only two people can really know the story and both our mouths are closed. From some incident or accident which I do not wholly understand, there is no longer any question of – that which you emphasised as the most determining cause of marriage.'[13] Already it seemed no child would be born.

The situation was not helped by Lady Welby, who was now telling everyone 'the facts of the case as she conceives them', from doctors to relatives, said Harry, 'and has completely alienated us from the Brownlows and others'. While Harry was reluctant to ask anything further of Balfour, he hoped he would point out to his mother-in-law that 'silence is best and that having fixed this future, she at least should if not help it, spare it'.

The fact that Harry had eventually done the right thing in marrying Nina did not mean the end of the matter. As George Curzon told Balfour, it was now necessary 'to save them from the consequences of his foolish delay', for he was facing questions from the Carlton Club and in the street about the odd marriage announcement.[14]

Curzon proposed that the story be that the affair had long been known to Harry's friends, who were not surprised he had cut 'the Gordian knot with this valiant slash', but his relatives had opposed it in the hope he might marry someone else. However, with only a few weeks holiday from Parliament and the *Gazette*, he had taken the law into his own hands and married Nina where he was free from opposition.[15] Curzon thought such an explanation would not impose on 'the innermost circle' but 'may shut the mouths of the public'. If Balfour approved of it, Curzon asked him to forward his letter to the Tennants at Glen 'to enlist their alliance'.

But the couple's families had other ideas. Nina's brother Charles gave Balfour the 'official' explanation for the suddenness, as agreed by the Brownlows and the Welby-Gregorys. There was 'an old attachment' between the pair, but Sir William disapproved of the marriage because of Harry's 'entanglements with married women' and because he had no certain income to support a wife. Lord Brownlow would not provide an income because he too was critical of Harry's conduct and was aware of Sir William's disapproval. However, as Harry currently had 'a fair income as Editor', he and Nina had 'made up their minds at last to marry at all hazards'. In her duty as a mother, Lady Welby wanted 'to ensure the wellbeing of both' and so had attended the wedding, although Sir William did not, and while he refused to make any marriage settlements, he had agreed to make Nina a suitable allowance. It was, said Charles, 'a thin veil at best'.[16]

That the couple had friends and family who, notwithstanding their own disapproval, wanted to save them from scandal and potential ruin was fortunate, yet it must have been humiliating for Harry. As one newspaper reminded its public, he was a rising star in Parliament and the 'best editor that the *Pall Mall Gazette* ever had', and yet he had to stand by as others fabricated stories on his behalf. Finding his own salvation was not an option this time.

Nina was desperate that no blame be heaped on Harry, telling Balfour she was worried that, in taking her problem to him, she had caused him to lower his opinion 'of the man I love, who is now my husband'. Harry was 'in utter misery' and 'bravely trying to redeem the past'. It was she, said Nina, who was 'unwillingly & unwittingly the cause of it all & deserving any & every punishment', yet Harry was 'now perfect in kind thoughtfulness & care … and yet all can guess how much it must cost him'. His one thought was her welfare. She wanted Balfour to encourage him back for the opening of Parliament. 'I could not live with the thought that I had ruined his career also.'[17]

A plethora of ambiguities and a rage of conflicting sentiments clouded the situation. Charles Welby told Balfour that their cousins, the Wharncliffes, were spreading a rumour about 'PW' (Pamela) and suggested he check it out before warning 'the W[yndham] family'. Lady Brownlow had said and written bad things about Nina, for which she had since apologised and forgiven her, 'which, whether really sincere or not, we know she still thinks evil – makes it more difficult to attack her on the subject', said Charles.[18]

What happened to the pregnancy has never been answered with certainty. One possibility is that it was a faulty diagnosis, resulting from Nina's panic and compounded by a doctor's misjudgement. If she suffered from a gynaecological problem, as seems likely, such as endometriosis, conception may not even have been possible without treatment. An abortion has been suggested, forced on her by Harry, but apart from such a course of action being undesirable and dangerous, it would have made the marriage unnecessary.

Alternatively, she might have suffered a miscarriage. A letter from Charles Welby to Balfour relaying news from their mother, who had gone to France, suggests this possibility. Nina had been fainting and was 'in a very low & depressed state – physically & mentally … Doctors say this illness is generally followed by a period of great mental depression – how much so with her!'[19] Welby said that Harry was now like 'Jekyll & Hyde' and had been reproaching Nina 'about his ruined life … He is evidently a man of sudden & violent moods – one hour gentle, thoughtful, almost tender, the next full of passion, disappointment & hate.' He wanted Balfour to impress on Harry the importance of being self-controlled and considerate to his sister. 'You have a better influence over him than any man,' he entreated.

But Harry was in despair, turning to Sibell Grosvenor, Wyndham's wife and Pamela's sister-in-law. He was suffocating, he said, and felt there was no one else who would understand. Although he did not want her to tell Pamela, 'I sometimes feel simply mad and murderous and have to cling close to Pamela's darling hand to help and save me as always'. Every minute he felt the presence of 'the one pure perfect love of my life, always with me, filling my heart and all my mind and all the room of all my love'.

There was one thing he did want Pamela to know. 'Except by English law I am not one bit married save to Pamela only. Not before God and still less before my legal wife: of all the ways of married men and women, of merest touch of hand or glance of eye there is not the faintest possible remotest question.' The joy of intimacy and closest friendship 'belongs of right to Pamela, and if I may not give it to her none other shall ever have it'.[20]

Such anger might be understandable if Nina had deliberately deceived him or even if she had grounds to realise she could not be pregnant, but the fact was that he had compromised her honour and the proper course was to marry her. It did not bode well.

Margot Tennant, who said she had known the story since September, considered it 'tragic'[21] and asked Balfour not to allow people to abuse Violet Granby. 'I know from herself the extent of the foolish part she has played in all this – but she is in low, <u>very</u> low water & you will be nice about her, I know.'[22]

However, it was not long before others outside their group formed a view. While the women of the Souls were noted for their aesthetic sensitivity and intellect, they were not noted for their contribution to women's rights. With no direct experience of the tribulations of ordinary women, female suffrage was not on their agenda. In this way, ironically, their beloved Balfour differed from them and from other politicians in their circle, particularly Curzon and Asquith. Balfour had an ally in his formidable sister-in-law, Lady Frances Balfour, wife of his brother, Eustace, who had begun her work for female suffrage in 1889 and was now the constitutionalists' main liaison with Parliament. As the daughter of a duke, she was one of the highest-ranking women to campaign for women's rights.[23]

While Harry and Nina were still abroad, Lady Frances attended a conference to discuss the position of women, 'much that was full of horrors. It is a painful world.'[24] Afterwards, she visited Balfour and found that 'Many things have stiffened him up against Harry, among other things I discern a sense that Harry has lied to him & consulted many other people. The Brownlows are going to receive them on their return a fortnight hence but not with cordiality!'

When Lord Salisbury heard about the fiasco, he reacted impatiently to the suggestion that Harry might lose his seat in Parliament, saying that public conduct and private morality were quite different, although as Balfour pointed out to Frances, his uncle had one code for the world and another for his family. Nevertheless, it was a view Balfour would adopt. He had 'never got over the Irish & English treatment of Parnell' in the O'Shea affair. 'How strange the world is,' Frances concluded sagely, 'and how inconsistent its judgments.'[25]

With some trepidation, the Custs arrived back in England in late November and tried to establish some kind of modus vivendi. Consequences began immediately. Lady Brownlow was furious with both of them but, it would transpire, mostly with Nina. Lord Brownlow told Harry he was not willing to support his Stamford seat in the next election: it was a tricky time politically when the Conservative–Liberal Unionist alliance was weakened by gains in the main Liberal Party. The Earl of Pembroke was no longer inclined to doggerel and instead condemned Harry as a man of dishonour. Margot thought Harry 'and his blood relations' had damaged the friends, for 'everyone has found out something against someone they have liked & trusted'.[26]

While Harry remained the main villain of the piece, Nina evoked a range of responses, most strongly from other women. That she was not having a child after all elicited sympathy in some quarters, but the main issue was that she had let herself be compromised in the first place. Alfred Lyttelton's second wife, Edith, known as 'DD', another suffrage supporter, spent time with Nina and feared that, because of the shame, she might will herself to die. 'I don't want her to,' she wrote, 'though I generally feel it to be the only solution.'[27] Betty Balfour, another of Balfour's sisters-in-law, felt tenderness: 'I think I admire her almost as much as I pity her; and her wretchedness seems to put all other sorrow in the shade'.[28]

Balfour himself was softening again. He had been a recipient of the righteous indignation of Edward Talbot, an academic and Vicar of Leeds, whose wife Lavinia was Alfred Lyttelton's sister. The couple had founded Lady Margaret Hall, the first Oxford college to admit women, at a time when many of both sexes opposed higher education for women.[29] Not only did they know Balfour and by association Harry, but Dr Talbot was also related to both Lady Welby and Lady Brownlow.

Talbot considered it was his duty, with Balfour, to consider the 'public ethics' of the situation.[30] When he heard there was no longer a pregnancy, he wondered if the Custs were 'responsible for it', which would be 'cold-blooded & selfish'. He mused on how to deal with 'such an accomplished liar … in him, & her subservience to him, and long training in deceit'.[31]

But Balfour realised he needed to do all he could for them, for it was he who had helped bring them into 'the intolerable position' they found themselves. He knew it would be disastrous if Harry lost his position at the *Gazette*, and he arranged for him to have a meeting with Astor. He also encouraged Harry to try for the seat of North Manchester; Balfour himself was MP for Manchester East. As for Nina, he intended to tell Dr Talbot that his admiration for her had never been higher. She was a woman 'who in the first instance has committed a fault – I won't say it is a great or a small fault but at any rate it is generally admitted to be a fault', but ever since had shown 'the noblest self-abnegation … the most unflinching faithfulness'. If anyone asked him for whom he had the greatest admiration, Mrs Cust or the ladies in society who were now trying to throw stones at her, he 'would unhesitatingly say the former'.

Balfour was aware of the hypocrisy. The only person who had spoken to him in the same vein as Talbot was Lady Londonderry, 'a woman who has had three lovers & one illegitimate child'.[32]

The story began seeping out of the Custs' inner circle, swept along by rumour and hearsay and facilitated by connections. Alfred Lyttelton's brother, Arthur, was a clergyman, whose wife Kathleen was a friend and supporter of Millicent Garrett Fawcett, the leading light in the suffrage movement. During 1893, Arthur and Kathleen Lyttelton moved to Eccles near Manchester, where he was appointed vicar, and in November, as the Custs returned to England, Kathleen entertained firstly Lavinia Talbot, then Fawcett. The opportunities for gossip were plentiful.

As 1894 dawned, and with it a future that looked uncertain both professionally and personally for Harry and Nina, the press reported that his association with the *Gazette* had terminated, but it was without foundation and published while he was busy with the annual Christmas party for 10,000 children. In the circumstances, it was too soon to attend the annual Grantham Hospital Ball (Harry donated the damages he won from his libel action instead), but the Custs were pleased to be invited to socialise with those who did not forsake them at a difficult time, among them the Duke and Duchess of Portland.

While Harry's emotions were still in a heightened state, he wrote the poignantly beautiful poem, '*Non Nobis*' about lost love and sacrifice.* He first published it anonymously in the *Gazette*,[33] but later it was published (and credited to him) in *The Oxford Book of English Verse*. Meanwhile, he took up Balfour's suggestion and applied for the seat of North Manchester.

In early February, at a specially convened Conservative meeting in Lincolnshire where he was observed by his new father-in-law and brother-in-law, Harry announced that, with 'great reluctance', he had decided not to offer himself again as Stamford's candidate in the next General Election, although he did not preclude the possibility of standing for a seat 'requiring less constant attention than a large county division'.[34] *The Gentlewoman* considered him 'a clever, capable man, with big opportunities of making a name in the future'.[35]

Shortly afterwards, he was enthusiastically adopted as North Manchester's candidate. The *Manchester Courier* was delighted, 'We greet Mr Cust, not alone as representing one of the most virile and honest of English journals, but also as a politician of the greatest promise. He strikes the key note of Imperialism. With such men the "Little England" doctrine recedes into its proper insignificance.' With misty-eyed flourish, it declared, 'If Troy is to be saved, these are the right hands to save her.'[36] How positive was the endorsement and yet how soon Harry would look back at it wistfully.

The *Gazette* kept him busy and helped distract him from his misery, but sometimes it overwhelmed him, as H.G. Wells discovered when he met him that spring. While seeking an entry into journalism the previous year, Wells heard that Mr Cust was making the *Gazette* 'the most brilliant of recorded papers', with more space devoted to literary matter than in any other evening paper and paid good rates. After publishing his articles, Harry gave him a reviewer's job and in 1894, invited Wells to meet him at his office. It was 'a magnificent drawing-room', Wells remembered, with at least one grand piano and a vast editor's desk, 'marvellously equipped, like a desk out of Hollywood'. As Wells walked across the room, he became aware of sobbing 'and realized that someone almost completely

---

* See Appendix 2.

hidden from me lay prostrate on a sofa indulging in paroxysms of grief'. He thought it wise to cough:

> … whereupon the sound from the sofa ceased abruptly and a tall blond man sat up, stared and then stood up, put away his pocket handkerchief and became entirely friendly and self-possessed. Whatever emotional crisis was going on had nothing to do with the business between us and was suspended.[37]

Wells was impressed by Harry's knowledge of literature and the world, and the fact that he immediately made him feel at ease. 'He combined the agreeable manners of an elder brother with those of a fellow adventurer,' he recalled. 'It wasn't at all Fleet Street to which he made me welcome but a Great Lark in journalism.' Wells was encouraged to use his scientific knowledge to write stories, and he would credit Harry and the *Gazette* with launching his career.

Kindness was a characteristic of Harry's that has been overlooked but was familiar to those who knew him well. In February, W.E. Henley's only child, Margaret, died of cerebral meningitis at the age of 5. Henley and J.M. Barrie, the author of *Peter Pan*, were good friends. Margaret called Barrie her 'friendy-wendy', which he adapted for his character, Wendy Darling. Harry was deeply moved by the pain of his friend and mentor and provided a burial place for her at Cockayne Hatley. 'We buried her in Cust's garden', Henley told a friend, '& left her piled high about with flowers … It is annoying (& delightful) to reflect upon the hold the exquisite creature had on one's hearts & minds.'[38] A friend of Henley's said that of all the people who knew and liked him, he found Harry 'the most elusive', adding that his kindnesses to Henley and his wife were 'countless'.[39]

Emotional drama was continuing elsewhere in the Souls. As the Custs returned to England, Hermione Leinster was reunited with the duke in Ireland – young Edward would be legally treated as his son. But a month later, the duke died of typhoid, aged just 42. Pained with guilt for not loving him more, Hermione sank into depression, telling Hugo's sister, Evelyn de Vesci, 'Do pray that I may become a little less ignoble and selfish … Do pray God for my little children Evelyn, that I may love them right'.[40] The eldest, Maurice, was now duke at the age of 6, the Leinster estate to be managed by trustees.

With her three sons, Hermione visited her sister, Lady Cynthia Graham, then took a cottage in Surrey to be near her art tutor, G.F. Watts. But she was 'haunted by the terror of going mad', she told Evelyn. Soon her physical health also began to cause concern. The Countess of Fingall described Hermione's beauty, with soft brown eyes, delicate retroussé nose 'and brilliant, pouting lips. It was before the days of make-up and her wonderful colour was her own. Alas! That colour told its own tragic story. It was the beauty of the consumptive.'[41] Her ill health, though, would not yet remove her from Hugo and Mary's lives.

Hugo's pursuit of Ettie, meanwhile, had been interrupted by her trip to India with her husband in 1891, and when they returned in 1892, it was the turn of Hugo's younger brother, Evan Charteris, a barrister, to fall deeply in love with her. In passionate letters, he expressed his feelings as though he were talking of his love for another woman in case someone else should read them, although he confided in Lady Wenlock, telling her that his involvement with Ettie illustrated the saying that 'the desire of man is for a woman, the desire of the woman is for the desire of the man'.[42] Somehow, Evan found the emotional energy to woo Margot too, as Asquith was doing. Earlier, she had fallen in love with Peter Flower, a good-looking, sporty man, who adored her but was a gambler with a complicated personal life.

In the summer of 1893, 'tired of love making' and seeking 'a quiet domestic life', Margot discussed her situation with Wilfrid Blunt. She sought a companion who would be sympathetic to all the things she loved, 'intellectual things & artistic things & sport too'. She was not in love with either man, she said, but each had his attractions. Asquith was more intellectual, although he had 'no artistic sense & cares nothing for the open air',[43] while Evan was less intellectual but more artistic, enjoyed the outdoor life and was a good companion whom she missed when he was not there. He was also the same age as Margot, whereas the widower Asquith was twelve years older.

Notwithstanding Evan's adoration of Ettie, Blunt advised Margot to accept him, for they were 'of the same world', and their families and friends liked each other. She ignored his advice, and in February 1894, her engagement to Asquith was announced, much to the surprise of Queen Victoria who, when Asquith asked if royal consent were needed, said that if it were, she would not give it, as she considered Miss Tennant 'most unfit for a C. Minister's wife'.[44] Later, Margot would write bitterly that she wished she had been born a man.

Blunt thought that the 'hideous scandals connected with Harry Cust' were having a constraining effect on the Souls' behaviour: 'Harry, if not virtuous himself has been the cause of virtue in others'.[45] While the Souls felt tainted by Harry's conduct, Blunt was thinking particularly of his own experience. One of his lovers was Margaret Talbot, who became frightened of the consequences if their affair were exposed and ended it. That her husband was Reginald Talbot, Adelaide Brownlow's brother, doubtless brought the Cust affair a little too close to home and compounded her anxiety.

For Harry and Nina, still coming to terms with their new situation, anxiety was just beginning.

10

Fallout

In the wake of events that followed his marriage, Harry has been dismissed as the maker of his own misfortune, attributed to a lack of self-restraint. But the seeds of social change were being sown, and double standards were inevitable while society worked itself out. He was a high-profile personality, an MP and therefore, crucially, a man, just as the campaign for women's suffrage was gathering steam.

Millicent Garrett Fawcett's meetings with Lavinia Talbot and Kathleen Lyttelton had convinced her that Harry should not be allowed to stand again for Parliament. Fawcett's antagonism stemmed from her belief that private immorality (as she interpreted it) should be incompatible with public influence for men, as it already was for women. Aged 46, she was already a tireless campaigner for women's issues, and with Lady Frances Balfour and others had formed the Liberal Women's Suffrage Society. Her late husband, the blind Henry Fawcett, had been Professor of Political Economy at Cambridge and Postmaster General in Gladstone's government, the head of the postal and telegraph system. Her elder sister, Elizabeth Garrett Anderson, was Britain's first female physician and surgeon.

Fawcett's ultimate success in helping to secure the vote for British women is a legacy for which all praise is due and is commemorated in the twenty-first century by her statue in London's Parliament Square. Nevertheless, on the road to any reform, personal conviction can lead to overzealousness, with good intentions mired in the collateral damage caused along the way.

Fawcett's campaign against Harry was based largely on hearsay. As she told Arthur Balfour, 'In November [1893] I was told in circumstantial detail a most ghastly story about Mr Cust, and I heard the main drift confirmed by the way people were talking about it in London.'[1] She considered that Harry's conduct 'struck at the root of everything that makes a home and marriage sacred, and that to place such a man in a position of public honour and responsibility would have a very bad effect, especially on all young people whose characters were still in the making'. A Liberal Unionist, and thus allied with the Conservatives on the matter of Home Rule, she also wanted to save the Conservative Party from the 'damage and discredit' that Harry's candidature might cause, as it would be accompanied by his appearing on platforms for 'promoting religious education, laying foundation stones of churches' and the like.

By the time Fawcett explained herself to Balfour, her friends and supporters were already rallying to help her prevent Harry's candidature in North Manchester. Kathleen Lyttelton was well placed to keep her ear to the ground, although initially she told Fawcett she was 'rather unwilling' to make the first move, as it would 'come badly from me as a Liberal & there are also strong personal reasons. Still, if it can be done in no other way, I will do it'.[2]

Kathleen had suggested that the Manchester Women's Liberal Unionist Society would be the best people to take up the case, but they refused, referring to politician Sir Charles Dilke, who had been forced out of Gladstone's Cabinet because of a sex scandal and yet remained an MP: they thought he might make Cust look comparatively respectable. The mention of Dilke would have struck a chord with Fawcett, for they had long been friends and correspondents until his trial, after which she ceased contact with him.

Instead, on 19 February 1894, Fawcett wrote to Leigh Maclachlan, the Liberal Unionist agent for the north-west counties. In her (inaccurate) statement, she told him that Harry had 'seduced Miss Welby, a young girl' (she was 26), who became pregnant; he 'deserted her and offered marriage to another girl, a daughter of a well-known Conservative MP'; and Miss Welby wrote him 'a despairing, imploring letter, which he spoke of or showed to other men at the country house where he was staying, with odious remarks intended to be facetious', with the result that his friends called him 'a cur'. Fawcett said the matter was made known to the family of the girl to whom Cust 'had engaged himself' and there was 'a great dispute and finally a sort of family committee' presided over by Lord Brownlow.

The result of the 'investigation' was that Cust was told if he did not marry Miss Welby at once, the whole thing would be made public. He did marry her, 'and she almost immediately after, in France, had a miscarriage. Lord Brownlow won't have Cust stand again for Lincolnshire but he is thought good enough for North Manchester'.[3]

Fawcett sent the same statement a few days later to Dr William Armstrong, Chairman of the North Manchester branch of the Liberal Unionists, admitting later that she had wrongly thought he was a Conservative.

Maclachlan retorted that Cust was already adopted as a candidate for North Manchester and it would be sufficient answer for him to say that the lady is now his wife, also, 'the bare fact of his having seduced a lady whom he later married would not I think prejudice him much in a Lancashire constituency'. Nevertheless, he thought the story was 'certainly a horrible one', and he felt a duty to tell Sir William Houldsworth MP, President of the Manchester Conservative Association, who had supported Harry's candidature.[4] Thus the campaign began, with help procured from some who knew Harry and others who did not.

Even those who had reasons not to take up the cause were condemnatory, not only towards Harry but Nina too. Mary Forster told Fawcett she could not do anything because her husband had known Harry since childhood and she and Nina's family were related. Nevertheless, she was disappointed that some seemed less concerned. 'The London people simply don't care,' she complained. 'Among "smart people" & in leading political houses he and his wife are received rather more cordially than if their record was stainless – Manchester people can hardly take such a line, one would think.' Despite their being accepted elsewhere, she would still renounce them: 'Of course, we shall not know them henceforward. It is all most painful & wretched & has made me miserable.' She shared Fawcett's view: 'It is utterly wrong that a man with a bad record like that should be whitewashed & sent to Parliament but until we have suffrage I suppose it will happen, unless the constituency can be warned & things made too hot for him on the spot.'[5]

Charles Hurst, a Manchester barrister, was one of many people contacted by Fawcett's supporter, Isabella Tod, an advocate of female suffrage and education in Ulster. While Hurst recognised Fawcett's information might be the repetition of 'an exaggerated malicious story', he was still judgemental. If the smoke-room story were true, he said (referring to the club where Nina's letter was read out), then Cust was a cur, 'who deserves to be kicked. Of course, I will not meet nor work for such a man.' Nevertheless, of all those to whom the story was disseminated, Hurst was perhaps the only one who gave any consideration to Nina's position: 'We must remember that no matter under what circumstances Mr Cust married Miss Welby, she is now his wife & any public exposure of him would be a still more painful one for her.'[6] Isabella passed Hurst's letter to Fawcett, but his concern made little impact.

Fawcett's action amounted to a whispering campaign, with no attempt at the outset to give Harry the opportunity to reply to the allegations. On 5 March, he informed Fawcett that 'a strange and vexatious rumour' had reached his ears that a letter signed by her was being circulated in Manchester 'containing very false, libellous and damaging statements about myself and others'. He seldom paid much attention to 'subterranean attacks', as he always found contempt the most effective answer. On this occasion, however, other names were being introduced, not least hers, so he felt it fair, especially 'in memory of my pleasant relations with your husband in Cambridge', to give her the chance to provide 'an early disclaimer'.[7]

It cut no ice. 'As a woman I naturally have the strongest feeling against men of known bad character being elected to the H/C,' she replied, 'and as a Unionist I have a special interest from the political point of view.'[8] She would see him if he wished, but she was not free until the following Saturday.

He tried again. His friends in Manchester had tried to obtain a copy of her letter to Armstrong but, said Harry, 'there appears to be a great unwillingness to disclose any tangible or effective evidence of the very malignant libels which you have thought it your singular duty as a woman and a Liberal Unionist to put into active circulation'. He also requested the sources of her information, because 'If you set yourself to blast a man's life, it is, let alone fairness and decency, wise and prudent to face that man and hear his defence before you pass your condemnation'.[9]

Fawcett denied she did not want to see him and said she did not make the statements 'without being convinced of their truth. Evidence as this reached me from many sources including members of almost every family directly concerned in the painful business immediately preceding your marriage.'[10] She repeated that she could see him on Saturday or any time on Monday. Harry said he had to leave London but would call on her the following Tuesday at 1 p.m. and bring a friend to witness the interview. He reiterated his request for a copy of her statements and the names of her informants.

She replied that a prerequisite of any meeting was that it be in front of a witness, but she was not in town on Tuesday, and she asked him to address any further communications to her solicitor (her brother). Still no copy of her statement or her sources was forthcoming and no meeting with Harry ever materialised. This was contrary to her brother's advice. He told her not to send her statement to others because some letters copied within it were marked 'private' and would need the parties' consent, but instead to invite Cust to her office and to send him a copy of her original statement.

Dr Armstrong said he would help her if he could but Conservative Party leaders in Manchester were saying Earl Brownlow denied that a 'committee' had been formed and would support Cust on the platform. Also, Mr Wyndham was denying any proposal had been made to his sister, and the smoking-room incident was also denied. Armstrong said the only fact admitted was that Mrs Cust was pregnant, 'but <u>they</u> say it is condoned through marriage'.[11] He asked if Fawcett could provide him with full names or come and meet their committee: Cust would be there the following week. However, Kathleen Lyttelton told Fawcett she was finding it hard to prove Cust had proposed to Miss Wyndham. Yet again, no meeting took place.

Balfour was reluctantly embroiled in discussing the situation with others. Dr Talbot said Cust's successful candidature would be 'a horrid blow to morality'[12] and, while admiring Balfour's chivalry in carrying out his promise to support Cust, nevertheless criticised him, suggesting that, having encouraged them to marry, Balfour was now protecting his back. Cust should not be standing for a new constituency, said Talbot, so 'if you see a chance of scotching the candidature, take it'.[13]

Balfour updated Mary Elcho. Harry had taken advantage of the errors of facts in Fawcett's statements, appearing before his committee in North Manchester and denying everything except the seduction. 'He promised to get Lord Brownlow's testimony and George Wyndham's support, and then put himself in their hands.' The committee believed there was nothing against him but the seduction and agreed to retain him as their candidate. They then arranged public meetings for the same night, so Harry telegraphed Wyndham and asked him to speak at the meeting without telling him about Fawcett's stance on Pamela.

When Wyndham found out, he was upset but could not see his way to withdrawing. Balfour hoped Wyndham's appearance might have the effect of 'crushing out all that part of Mrs F's attack which drags in Miss P's name: if so, he will have acted wisely'. The real question, said Balfour, was how far Fawcett was mistaken. He hoped she had 'blundered sufficiently in her particular facts to discredit her general statement: for deeply as I blame H.C. I think Mrs F's uncalled for intrusion absolutely unwarrantable'.[14]

Harry was warmly received at his first public meeting. He paid tribute to the recently retired Gladstone (replaced by Lord Rosebery) and proposed a motion of support for Unionist Party leaders and for the endorsement of Lord Salisbury's action as Leader of the House of Lords in rejecting the Home Rule Bill. The motion was seconded by Wyndham, who, if he was annoyed with Harry, showed no sign and raised cheers from the crowd. Although it was acknowledged that they had a hard battle to fight for North Manchester, they were glad to have Cust to do it.

It was Balfour's sister-in-law who put the pressure on Fawcett to produce her statement. 'I am afraid you have earned the distinction of being the best abused woman in London!' Lady Frances Balfour told her fellow suffragist. She had always feared this might happen. Cust was now seen as 'the victim of a personal persecution'.

Lord Brownlow had written him a supportive letter and Wyndham had spoken on his platform. Rumours were now circulating about the nature of Fawcett's accusations: that she had mentioned Miss Wyndham by name; that she was asserting Cust seduced his wife after proposing to Miss Wyndham; and that Brownlow had turned Cust out of his clubs. Further, the families were denying the proposal. Arthur 'disapproves of your whole proceeding', Frances said, 'but the point he thinks you have been specially wrong on is not allowing Cust to have a copy of your letter to Mr Armstrong … he thinks every person accused ought to know the terms of the accusation'.[15] She suggested that Fawcett give Balfour a copy.

Fawcett did so, telling him in her letter of 19 March that she herself had never mentioned the name of the 'second lady' referred to but admitted there had been some 'minor inaccuracies' in her original statement to the Manchester people, namely that she was not the daughter of a Conservative MP and Lord Brownlow was not one of those who investigated the facts, although she said he shared the view of other men who knew Harry, that his conduct was 'atrocious'.[16]

Fawcett stood by the rest of her assertions, referring to the 'cruel desertion' of Nina and Harry's 'overtures to another woman which coming from an honourable man would have been equivalent to an offer of marriage', saying he only yielded to marriage with Nina after having 'heaped all kinds of insult and words of hatred and loathing on the poor woman who is now his wife'.

Fawcett's position was that if, after hearing the facts, the constituents still decided Cust could suitably represent them, that was their choice, 'but the responsibility is theirs and not mine'. She said Lady Frances told her it was he, Balfour, who had really made Cust marry her and, feeling responsible for helping the marriage succeed, thought being in Parliament would help.

Balfour elegantly but forcefully attacked Fawcett's arguments. In concluding that certain alleged episodes in Cust's private life made him unfit to perform the public duties of an MP, she had felt bound to tell his would-be constituents, who normally would never have heard of them. In doing so, she had 'made public, through the length and breadth of Manchester, the unhappy story of a most unhappy woman. [Nina's] shame has become the common topic of political gossip.'[17] Errors which, after marriage:

> … are usually committed to a kindly oblivion have been turned into subjects of party controversy; and worst of all, she has once again been made to feel that she is the chief obstacle in her husband's path. Perhaps you will say she deserved it. It may be so, but she must be wicked indeed if she has deserved all she has already suffered.

Fawcett had also made others suffer undeservedly. Although she denied mentioning the name of the lady to whom Cust allegedly proposed, it was certain that her action had made it 'the subject of general conversation in political circles'. Houldsworth, the Conservative President, had told Balfour she was named in Fawcett's letter, yet she had done nothing to be 'dragged into this disgusting story' and neither had her brother, yet they were helpless to do anything.

Balfour anticipated Fawcett's view that public interests were more important than private and must override them, 'even at the cost of much individual suffering'. However, he wondered what public interests were served by dragging these private scandals before a constituency. No doubt she would say morality. Of the two charges against Cust, the first was seduction followed by marriage, which Fawcett had told Lady Frances she did not think was sufficient reason to exclude a man from public life. The second was events alleged to have taken place between the seduction and the marriage, such as showing Miss Welby's letters to men in a country house and proposing marriage to another woman. But even if that charge were true, he would still not think the facts to be of a kind to be made public property or the grounds for public attack.

Moral judgement was, after all, subjective. Such actions may be disgraceful, said Balfour, but bad as they were, they were not worse than many offences of which it is impossible, and therefore undesirable, to take public note. He gave examples of men in their private lives whose conduct was heinous but harder to see, men whose conduct to their wives, using Fawcett's words, truly 'strikes at the root of all that makes home and marriage sacred'.

Even in the 'interests of public morality', he did not think her intention could be to pry into the private lives of individuals, for she would surely feel 'the difficulty of getting to the facts' and of judging them without the kind of knowledge that no outside enquirer could ever obtain. Also, the subject of attack is 'never in a position properly to defend himself'. She would surely realise how easily 'a procedure, honestly used in the first instance to serve the interests of morality, can be perverted to serve the purpose of personal malignity or party rancour'.

Balfour believed that as the duties of an MP were public ones, the ability of a candidate to perform them should, in most cases, be the sole ground of his selection. However, he recognised that if evidence given through proper channels, such as a Court of Justice, brought to light facts which shocked 'the moral sense of the community', then of course they should not be prevented from being 'important factors in the decision of the constituencies'. That was not the case here. The facts she was claiming pertained to Cust in his private life and were not for public scrutiny. The only admitted fact was Mrs Cust's pregnancy, and he had married her.

Fawcett said her aim was 'to get Mr Cust withdrawn by his own party in London and Manchester with the least annoyance to those innocently mixed up in the story, and the least amount of discredit to the party'. She said she had limited her correspondence to Maclachlan, Armstrong (erroneously) and Frances Balfour. Only when it seemed withdrawal was not happening did she write to two friends in North Manchester engaged in 'social and religious work' and to a friend whose husband occupied 'an influential position in Manchester'.[18]

Yet she knew her supporters were disseminating the story on her behalf, sending her the names of people they would contact, from the Primrose League Committee to bishops. Kathleen Lyttelton had found several churchmen willing to take up the matter. The fall of Parnell had seen Nonconformist churchmen coin the phrase 'pugnacious righteousness', which expressed their moral attitude towards Harry. Fawcett herself encouraged F.W. Crossley, a Christian philanthropist, to talk to the Bishop of Manchester.

As for Mrs Cust, Fawcett concurred that 'her punishment is already far beyond her desserts' but disagreed that she had made her feel once more that she was an obstacle. That was the fault of Cust, who had accused Fawcett of 'blasting his life' but had done so himself. Mrs Cust's 'additional suffering' was the fault of all those who had encouraged her husband to stand for North Manchester. After all, not even her best friends would urge her to stand even in a semi-public capacity, for such a candidate 'courts public enquiry and invites criticism'. She said Harry should have stood aside from a public career for four or five years, by which time the innocent names would have been forgotten by the public. While the Wyndhams had acted honourably in difficult circumstances, Fawcett nevertheless thought the brother 'very ill-advised' to speak on Cust's behalf, for the effect was to underline a name which should have been forgotten.

Significantly, she felt the present time to be a particularly important one in such matters:

> Up to our generation the whole of the social punishment in these cases has fallen on the woman and none, or next to none, on the man. But

> now whether we like it or not, a movement is making itself felt towards equality. If we don't level up we shall have to level down.

Fawcett wanted to 'level up' severely enough to minimise:

> … the temptation to lapses of this kind. If for the last four or five generations all the H Custs of the world had been disciplined by a healthy 'coercion' of law and public opinion, the whole of this pitiable business might have been prevented and two lives at least saved from going to shipwreck.

Therein lay the crux of Fawcett's view. Men and women were not the same: each had different abilities and could bring something different to public and political life. Women, being more loving and nurturing, had higher moral standards. If Nina's conduct would have prevented her from standing for public office, then it should prevent men, too. Fawcett saw the answer in forcing men to 'level up' to women's higher standards. But this notion of the morally superior woman meant that if she fell off that pedestal, judgement would be harsh.

Despite discouragement and entreaties Fawcett persevered, even though she knew there were men in public life whose private conduct, as Balfour had said, was worse than Harry's but harder to see. She had supported the former *Gazette* editor W.T. Stead when he was imprisoned during his campaign against child prostitution and had seen his accounts of abuse by princes and prominent public men. One whose conduct was known about by some in society was Loulou Harcourt. He had served as private secretary to his father when he was Home Secretary (and would become an MP and hold other public positions), yet he was a sexual predator of children of both sexes, before and after his marriage.[19]

But it was Harry she was aware of. Marrying Nina was not enough. Fawcett wanted to show he had made her suffer, even if she suffered more in the process. She also believed Nina knew that Harry had (allegedly) said he hated her. Marrying him under those circumstances made her situation like 'legalised prostitution'.[20] Having fallen off the moral pedestal, Nina was guilty too.

Meanwhile, Harry spoke at meetings and was as well received as he had been in Stamford. But still the campaign continued. Dr Armstrong thought the moral attitude of the voters was stronger than party leaders seemed to think. With a good candidate, the Conservative–Liberal Unionist alliance might stand a fair chance in North Manchester. As Cust had been put forward by the Conservatives at a meeting to which the Unionists were not invited, Armstrong wanted to hold a meeting of local party leaders to discuss the matter. He informed Balfour that if Cust brought a libel case against Fawcett she would subpoena all those with any knowledge of the case, including Balfour.

Balfour was annoyed that Armstrong had interpreted his letter to mean that private character was of no importance in public men, telling Fawcett, 'I need not tell you that I hold no such opinion. I trust Mr Mercer will not fall into the same mistake.'[21]

The Reverend J. Edward Mercer, a Liberal Unionist, was rector of a large Manchester parish and a prominent member of the Christian Social Union (CSU). He knew the Conservatives would not turn out Cust without evidence. Lord Brownlow was denying having caused his withdrawal from Lincolnshire and sent him his good wishes and, as Cust now also had Charles Welby's support, Mercer concluded that 'the chief parties concerned have conspired to see Cust through at any cost'.[22] He asked Fawcett's permission to show her correspondence to the Purity Committee of the CSU, and in an unpleasant letter told Balfour he was bringing the matter before the Social Questions Union.

Mercer said that if the Conservative Party continued to press Cust's candidature, he would 'use every possible means, public as well as private to make the circumstances known, sparing no details or names'.[23] He knew 'for a fact' that some influential members of the Unionist Party in Manchester were 'exceedingly indignant at the way Mr Cust is being forced upon them & that they feel they are in the hands of two or three unscrupulous local politicians, who are hand in hand with the clique in London'. The conflict between local versus national politics, together with the sanctimony of the churchmen, was a toxic combination.

Balfour showed Mercer's letter to Sir William Houldsworth, the Conservative President, who passed it to Iwan-Müller. He was not only Harry's sub-editor but, as a Manchester man, had introduced him to the constituency. Houldsworth said he suspected Mercer was not acting alone and he feared that if he carried out his threat, possibly with exaggerated and fake details gathered on the way, Cust's prospects of success would be seriously damaged, which would also be bad for the division. Iwan-Müller told Balfour he was furious at 'these sole purveyors of chastity and charity' and said Harry would be happy to meet him to discuss it; he was only avoiding him 'because he is conscious that his affair must have become a weariness to you'.[24]

At the joint party meeting that Armstrong wanted, the Unionists agreed to support Cust. Armstrong told Fawcett that her original letter to him should be submitted to counsel, and if he considered it libellous, Cust should be asked either to take action against her or to retire. He asked Fawcett if she could do 'any more in the way of bringing pressure to bear upon the Conservative leaders in town'.[25]

The Reverend Arthur Lyttelton, Kathleen's husband, had a go, telling Houldsworth that although he had private reasons for not interfering, as well as being unconnected with the constituency, he wanted 'to prevent further mischief being done'. He had 'very full knowledge' of the circumstances of Cust's marriage and if his candidature continued, it would publicly expose 'many innocent or at least less guilty persons … no means should be left untried' to get him to withdraw, which would be 'a great benefit to the cause of public morality'.[26]

Houldsworth asked Lyttelton for more information, whereupon he took refuge in replying that, as his knowledge came from the confidential statements of relatives and friends, he did not feel he was justified 'in making even a quasi-public use of it'.[27] He suggested Houldsworth contact Fawcett, which might enable him 'to intervene with effect'.

Lyttelton's input was one of many examples of interference. Fawcett invited Houldsworth to lunch with her and Kathleen, who could give him the story in detail. Houldsworth offered them a tentative appointment but said he refused to interfere.

Councillor Needham, a Conservative, asked Fawcett to meet with him and Cust, although as usual when a meeting with Harry was proposed, it did not happen. Instead, she told Needham that all she wanted to do was 'to put the circumstances of Mr Cust's recent career before North Manchester … as I would imagine every political organisation would prefer a candidate with a good record of conduct & character'.[28]

At Balfour's request, Richard Haldane, a philosopher, Liberal politician and friend of Harry's, asked Fawcett for a meeting, which took place on 11 May. Haldane did his best to speak for Harry, and while he may have made matters worse in some respects, Fawcett's note of their conversation demonstrated how much about the Custs and Pamela had reached her and how unwilling she was to acknowledge evidence contrary to her view or to accept that the political parties were still willing to accept him.

Haldane spoke 'in the highest terms of Mrs Cust', noted Fawcett:

> [Mr Cust] was at all times not so much immoral as amoral – without morals, & that from about last August or some time not exactly specified he had been practically insane & might not be judged by the standards by which sane people are judged. I, of course, rejoined that this was an additional reason for his not being in Parliament.[29]

Haldane's main wish was to 'save two lives from absolute & irretrievable ruin'. Fawcett said that was laudable, but the chances would be greatly improved by Cust's retiring from his candidature and avoiding the greater publicity that would otherwise arise. Haldane asked what the 'worse things' were that she had referred to in her letter to Balfour. She replied that the connection with Miss Welby 'was not the case of a night of temptation & fall, but had lasted over a long period into years'. There was also Cust's 'insulting language etc about his wife. I did not refer to anything else I had heard about Cust's other immoralities.'

Even the Wyndhams did not escape censure. Fawcett denied believing or circulating a report that was detrimental to Miss Wyndham's reputation, although she 'considered the conduct of the Wyndhams in sending her to India & of Mr G Wyndham in speaking for Cust at Manchester extremely foolish and ill-advised in view of the probability of such reports'. Afterwards, she sent copies of her meeting with Haldane to various people, including Reverend Mercer.

As it happened, George Wyndham had just seen Wilfrid Blunt and told him that Pamela had 'quite recovered her spirits' and that it was no use being angry with Harry, who 'had not behaved as badly as was said'. In marrying Nina, he had done all he could in the circumstances, and it was unfair that people should treat him as a 'mere heartless seducer'. Wyndham blamed the Brownlows who, after approving the marriage as reparation, became indignant at the 'too general and complete forgiveness of the sinners'. Now Fawcett was raising a storm about his ears 'in the name of the nonconformist conscience; all this was unjust'.[30]

After his meeting, Haldane told Balfour he did not believe Fawcett would take any further action except with a view to moderating the zeal of her friends. He believed she realised that the chances of the Cust marriage succeeding depended on Harry being allowed to do his work in life.

It was rather an optimistic view. Kathleen Lyttelton was still stirring up the churchmen. One sent Harry an ultimatum, saying he must bring a libel case or withdraw, otherwise there would be a public meeting of the clergy. When Fawcett told Kathleen what Haldane said about Harry's mental state, Kathleen said he might well be mad because he had 'had a fall', which left him 'with what are called fainting fits', a crude reference to his condition.[31] Their mercilessness continued.

Harry Cust. (Courtesy Artemis Cooper)

South front of Ashridge House, Hertfordshire, *c.*1870s.
(Hult Ashridge Executive Business School, Ashridge House)

Emmeline ('Nina') Mary Elizabeth Welby-Gregory, Mrs Henry John Cockayne Cust (1867–1955), by the Ho John Collier (London 1850 –Hampstead 1934), Belton House. (© National Trust)

Margot and Laura Tennant. (Courtesy Lord Crathorne)

Arthur James Balfour. (Manuscripts and Archives Division, the New York Public Library Digital Collections)

ary Elcho, née Wyndham. (Courtesy the Earl of Wemyss and March)

Belton House, September 2020. (© Trevor Morecraft)

George Wyndham MP.
Look and Learn/Illustrated
Papers Collection/
Bridgeman Images)

Ettie Grenfell, later
Lady Desborough.
(Courtesy Ivo Mosley)

Violet Granby, later Duchess of Rutland. (Permission of Jason Cooper)

Hermione, Duchess of Leinster. (Courtesy the Earl of Wemyss and March)

Lucy Graham Smith, née Tennant.
(Courtesy Lord Crathorne)

amela Wyndham, watercolour
by Lucy Graham Smith.
(The Loder Collection)

George Curzon, watercolour by Lucy Graham Smith. (The Loder Collection)

Charty Ribblesdale (née Tennant) with daughters Diana and Laura Lister.
(Courtesy Lord Crathorne)

Gay Windsor-Clive (later Countess of Plymouth), from the photograph album presented by the Souls to George Curzon in 1890.

Lord and Lady Elcho (Hugo and Mary) in 1900 with children and chow chows. Back row, L–R: Ego, Hugo, Guy. Front row, L–R: Mary, Mary Elcho, Yvo (on knee), Cynthia. Chow chows: Cymru (formerly the Duchess of Leinster's), Ching, Siegfried. (Courtesy of the Earl of Wemyss and March)

The Shah of Persia at Ashridge, 1889. The Shah stands fifth from left, between Lady Brownlow a[nd] Prince Albert Victor, 'Eddy' (later Duke of Clarence), who holds a hat. Behind Lady Brownlow and the Shah is Harry Cust. The Persian Ambassador is third from left, between Lord and Lady Brownlow. (Hult Ashridge Executive Business School, Ashridge House)

11

For Love's Sake

The Custs were trying to achieve a semblance of married life in their Westminster house, St James's Lodge in Delahay Street, overlooking the lovely gardens of St James's Park, and busied themselves in work. When Harry was not at the *Gazette* or entertaining his contacts, he was usually to be found at the Carlton Club. Nina helped to host his friends, including the Henleys.

Unlike the Souls, Henley had firm ideas of what could be discussed in front of women and insisted on his wife, Anna, whom he adored but who was less intellectual, being in another room. Nina resented the fact that they had to sit separately from the men, 'making shy, irresolute attempts to talk to one another'. Anna was unconcerned, but to Nina, with her 'sensitive and cultivated intelligence, this was exasperating in the extreme', noted a friend.[1]

Nina skilfully reviewed books for the *Gazette*, although without pay as the editor's wife, and discovered that, while he welcomed female contributors, Harry had boundaries: 'My husband was strongly averse to female influence in the office.'[2] She might otherwise have welcomed a move to equality but soon found herself answering to Fawcett.

Lucy Clifford, a friend of Lady Welby's and a successful novelist with wide connections, knew Fawcett and tried to appeal to her, woman to woman. Mrs Clifford asked to meet Fawcett, for whom she had made notes 'to the good that I have remembered about Mr Cust – just to show you that after all he is not all bad'.[3] People were effectively ruining his career, 'for to dismiss him with disgrace from Manchester … will be to prevent his standing for any other place' and may lead to his dismissal from the *Gazette*.[4] 'He could not have been more severely punished if he had seduced ten women & refused to marry any one of them.'

She had many examples of recipients of Cust's kindness: the mother of Algernon Webb after his suicide; a German woman whose daughter told Nina 'what an angel' he had been to her late mother; the French family with whom he lived in Paris, whose mother 'worshipped him' for paying her son's debts and put him in the top room 'near the sky & heaven for which he was fitted!!!' There was also a well-known man in London whose identity she could not disclose, 'whom he pulled through a terrible crisis'. Nina told her how good he was when she was ill after their marriage, bringing her flowers and fruit and staying in all day to carry her up and downstairs.

Mrs Clifford also relayed what Nina had told her about the situation.[5] In late August, she thought she was pregnant, although Mrs Clifford had not suspected her intimacy with Cust. He was pressing Nina to marry him privately at a register office, but she refused, so they agreed she would go home and tell her parents not the whole truth but that she was engaged to Cust and he was coming soon to ask their consent. He would go to the Brownlows and make a similar announcement. However, he did not arrive at her home and sent telegrams making excuses, and Nina was in agonies of wretchedness. Eventually, she told her brother she was pregnant, and he immediately saw Cust with a view to making him marry her.

Meanwhile, said Mrs Clifford, Cust had told Lady Brownlow about the pregnancy and said he intended to marry Nina at once. Lady Brownlow urged Cust strongly against marrying her and said she could have the baby abroad. She also said Nina was 'an undesirable wife because she never could give birth to a child'. (Fawcett noted that 'these inconsistencies were unexplained' and then crossed that whole part out at the suggestion of Mrs Clifford, to whom she showed her notes a few days later. Perhaps Mrs Clifford was unsure if she was relaying Nina's account accurately or, alternatively, maybe she feared it might imply Nina's pregnancy was not real.)

Then, said Mrs Clifford, came Cust's visit to the Wyndhams (although no dates were given). Nina had never heard it said that Cust declared his hatred of her, 'he never spoke to her with hatred and contempt'.

Although he 'did not pretend to affection for her, he treated her with kindness and gentleness since their marriage'.

Fawcett made a note that Mrs Clifford urged her 'with tears and entreaties … to act in some way to make the Manchester people believe I had been misinformed and had overstated the case against Cust in some material point. I did not feel I could do this.' Fawcett considered that even if Cust honestly intended to marry Nina in August, 'it does not seem to me to make his conduct really better taking it as a whole'. To send Nina to her parents to announce their engagement and promise to follow, then 'make love to another girl seems so bad that it is almost incomprehensible except on the hypothesis of insanity or downright scoundrelism'.

In respect of Manchester, Fawcett was now doing nothing. 'I had told the truth as far as I knew it to four people in important political positions in Manchester and I now considered the responsibility was theirs and not mine.' But she had not told 'the truth' to only four people. A list exists which she drew up, containing the names of others she had written or spoken to, with the date and detail of what she had imparted next to each one.

In what bears similarities to her view of Nina as expressed to Haldane, Fawcett told Mrs Clifford that the version of the story currently circulating 'was to the effect that Mrs Cust was no better than a prostitute who had forced herself on HC, that his feeling of loathing for her was therefore natural, as that of a pure minded man towards one who had caused his fall'. Mrs Clifford 'of course expressed great indignation at this'. What Fawcett thought would be achieved by repeating this disparaging view of another woman can only be surmised.

Mrs Clifford said Lord Brownlow had promised to support Cust in a libel action, and she was prepared to swear that Nina told her he was willing to marry her in August. Fawcett noted that Mrs Clifford had been pleasant throughout and motivated by compassion for Nina. Fawcett, too, felt 'deeply sorry' for Nina, mainly because she was married to Cust, who said he hated her and had proved to be 'thoroughly contemptible'. She also considered they had both been wrongly advised by those who had encouraged him to stand as candidate. Fawcett did not address the dilemma that Nina and other women in such a situation faced: that if she had *not* married him in the circumstances, she would have been condemned even further.

On seeing her notes later, Mrs Clifford released Fawcett from her promise of secrecy but begged her not to mention her by name. She also thought, perhaps unwisely, that it would be better if Fawcett and Nina met face to face, and although she feared Nina might break down, 'It will convince you of her truthfulness'.[6] Fawcett did not need to act on anything Nina said; she just wanted the chance for her husband.

Fawcett agreed to see Nina but only with lawyers present. Mrs Clifford begged her to see her alone, for Nina had said 'it would be so difficult to talk of one's most sacred things to one lawyer but to two would be impossible ... besides, I could not say some things except to [Fawcett] alone'. Nina had not envisaged a formal meeting, only 'an interview given privately by one woman to another in some distress'. Nina would be attending without Cust's knowledge, so Mrs Clifford told Fawcett she had reassured her that 'out of the tender feeling one woman has for another you will keep her visit a secret'.[7] But there was little sense of sisterhood here.

Fawcett reluctantly agreed to meet Nina on 26 May but insisted her sister Agnes be present, so Mrs Clifford came too. Fawcett's reason was in case there were legal proceedings, for she 'could not, under all the circumstances, consider Mrs Cust incapable of duplicity'. She could not have been Cust's mistress for all that time 'without acquiring a considerable power of dissimulation, and probably not without telling a great many lies to conceal the truth'.[8]

In the two-hour meeting, in which she found Nina 'ill and worn', Fawcett explained she wanted to counter the 'falsehoods' that were circulating about what she, Fawcett, had said and done, and read to Nina the correspondence between Balfour and herself. Nina spoke about how willing Cust was to marry her as soon as he knew her position, saying she had never heard of his expressing reluctance. He had never had the least idea of marrying anyone else. The delay, said Nina, was only caused by his desire to win over Lady Brownlow.

Why, asked Fawcett, did he go to the Wyndhams? Nina said he had never been there between August and the date of the marriage, and repeatedly said he was 'kind and gentle' to her. How could she reconcile her statement about his never swerving from his wish to marry her, with Lady Frances's claim that Balfour had made him? Nina asked if Fawcett had heard that from Balfour's own lips. She said she had not, but he had not contradicted it in her letter, and neither had Haldane.

Nina said Lord Brownlow had not wanted Cust to stand again for Lincolnshire, although he had been very kind to them both. She wanted Cust to bring a libel claim against Fawcett, for which Brownlow had promised to pay. It was Lady Brownlow towards whom Nina felt bitterly.

Fawcett and Agnes felt they could not keep on showing Nina proof of Cust's resistance to the marriage and his insult to her because 'whatever he is, she is married to him'. Fawcett decided not to act on Nina's responses, because 'strange as it may appear, [she] still loves him; her love for him is the only thing that makes her position tolerable'. However, she felt Nina was in error, 'whether wilfully or not I cannot say', in saying he always wanted the marriage, and thought she was prepared to say or do anything to make things better for him, even enduring 'the unpleasantness of coming to see me'.

If there were inconsistencies between what Nina told Fawcett and Mrs Clifford's account, it is understandable. Truth may have fallen through the cracks of interpretation and memory, while a desire not to believe the worst of the person she loved and sought to protect was Nina's protection, too. None of it, however, should have mattered. Fawcett may have recognised true, if obsessive, love, and that should have been enough. But it was not.

The parties agreed to keep the meeting between themselves, but two days later Nina told Fawcett that she felt 'so distressed' at having kept a secret from her husband that she wanted to tell him and hoped Fawcett would not object. She also wondered if it might do some good for Fawcett to make it known in Manchester that she had seen her. They had been 'gentle and anxious to be kind' at the meeting, and Nina wanted them to know 'that what I am asking for my dear one is only justice'.[9]

Later that day, Nina decided not to tell Harry after all, unless there was likely to be a benefit, for he would 'very greatly mind'. She felt that almost every action of hers to her 'intense misery [has] been interpreted to <u>his</u> discredit. I now greatly dread lest even this should prove somehow a fresh source of abuse of him in the minds of those who hear of it.'[10]

The sisters agreed not to tell anyone of her visit. Fawcett told Nina that she had 'only' told a friend in correspondence that an unnamed lady had visited them and said Mr Cust wanted to marry Miss Welby from the start, and that in reply, 'I had mentioned the reasons which appear to me conclusive against this view to which she gave (in my opinion) no satisfactory answer'. Fawcett ended, 'I do feel very strongly that truth & courage would be best; indeed, your only guides out of this labyrinth.'[11] But the labyrinth was not of Nina's making.

Fawcett may have been gentle in the interview but, for all her private acknowledgement of Nina's love, she was not going to be moved. Not only did she believe Nina was lying but she had married a man who said he disliked her, and for that not only was he culpable, but she was too, and would have to accept the consequences. The issue had moved from Cust's fitness for public office into an intrusive appraisal of Nina's judgement in marrying the man she loved, the man to whom she had given herself, imperfect as he might be, as unpromising as their marriage might seem to outsiders.

The Custs did not attend Margot's marriage to Asquith in May that year, an occasion at which four prime ministers signed the marriage register: Gladstone represented the past, Rosebery the present, and (although it was not anticipated) Balfour and Asquith the future.[12] Violet was there, Blunt noting, 'Lady Granby older much than last year. The Cust scandal must have caused her trouble.'[13]

Elsewhere, they engaged as normally as they could, such as at the Duchess of Rutland's reception at the Grafton Galleries, where the chief guests were HRH Princess Louise and her husband, the Marquis of Lorne, an event at which they could not avoid seeing Violet.

The scandal that Harry had caused resonated in society. Mothers of unmarried daughters became more anxious than ever that their darlings should be chaperoned. When Princess Louise introduced a niece to society that year, her sister-in-law, Lady Frances Balfour, pointed out that affairs were confined to married women because 'they know the game, & can play it either way, but not so the girls'.[14]

When Fawcett's campaign showed no sign of stopping, Harry turned to Balfour. Making it clear that he was advising only because Harry asked him, and that it was in a private rather than a professional capacity, on 1 June Balfour reluctantly said he could see no way forward other than to retire from North Manchester. He advised against bringing a libel case, not because Harry could not 'expose the falsity of the stories' but because he would cause more pain to innocent persons. He would not advise Harry *not* to appear before his council to answer the charges against him, neither would he press him to withdraw if his council supported him as the 'ill-used man' that he was. However, Balfour thought Harry would find it impossible to make an effective reply to the charges other than a bare denial. Neither could Harry stop the personal attack, of which he may not be the only victim. Further, he would be unable 'to bring to the poll anything like the full strength of the Unionist party in the Division'.[15]

It was hard to see what advantages, private or public, would come from continuing a contest that had become 'hopeless from the beginning'. Balfour had conveyed to those responsible his strong disapproval of Harry's treatment, but their conduct was no longer the issue. The questions were whether continuing the struggle would make it worse in future if he canvassed another constituency; whether people would remember things that might otherwise be forgotten; and whether a serious defeat, attributed to those stories, might 'give them an authority which they would not derive from a voluntary retirement'. Harry might also be the object of resentment in Manchester if it were thought he had contributed to a party defeat. Balfour recognised Harry's position was one of 'extreme undeserved difficulty' and he was deeply aware of the embarrassment in which he was placed.

While Harry pondered, Fawcett's followers became increasingly entrenched in irrelevant details in response to attempts to make her withdraw her allegations. The Custs' friends still tried to help, sometimes eliciting contempt. Mrs Galloway, wife of another Conservative candidate, visited Kathleen Lyttelton, who told Fawcett afterwards that she was 'the supremist idiot I have ever come across'.[16] Kathleen was also in touch with Reverend Mercer's wife but was reluctant to send her Mrs Clifford's correspondence because she thought it exonerated Cust more than was just.

When, in July, Fawcett found herself at a dinner with Sir Henry Howarth MP, he said it had been 'infinitely stupid' to put Cust forward as a candidate, given that incidents in London were being talked about in Manchester. However, he had heard that the Brownlows, Mr Wyndham and Sir William Welby-Gregory were prepared to appear on Cust's platform and 'Lady Brownlow strokes Mr C's hair & says "poor Harry has been so ill used"'. He wondered if Fawcett knew she had made herself unpopular. 'I replied that I had heard so but that I didn't care in comparison with the interests involved – if women did not protest, who was to?'[17]

Harry escaped to Norway for a few weeks, the press reporting that it was for health reasons due to the combined stresses of Parliament and journalism. On 22 September 1894, the *Manchester Courier*, which just a few months earlier had heralded him as the saviour of Troy, published his letter of retirement from North Manchester. Using his health as the reason, he deeply regretted that such warm and promising relations with the men of Manchester had come to nothing. The division publicly expressed its regret at losing such an able candidate. In his copy of Goethe's poems, Harry wrote disconsolately in the margins, 'Crooked eclipses 'gainst his glory fight'.[18]

As Harry reeled, Kathleen Lyttelton wondered, sarcastically, if he intended to recover his health before the General Election in order to stand elsewhere, and hoped not, for Fawcett's sake. 'But at any rate, the battle is won here & looking at the whole thing now, I am sure that much good has been done & little if any harm.' She was aware that some people were 'very angry' with both her and Fawcett, 'but as I am sure they are wrong, I do not care'.[19]

The year 1894 was a difficult one for other Souls too. At Cockayne Hatley in September, Violet Granby suffered a tragedy when her eldest son, Lord Haddon, died suddenly at the age of 9, after an operation for an intestinal obstruction. His life had hung in the balance for several days and her desperate letters to Gay Windsor and others, asking them to pray for her, were in vain.

Violet began sculpting an effigy for the mausoleum at Belvoir Castle – a little boy lying on top of the tomb as if sleeping, wearing a loose nightshirt with a blanket around his shoulders and curls of hair falling across his face. The inscription she carved on the plinth begins, 'Hope of my eyes/ Something is broken that we/ Cannot mend'. In her grief, she would seek Harry's words of solace, for her love for him would continue, the pair bound inextricably with their daughter, Diana.

To survive their new life as a couple, when Harry resented it and Nina was desperate to make amends, required them to live separate lives where possible, although socially they often presented a united front. Nina had to accept his frequent absences, but even his limited presence was more than she had enjoyed before. Harry's salvation was work and other women.

In the early part of his marriage particularly, he seemed to flail around emotionally, incoherently. He still pursued Lucy Graham Smith, sending her a box of fine furs from Norway, which she promptly returned. He sent them to her again that Christmas, with a letter saying, 'I should love to think I had begun to enter into and to mix with all your life and that whether present or absent we were always close together in thought and interest'.[20] Again she returned them, telling him, not for the first time, that their part in each other's lives was over. 'He is married,' she told her diary. 'To write or meet would be disastrous to both. I have no temptation to do either.'

Her mother, Emma, was ill, casting a shadow over the Tennant family about which Harry wrote sweetly, wishing Lucy would let him help her. She found his words of sympathy 'tender and devoted and patient and gentle'. He was, he said, waiting for his 'gentle angel to turn and save and love and make me'. He relived the happy Christmas of 1892, a 'merry and happy occasion', while 'the dear thought of her never leaves me night or day'.[21]

Yet this difficult time with her mother had convinced Lucy 'of the madness of living for one's own indulgence. He must build up his life, good name and private happiness as bravely as he can.' She knew it was not in her power to help Harry and she felt strong enough to resist his appeals to change her course. She thought of 'his lonely, sad and discredited life and of the great change from what it was. This tears daily at my heartstrings and inflicts nightly pangs', yet she was not tempted to comfort him. This gave her confidence in her resolve, which, with the approval of her family and friends, was 'a small return for what it costs to inflict pain and be judged heartless and shallow'. With a religious strength that her sisters shared, Lucy prayed 'that God will inspire his soul to stretch forward beyond the immediate darkness, that He will increase the unconscious good that is in him and bless him with His widest and most beautiful blessings'.[22]

Harry had no desire to live a 'discredited life', and in the journalistic world he was much feted. But the rising star who had been predicted to become prime minister had to rebuild his image if he wanted to regain political power. He could still involve himself in national and global issues through the *Gazette* and his many contacts.

One of his achievements was the co-founding of the Navy League, a non-political organisation. At a time when every European country feared aggression, the Naval Defence Act 1889 had embodied the need for the Royal Navy to be kept strong to ward off rivals to Britain's world position. Defence had long been a concern of Harry's, and in late 1894 he published in the *Gazette* a series of articles by a military expert to raise the public's awareness of the importance of the sea to Britain. With the aim of maintaining awareness, the first council was formed, its members comprising Harry and Earl Brownlow, admirals and other military figures. The league would continue to maintain much influence over naval affairs. Soon Germany and other countries followed suit, forming their own national groups.

In the spring of 1895, Harry travelled to Constantinople to interview Sultan Abdul Hamid II about the atrocities in Armenia, where thousands had been massacred in response to their pushing for more rights in the Ottoman Empire. Harry's attempt was viewed with great scepticism by the journalistic world, but he managed to secure both an audience with the Sultan and permission to enter Armenia. However, the Sultan refused to let him enter Sassun, where the worst violence was said to be happening. While he did not accomplish his main goal, he was widely, if grudgingly, admired for his audacious attempt to do what no one else had.

Harry recruited brilliant journalists for the *Gazette*, who were intrepid in their investigations and sharp in their delivery, among them George Steevens, the distinguished war correspondent, whose book, *With Kitchener to Khartoum* would vividly describe the Anglo-Egyptian conquest of Sudan. With Harry's ear for a good story, the *Gazette* started publishing the dramatic adventures in Darfur of the Anglo-Austrian soldier, Slatin Pasha, which became the classic book, *Fire and Sword in the Sudan*.

But his skill lay not only in procuring great copy but in creating it. Staying with Nina's relations, the Wortleys, in Yorkshire, they were entertained by a group of local Morris dancers whose part in English folklore was barely known outside the rural areas where they lived. Harry was fascinated by them, 'miners, quarrymen, moulders; men soaked in nineteenth century democracy and free speech and thought, and all our diseases, and yet inheritors of old renown and mystery'.

Dressed in brightly patterned short jackets and long, dark trousers, their leader wearing a large rabbit-skin cap with a small rabbit's head in front, they 'danced assuredly and did strange things', wielding swords and playing hornpipes, and by the end of the evening, Harry had made note of their songs and elicited from one dancer, surprised by his interest, some detail of their craft. None of them, though, even those whose grandfathers had been Morris men, could tell him where the custom originated, and it was this sense of strangeness and history that imbued a sensitive and lyrical piece Harry wrote for the *Gazette*, evoking the beauty of the local moors, where 'in that free wild country, progress and primitiveness meet together, and science and simplicity kiss each other'.[23]

An event of heartening note came that year, 1895, with the second marriage of Harry's sister, Barley, who had been widowed young after the slow death of her husband following his head injury. Her second husband was Charles Collier, a promising surgeon and sportsman who was fifteen years her junior. Her siblings wondered what they had in common and, with characteristic Cust wit, would describe the marriage as 'the Great Colliery Disaster'.

Before the wedding, Harry stayed with Barley in Shropshire with another guest, Sir Henry Colvile, who had been a ladies' man in his youth. When Harry wished him a good morning, Sir Henry said he had risen early to welcome the dawn. Quick as a flash, Harry got to work, and when Sir Henry came into breakfast, he found lines upon his plate:

Since Venus will no longer break
Her nights for me, though I adore her,
I leave my lonely couch and make
Rheumatic love to rouged Aurora.[24]

Whatever was going on in Harry's emotional life, his wit was never extinguished.

Love blossomed elsewhere in the Souls that year. A love match was cemented in April when, after a long courtship conducted largely at long distance, George Curzon married Mary Leiter, the beautiful daughter and heiress of a wealthy American merchant.

He had met her in 1890, at the Duchess of Westminster's Ball, and was struck by her grace and social confidence despite her youth: she was 20, Curzon 31. Well-read and cultivated, she was accustomed to moving in White House circles in Washington and was becoming an accomplished political hostess. They met again at Ashridge, and when the next day she took the rather forward step of sending him a pearl from her necklace, set in a gold tie pin, Curzon realised she felt something for him.

Mary returned to Washington but visited London every summer. However, she and Curzon met very little over the next few years for he was constantly travelling – to India, Afghanistan, the Far East – so she kept his interest alive with letters. She had other suitors but rejected them for Curzon.

At last, at a brief meeting in 1893, she told him she had waited for him. He told her he had always felt they were meant for each other but had dared not commit, for he did not think the work he had to do would make a wife happy. That night, they became secretly engaged on the basis that he would be free to complete his tasks before they married.

In 1894, she persuaded him to let her tell her parents. He then carried out another perilous trip to the Pamirs and Afghanistan, before they officially announced their engagement in March 1895. The wedding took place in Washington, and they returned to England in May, to a house her father had rented for them in Carlton Gardens.

But if the Souls were happy for Curzon and delighted to gather at his wedding, the following month brought the shock of the death of George, Earl of Pembroke, aged just 44. He had never been robust, and at 6ft 4in, was unusually tall. After an operation, he had gone to Germany with Gity to recuperate and died shortly afterwards.

His was the first death in the Souls since Laura's in 1886. His funeral at Wilton involved hundreds of tenants, nobility, schoolchildren and staff. Harry was still in Constantinople, but it was perhaps just as well he could not go, for among the Souls was a smattering of Lytteltons and Talbots. Gity Pembroke, now 54, was also absent, forced by exhaustion to stay in Germany for the moment with her sister and brother-in-law, the Brownlows.

In the absence of children, George's brother, Sidney, became 14th Earl of Pembroke and, as was the custom with landed estates, Gity, now dowager countess, moved out of Wilton and next door to the Brownlows in London. There they could keep an eye on her eccentricities, which sometimes got her into trouble. On one occasion, after selling tapestries to a leading art dealer, she was appalled to learn she could have got a much better price, so she told her servants not to allow the dealer in to collect his goods. He successfully sued her and won his legal costs.

To have her sister living next door must have been slightly worrying for Adelaide Brownlow, who, as her relation George Leveson Gower noted, was too easily distracted by petty matters to be able to focus on anything worthwhile, and the main distraction was her family. 'She is more weighed down by her brothers and sisters than many women by a large family of their own,' he noted. When she moved to Ashridge upon marrying, her siblings had descended on the area. 'I believe that, if there were no chance of her seeing any Talbots for a month,' said Leveson Gower, 'she would settle down and develop amazingly.'[25] For all her largesse, Lady Brownlow was said to be disparaging of those she considered frivolous and worldly. It would partly explain her antagonism towards Nina, whose 'immoral' conduct she saw as ruining Harry's life.

That year, a chance came for Harry to try again for Parliament, for another General Election was to be held in the summer. Harry's former constituents praised his 'exceptional ability as a politician, a man and a statesman', the latter because 'he would ultimately climb the political ladder and would take part in the counsels of the nation'.[26]

But Fawcett had other ideas. Word was out that she would agitate again, and Frances Balfour was tasked with asking her if she would continue her campaign if Harry stood for another constituency. Frances hoped she would leave the matter alone, telling her:

> As far as Cust goes, your action with regard to Manchester means <u>now</u> that no constituency can take him in ignorance of his history, they will do it knowing all about him. The man is leading a decent life & his wife is contented.[27]

Frances pointed out that as a public character and as the leader of suffrage, Fawcett's 'persistence against Cust must mean the loss of front bench support … I must return your answer now to certain powers that be, & if you cannot say you will leave Cust alone if he stands there will be the devil to pay as far as suffrage goes'.

Her reply disappointed and angered Frances:

> The more I think about it, the more I feel that I cannot give you the assurance or pledge you wish for. I hope you will forgive me for saying that the way I see it makes my position that of a person who is being offered a bribe.

She felt she was being asked to buy off opposition to suffrage in return for promising to pursue a certain course. Further, she did not think the only front bench man who had ever given suffrage any help (Balfour) would be party to that. Fawcett invited Frances to send her letter to some impartial outsider, 'say Mrs Sidgwick or Dr Talbot of Leeds and ask for their judgement … I can only say that their opinion would have great influence with me and after hearing it, I would not act without duly weighing it'.[28]

Frances's reply was sharp. The request to ascertain Fawcett's intention had not come from Arthur Balfour but elsewhere. She had expressed her own opinion, which was that if Fawcett persisted, suffrage would suffer, 'not because anyone identifies themselves with Cust or would resent your action against him as an individual but [because] your action involves a policy about morals with relation to public life'. Frances had heard it said by those who supported them that 'if women are going to take this line, they are not fit to have suffrage'. As for offering a bribe, she was 'not a born idiot', and only told Fawcett what she had found to be 'a matter of fact' in the last year, adding, 'I must say I think you ought to consider the opinions of those who work with you, as much as the morals of H Cust!'[29] Fawcett replied in a brief sarcastic note.

When Harry's acquaintance, Lord Wolmer, told Frances days later that he too thought Fawcett was injuring the cause, she wrote to Fawcett again, her anger barely concealed. She would tell those who had asked her to make the enquiries that Fawcett was unable to bind herself to anything. Further, she felt so strongly on the matter that, if Fawcett took such action again regarding Cust's candidature, 'I shall feel compelled to leave the suffrage committee & state publicly my grounds for doing so. This supervision of morals was tried in the Puritan age & was not successful, &

I see no reason why it should end in any better way now.'[30] Fawcett made a note that she sent no reply at all.

The last word came from Kathleen Lyttelton. After seeing their correspondence, she sneered:

> I can only suppose that there is something in being an aristocrat & living in London society that confuses the moral stance. If women's suffrage is not to have the moral effect they seem to deplore, I for one hope it may not come. Are we to consider Cust as the prodigal son?[31]

Harry may have been making his way back from the social wilderness, but without the assurances from Fawcett he could not risk standing for Parliament again so soon. Instead, he gave his support to Stamford's candidate, who won in a resounding victory for the Conservatives. Lord Salisbury was returned as prime minister and formed an alliance with the Liberal Unionists with a large majority over Lord Rosebery's Liberal Party. Balfour was now Leader of the House of Commons and First Lord of the Treasury. From now on, the governing party would generally be known as the Unionist Party.

At least Harry's literary life remained rich, and he was also writing for the *New Review*, owned and edited by W.E. Henley. Henley soon realised that talent like Harry's came with a price, namely unpredictability, complaining to their friend Charles Whibley, the *Gazette*'s Paris correspondent, that he 'never answers letters & nobody seems to know where he is'.[32]

But Harry had other work pressures. He was seen at 7 a.m. every day in the *Gazette* offices in his shirt sleeves, cigarette in mouth, half-buried beneath papers, proofs and articles, his image captured affectionately in a *Vanity Fair* cartoon. The Lincolnshire papers thought Astor had made 'the cleverest man' in England his editor. The clever woman who reviewed books for him was less acknowledged, although their literary circle appreciated Nina's talent. Her first review was of Thomas Hardy's *Jude the Obscure*, with (ironically) its storylines of sex and entrapment. Henley was impressed and, aware of Harry's professional pride, remarked to Whibley, 'He'll be jealous of *her* next, I think!'[33]

Harry and Hardy rubbed shoulders in July at a dinner of the Omar Khayyam Club and mingled with other literary names, including

Edmund Gosse and Andrew Lang, although the honoured guest was the great novelist, George Meredith. Among the many speeches, it was Harry who 'provoked great mirth with a speech full of impromptu quips', of which the most successful was a parody of a verse from a well-known poem.[34] Clearly, he was on great form, in contrast to what must have been a melancholy mood two days earlier, when Pamela Wyndham got married.

Crises

Leaving behind the vibrancy and steamy heat of India, Pamela Wyndham had arrived back in damp England in April 1894. Refreshed by her experiences, although still unhappy about Harry, she was thrown into a whirl of social engagements calculated to keep her spirits buoyant and give her opportunities to meet other men.

That summer she was courted by the amiable Francis, Viscount Drumlanrig, brother of Oscar Wilde's lover, Bosie; their mother was a cousin of the Wyndhams. Known as 'Drummy', he was appointed secretary to the new prime minister, Lord Rosebery. However, Rosebery was a widower, prone to depression and was finding it hard to cope with his new role, and Loulou Harcourt spread a rumour that he was having a homosexual affair with Drummy. Drummy's father, the Marquess of Queensberry, believed the rumours and pursued his son to Germany, threatening to thrash him to the bone. He was saved only by the intervention of others.

Ironically, at around the same time, Queensberry's other son, Bosie, was staying with Wilde in the seaside town of Worthing, enjoying his company and that of local boys, in a relationship that would soon cause a notorious scandal.

The Wyndhams had reservations about Drummy, as did Pamela, and she broke it off with him. Soon afterwards, he became engaged to someone else. As the first anniversary of losing Harry loomed in October 1894, Pamela said the past year 'makes one afraid of living. The waking every morning – the needle of pain coming through sleep.'[1]

That month, she and her parents were visiting Mary at Gosford when the news came that Drummy had been found dead in what was officially said to be a shooting accident. However, Pamela was certain he had killed himself because of the rumours. She blamed herself, thinking she might have saved him by marrying him.

Pamela's decision to marry Eddy Tennant, assistant private secretary to the head of the Scottish Office, was met with delight by his sisters, Margot, Charty and Lucy, who had been hoping their sweet, steadfast, slightly dull brother might propose to her ever since she had visited Glen.

In the spring of 1895, Pamela and Eddy both visited Italy separately. She and her mother were invited to the beautiful Florentine villa of Lady Paget, whose daughter, Gay Windsor, was also there with her children. Pamela stayed on for a while and was joined by her brother. Lady Paget found Pamela 'as nice-minded as she is pretty, clever, too', while George Wyndham was 'very intelligent and good-looking and full of life' (an observation she would nurture for future reference).

Lady Paget invited Eddy to dinner and afterwards contrived to leave him and Pamela alone together. Her ruse worked. 'When Mr Tennant took leave of me that evening he bowed low and kissed my hand. I then knew that the balance had dropped on his side.'[12] But Pamela did not accept his proposal at once. Although Eddy was handsome, rich and kind, she looked down on the Tennants as being trade. However, the snobbery probably upset Eddy less than Pamela telling him that she would never forget Harry Cust.

The next day Eddy sent Pamela a letter, which had the desired effect, and they announced their engagement. Although the Wyndhams thought him a good man, they wondered if he was sufficiently spirited for Pamela but, given the unfortunate excitement she had already suffered, Eddy was safe and came with no obstacles, as her sisters noted. On 11 July 1895, Pamela, aged 24, and Eddy, 36, were married.

Pamela's marriage to a Tennant further joined the two main political parties. While the Wyndhams were Conservative, Pamela's uncle was married to Lord Rosebery's sister, and as Margot and Pamela were now sisters-in-law, Henry Asquith became part of the fold. It was unfortunate that shortly after the wedding came the disastrous Liberal defeat in the General Election, in which Asquith was replaced as Home Secretary and

Eddy lost his position. Fortunately, he had inherited his father's business acumen and was happier in finance than in Parliament.

Unsurprisingly, Harry and Nina were not invited to the wedding, but it must have served as a reminder of the irregularity of their own relationship: for Harry, life with a woman he had not chosen to marry and for Nina, the knowledge that she had no hold over him save legally. For all the Souls' bucking of convention, the Custs were nevertheless forced into the yoke of marriage that bound all others. And yet for Nina, the mere fact that she was Harry's wife seems to have been enough. After their marriage, she visited her friend Edward Burne-Jones. 'You do like my man, don't you?' she asked. He answered positively, but added to himself, 'May the Almighty forgive me.'[3]

Divorce was permitted only on limited grounds, which were different for each sex. Both had to prove adultery, but women also had to prove a compounding offence, such as cruelty or desertion. Divorce was therefore not an option except in extreme scenarios, where staying in a marriage would be worse than being cast into the social wilderness – Queen Victoria would not receive divorced people at court.

Unconventional domestic set-ups were more likely to be found among creatives such as writers, artists and actors. George Eliot, the female novelist, lived with a married man, yet her success made her acceptable company, even for royalty, who were not above courting scandal themselves.

As well as the Prince of Wales, other royal children sailed close to the wind. Princess Louise enjoyed a close friendship with her handsome, married Hungarian art tutor, Sir Edgar Boehm, an acclaimed sculptor, which continued after her marriage. She saw him the day he died suddenly of an aneurism in 1890, and rumours spread (largely by Wilfrid Blunt's ex-lover, 'Skittles', the courtesan Catherine Walters) that they were making love when he died.

While many still quivered with moral indignation over Harry and Nina, in 1895 Oscar Wilde became the subject of a far wider scandal when his transgressions became public. It started in April, with his court case for libel against Bosie's father, the Marquess of Queensberry. With his son Drummy dead, the marquess had found cause to be concerned about his other son's activities and had called Wilde a 'sodomite', which in legal and journalistic discourse was an 'unmentionable' crime.

In his role as a critic, Wilde had once commented on Balfour's book, *A Defence of Philosophical Doubt,* published in 1879 – 'one of the dullest books we know' – and on the effect that Blunt's imprisonment in Ireland, ordered by Balfour, had on his poetry: 'It must be admitted that by sending Mr Blunt to gaol [Balfour] has converted a clever rhymer into an earnest and deep-thinking poet'.[4] Wilde could not have imagined that he too would create his most memorable poem while incarcerated.

When his lawyer withdrew the libel case after days of sordid allegations, it was seen as an admission of guilt. Wilde was arrested and faced trial for gross indecency. George Wyndham tried to help Bosie by encouraging him to go abroad. Wilde was found guilty, and on 25 May 1895 began a two-year prison sentence.

Ettie Grenfell's husband Willie had supported Wilde in his libel claim, saying Queensberry's accusation was impossible as such vices could not happen. As the matter progressed, he changed his mind. Curzon had always looked down on him, but Wilde would have the last word. Later, exiled in Paris after his release, raging against injustice and nursing his genius, he saw a newspaper picture of Curzon as Viceroy of India (as he would soon become), in a state carriage with his wife, escorted by cavalry and cheered by crowds. Remembering the aggressive speech Curzon had made at the Crabbet Club (although Wilde had retorted brilliantly and later acknowledged that Curzon apologised), Wilde complained to his friend Frank Harris, 'Fancy George Curzon being treated like that. I know him well; a more perfect example of plodding mediocrity was never seen in the world.'[5]

He spoke also of Wyndham, 'with his beautiful face and fine figure … infinitely cleverer than Curzon but he has not Curzon's push and force … he was charming to me'. As the two Souls enjoyed power, Wilde was 'hiding in shame and poverty in Paris. The awful injustice of life maddens me … what have they done in comparison with what I have done?' But Wilde knew his talent would give him immortality.

Curzon's hour approached later in 1895 when Salisbury appointed him Parliamentary Under-Secretary for Foreign Affairs. Wyndham, still MP for Dover since the election but not yet in the office that would make his reputation, was venting his creativity by writing poetry and editing journals.

Lord Elcho also held his seat in Ipswich but his personal life that year underwent upheavals. Since 1894, Hermione Leinster had been dying of TB in France. Mary's sense of humanity meant that, regardless of what had happened, she felt Hugo should go to his sick mistress and stay until her death, then they would reconcile and have a child to cement their marriage. Hugo joined Hermione in October 1894, but two months earlier, Mary had entertained a group of Souls at Stanway, including Balfour, and unexpected visitors appeared in the form of her cousins, Wilfrid Blunt and Bosie Douglas.

Blunt had enjoyed an affair with her mother, Madeline, early in her marriage to Percy and maintained a warm relationship with her, while Mary, twenty years Blunt's junior, also thought him attractive. As her guests amused themselves in Stanway's lovely grounds, Blunt kissed her, and although she did not respond and returned to Balfour, Blunt wrote in his diary that the seed had been planted. For him, 'Passion was the element in which he lived, as a bird in the air or a worm in the earth, according to his mood'.[6]

In January 1895, while Hugo was still with Hermione, Mary and the children were invited to join Blunt, Lady Anne and their only child, Judith, aged 22, at their stud at Sheykh Obeyd near Cairo. Anne was used to Blunt's infidelities, and yet she was no ineffectual woman. The granddaughter of Byron and daughter of the mathematician Lady Ada Lovelace, Anne was multilingual, musical and a brilliant horsewoman. Judith was also very talented. While bitter disputes with her father lay in store, in which she would dismiss him as 'completely at the mercy of oriental deceit and Irish blarney and [believing] every woeful tale of oppression by the British government, however fantastic', she never denied his genius or the effect he had on people. He possessed 'a magic so powerful that no one could overlook him or forget him', with his 'hypnotic glittering eyes – strange eyes … which seemed to smoulder with fire'.[7]

Certainly, they exerted a powerful hold over Mary Elcho as she accompanied the Blunt family on a journey into the desert and towards the Red Sea, returning to the oasis's beautiful gardens to sit amid fruit trees and flowers, eat dates and drink fresh camel's milk. Mary adopted the flowing clothes of the Bedouin, in which Blunt always dressed, and did not discourage his attentions. One morning, while her children were sightseeing with their governess, she stayed behind. When Blunt knocked at her bedroom door, she let him in. 'She is an ideal woman for a life-long passion,' he wrote, 'and has the subtle charm for me, besides, of blood relationship.'[8]

Another trip into the desert followed, this time with Anne and Judith coming only for the first day, leaving Blunt and Mary with the children and servants: he called it 'their desert honeymoon'. When the camp was pitched at night, with the children supervised elsewhere and Blunt's tent set apart, Mary joined him. She told Blunt that relations between her and Balfour were 'not those of absolute lovers', yet he found she was 'pledged' to Balfour 'far more than to Hugo'.[9] Nevertheless, her promises to Balfour 'never to give herself to another' seemed to be forgotten. She felt entirely at home in the desert, as though her childhood roaming the countryside had prepared her for it.

What she was not prepared for was falling pregnant. Blunt was overjoyed – 'For me it is a pure gift from heaven' – but she was anxious. She had not slept with Hugo for six years after receiving her doctor's warning. Despite his own peccadilloes, Hugo was concerned at his wife's absence and sensed people were starting to talk about it. He made the decision to join Mary, but when he told Hermione that he must leave her for a while, she became agitated; she had tried to kill herself in the past. Nevertheless, he made arrangements for Egypt and arrived the day after Mary had told Blunt her news – Blunt noted scornfully that he was wearing a bowler hat. Hugo's presence provided a potential solution to Mary's state, but when he joined the family on a desert outing, Blunt would not facilitate him and Mary sleeping together, for in his mind, 'she is my Bedouin wife'. Instead, she slept in a separate tent.[10]

As Hermione worsened, Hugo returned to her. She died in March 1895, aged 30. He told his sister Evelyn, 'She died this afternoon – it lasted a long time, 24 hours and was terrible to watch … She was hardly conscious at all.'[11]

In the meantime, Mary had another desert excursion with Blunt, but when Hugo telegrammed to say he was unhappy and would await her at home, Blunt realised it was over. Mary went home in late March – Lady Paget thought she looked very frail – and confessed everything to her husband. 'If it had been Arthur I could have understood,' said Hugo. 'I shall forgive you, but I shall be nasty to you.'

Mary told Blunt – surely by way of excusing herself to Hugo, for she had not exactly resisted her host – that he had tried to wreck her life and the only thing that prevented her being utterly angry with him was that she believed he cared for her in a way. Hugo injected his own fury in a letter to him, 'You have wrecked the life and destroyed the happiness of a woman whom a spark of chivalry would have made you protect.'[12]

As for Balfour, he was not jealous of their desert trip, Mary told Blunt. Yet, initially, she dared not tell Balfour everything, in case his feelings for her changed. Eventually, she confessed to the child's paternity.

She and Hugo swore Blunt to secrecy about the baby, or they would reveal all. A scandal was averted, and in October she gave birth to Mary, without the problems her doctor had anticipated. To her daughter Cynthia, by then aged 8, the baby's arrival meant 'an utterly changed home',[13] while Judith Blunt was jealous of her new half-sister, on whom her father sent her to report; he provided for her through Wyndham.

Hermione's orphaned children went to live with her sister. Maurice, the Duke of Leinster, was 8, Desmond was 7 and Edward, Hugo's son, 3. It is believed Hugo had no contact with Edward but inherited Hermione's chow chow, Cymru.

A Soul who was less lucky that year in childbirth was Margot. Her first child with Asquith was due in April, but her pelvis was too small. The baby was sacrificed to save her own health.

The Custs, meanwhile, were forging a life that gave Harry freedom in a marriage he had not wanted, while satisfying Nina that he was hers. Writers have accused him of abandoning her, and sexually he may have done, but socially they were often together, although his cousin's wife, Sybil Cust, would sneer, 'Nina *in statu quo*, who clings closer than a limpet'.[14] A Lyttelton by birth and half-sister of those siblings who had made life difficult for the couple, Sybil was not going to start admiring Nina now.

Henley spent pleasant times with them, although it did not stop him turning his friend's love life into a verb. Of Iwan-Müller, who was involved with 'a pretty married woman with the vilest of husbands', Henley observed that 'he was Custing like hell'.[15]

They also kept their own sets, and Nina was still part of Violet's group. At a party for the composer Gabriel Fauré, *The Sketch* noted the two women were part of 'an artistic trio, both dressed very much alike in grey', the third being Mrs Tree (in yellow).

The American author Edith Wharton, the same age as Harry, met him at dinner at the house of his former lover, Gladys de Grey, now Lady Ripon, and was enthralled. She did not catch his name to start with, but:

> … within five minutes I was being whirled away on such a quick current of talk as I had not dipped into for many a day. My neighbour moved with dazzling agility from topic to topic, throwing topics to and fro like glittering glass balls, always making me share in the game, yet directing it with a practised hand.[16]

They discussed their favourite kisses in literature, Harry admiring Wharton's choice from a new novel by her fellow countryman, Henry James, while he quoted the last desperate embrace of Troilus and Cressida from Shakespeare's play, 'Injurious time now with a robber's haste/ Crams his rich thievery up …', its image of time lost as close as ever to Harry's heart. Only at the end of the evening did Wharton discover who he was, 'one of the most eager and radio-active intelligences in London'. After that, she rarely missed an opportunity to see him when she was in town.

The *Gazette* flourished, so in February 1896, when Astor asked Harry and Iwan-Müller to resign, his world collapsed. Undoubtedly there had been differences between the newspaper proprietor and his editor, not least Harry's sheer cleverness, causing Astor to say petulantly on one occasion, 'You always get the better of me on so many points that it makes me merry to score now and then'.[17]

Harry was extravagant with Astor's money, but he could justify it with the quality writing he published. He did not always manage the paper in the way Astor wanted, but his staff loved him, and he delivered great copy. He was a maverick, but he got results. Under Harry, advertising revenue doubled. The previous year, in a glowing commendation, Astor had told Harry he thought they were coming 'within sight of the greatest journalistic success ever accomplished in this country'. So, what had happened?

Making it clear that he had no problem with Harry's skills as an editor, Astor claimed he had refused to follow his instructions on some recent stories, particularly the 1895 crisis in Venezuela which had soured Anglo-American relations. An American himself, Astor wanted Harry to present the American standpoint, but to do so would be derogatory to the position Britain was adopting.

Astor also cited other occasions of Harry's alleged refusals going back three years. In light of the praise more recently heaped on him, Harry was baffled.

Astor insisted the men deliver their resignations within a week, and they would receive salary in lieu of notice. They both refused. 'I have endeavoured to follow your instructions whenever you have communicated them,' Harry responded, wounded, 'and have given the best of my life to make your paper a success.'[18]

It did no good. In the absence of their resignations, they received formal notice of termination and a cheque. Many saw the real reason for Harry's dismissal as Astor's ego, for he fancied himself as a writer and frequently sent Harry his articles, insisting they were to be published without alteration. Harry, however, considered them to be inferior and refused to do so.

Harry wrote to *The Times* with copies of the correspondence that had passed between him and Astor. While the press recognised that fault probably lay on both sides, one paper noted, 'It is the old, old story of the brilliant wayward editor and the compromised proprietor'.

The press widely lamented the departure of both men, pointing to one of their recent clever headlines, 'Rhodes-Easier'. Harry's finale was a typically stylish classical pun, '*Qui Cust-odit Caveat*' – 'who hates Cust, let him beware'.

His staff were so upset they offered to resign with him, and at the final parting where, in typically dramatic style, he joined them in singing the canticle '*Nunc Dimittis*', they presented him with an ivory paper knife, inscribed with an affectionate message. His office manager, Henry Leslie, a quiet, inoffensive man, could not trust himself to go to the official farewell, but told Harry he had found the whole wretched business 'unutterably painful … No period of the *Gazette* has ever realised more closely Thackeray's conception than your brilliant editorship.'[19] Katharine Tynan Hinkson, to whom Harry had given the 'Autolycus' column, said his departure 'was worse than a Cabinet crisis to our circle'.[20]

Despite her resolve not to see Harry, after hearing what had happened Lucy Graham Smith visited him on 8 February and noted, 'He seemed to be in excellent spirits', touched by his staff's allegiance although exasperated by Astor's behaviour. The next day at Easton Grey, she received a note on a *Gazette* card:

> These are the last words I shall write at the PMG & they are God bless & keep my darling darling love for ever & ever and bring her back to me. I love you darling I love you I love you & always shall, wholly & utterly I love you darling.

In her diary she wrote, 'So sad. Could not help tears. Twice to church. Played organ. Golfed with Ribblesdale and Graham [her husband] at Elmestree. Most dazzling day.'[21] Days later, she was pleased to learn from Ribblesdale that he, Charty and Margot had met Harry at Devonshire House, the London home of the eponymous duke, the Lord President of the Privy Council; Richard Haldane had suggested Harry talk to this popular and influential figure. Harry still seemed 'in an excellent and reasonable frame of mind generally'.[22]

He was always good at putting on a positive face, although his immediate concern was money. Without the *Gazette*, his main income source was removed, and while he had others, he had a wife to support. Although Nina received an allowance from her father, Harry could not abrogate his marital responsibilities. Recognising the unwarranted crisis in the couple's life, the Brownlows invited them to Ashridge where Harry could consider the future. As Earl Brownlow's heir, it is likely a financial arrangement was reached between them that would enable Harry to maintain their lifestyle until he found something else. Apart from the money, work was vital to his sanity.

Presenting a positive front, the following month he and Nina entertained an interesting group of Souls and others, which included Balfour, the artist James Whistler, Mrs Beerbohm Tree, the Duke of Leeds, Charles Whibley and the handsome David Lindsay (Lord Balcarres, a cousin of Violet Granby), who, at an earlier Cust dinner where alcohol was always plentiful, found that Whibley 'got very fond of me about midnight and persisted in giving me little hugs'.[23]

At least Harry was not only a contributor to, but also a director of Henley's *New Review*, with George Wyndham and Lord Windsor, husband of Gay. In July 1896, Harry left for South Africa in search of a story for the paper. The Second Matabele War was in progress, triggered by the revolt of the Matabele people against the authority of the British South Africa Company. His travelling companion was Lionel Decle, an Anglo-French explorer and expert on Africa. Harry secured an interview with Paul Kruger, President of the Transvaal, which furthered his understanding of the situation.

While he was away, other Souls were feeling restless. Hugo Elcho was the object of actress Mrs Patrick Campbell's desire. She was invited to Stanway for a week and stayed for three. 'She has flung herself at Hugo,' Mary told Balfour, 'to such an extent that I fear trouble will come of it.'[24]

George Wyndham was missing the excitement of great affairs of state and, according to Blunt, sought 'a *grande passion*'. In September 1895, Gay Windsor and her mother had hosted George and Sibell at St Fagans Castle in Wales, which he loved. Lady Paget had already noted Wyndham's charms in Florence. Now she saw he was 'clever and well-read, has an excellent memory but a mind which has not yet attained its full balance'. She wondered if he would 'ever do anything in politics; they seem too modern for him', for he seemed to belong to another age. 'He is aesthetic and romantic … enamoured of this Arthurian country, and believed himself to be a knight of the round table.'[25]

How very *au courant* was that image, for the Wyndhams' friend Edward Burne-Jones had just completed a series of tapestries with William Morris inspired by Malory's poem *Le Morte d'Arthur*, depicting the spiritual quest by King Arthur's knights for the Holy Grail. Like those knights, Wyndham would play a part in maintaining the peace of the kingdom. For now, though, the scene was set for a lady to hand him his shield, as Guinevere did to Lancelot – and it was not his wife. Lady Paget thought Sibell 'perfectly angelic', and there was the rub. 'Sometimes when she took your hand in that warm soft clasp of hers,' recalled a friend, 'one felt she did not know whose hand it was.'[26]

Instead, the lady would be Gay, as perhaps Lady Paget anticipated. In April 1896, Wyndham told Blunt he had never been so happy, by which his cousin inferred he was in love. But if it was with Gay at that point, he would have to wait a little longer for her.

Wyndham also had another close female friend, Lady Sybil Eden, mother of Britain's future Prime Minister Anthony, who although not part of the Souls, often socialised with them. 'In those days it was rather the fashion to belong either to the racing set or to the society circle or to "the Souls" … very literary and artistic folk', she said.[27] Although her husband was part of the racing set, they dipped in and out of other groups, but it was the Souls who interested them the most, of whom Sybil considered Wyndham to be one of the 'shining lights'.

Sybil Eden and Wyndham were undoubtedly very fond of each other. Aware of their closeness, and bearing a physical resemblance to him, Anthony Eden always wondered if Wyndham was his real father, pondering the possibility until his own death. Although that would mean drawing the distasteful conclusion that his mother had been unfaithful, it was otherwise an attractive prospect. Wyndham was the antithesis of the unpredictable Sir William Eden, a clever, aesthetically aware but foul-mouthed man, whose 'turbulent spirit',[28] which manifested in terrible rages, made it difficult to live placidly around him. In 1896 he was attracting publicity for the legal battle he was fighting against James Whistler concerning the artist's painting of Sybil. She had first sat for him in Paris in 1894, but a contractual dispute arose between him and Eden that dragged on in the French courts until it finally concluded three years later.

Sybil was said to have a Madonna-like beauty. 'Lady Eden and Mrs George Curzon stand alone among the beauties of the day by reason of the almost Puritanical simplicity of their coiffure and attire,' enthused *The Gentlewoman*[29] and quoted the Prince of Wales, who said Sybil reminded him of a beauty of bygone times, 'with her hair parted in front and worn plainly down on either side'.

Born in 1867 in Calcutta, she was a great-granddaughter of the 1st Earl Grey and daughter of Sir William Grey, formerly Lieutenant Governor of Bengal and Governor of Jamaica. Her mother was Georgina Chichele-Plowden and her first cousin was Pamela Plowden, Winston Churchill's great love. Sir William Eden was not Sybil's first choice of husband, but her father died when she was 11, leaving her mother with four young children, so marriage may have assumed more importance than usual.

After coming out in 1885, Sybil met Sir Francis Knollys, private secretary to the Prince of Wales, and although she was 18 and he 48, they fell for each other. 'He was greatly attracted to me and I completely lost my heart to him,' she wrote, 'and had he proposed would certainly have accepted him.' However, someone interfered, she said, and the Prince of Wales told Knollys it could not happen, 'so he disappeared out of my life'.[30]

Instead, in 1886 Sybil married Eden, aged 37 to her 19, whom she had known for a very short time. He seemed impressive: strong and handsome, a good sportsman, a traveller and a talented watercolourist, with an estate at Windlestone, in County Durham.

The following year, Knollys married the Hon. Arden Mary Tyrwhitt, whose brother was a friend of Eden's. It is tempting to speculate whether some manoeuvring had gone on in Eden's favour. He professed his undying love for Sybil in elaborate letters, but it was a strange match. Although she would recall their early married years as happy, his behaviour would become increasingly difficult.

George Wyndham and his wife were among Lady Eden's dearest friends. Sibell was 'delightful', he was 'handsome and debonair … a great personality with the soul of a poet'. He called Lady Eden 'copper head' because of the tints in her hair. Wyndham would become godfather to her youngest son, Nicholas, born in 1900, while she called him her 'political godfather', having initiated her into politics, a subject in which her husband had no interest. Wyndham also introduced her to the beauty of literature.

'I don't think there has ever been anyone in the world quite like him,' she marvelled, 'such good looks, such vitality, such an imagination and so generous a disposition.' Sybil loved his visits to Windlestone, and she and Eden dined at Wyndham's London house, where he would read aloud 'in his beautiful voice' from Shakespeare's sonnets or from his own book on the poet Ronsard. 'Those were golden moments in my life,' she said.

Her description of Wyndham fitted his self-image, 'He spent his life in chivalrous endeavour to help and to heal'. His gallantry expressed itself in a poem he composed at Windlestone and copied into Sybil's day book. Entitled '*Arx Amoris*', it speaks of protecting his 'adored' from death, 'I will build a city that shall last forever/ And fight for it with my sword'.[31]

Despite the beauty of Windlestone and the sporting attractions of the countryside, the Edens often spent time away and apart. In 1894, three years before Anthony's birth, for example, they spent the winter in Paris with their daughter and two sons before Eden went off to hunt in India and Sybil remained in Paris with the children until the following spring.

Anthony was the fourth of Sybil's five children, born on 12 June 1897. Sybil said he inherited the Eden temper, the biological inference of which is clear, although such indication of paternity could serve as a cover for any contrary truth. Sir William saw little resemblance between himself and Anthony and thought him more Grey. According to the press, earlier in 1896, the year Anthony was conceived, Sybil was very ill after an operation, the details of which were not disclosed. By July 1896 she had recovered sufficiently to return to society, although temporarily in a bath chair.

Given the date on Anthony's birth certificate, and based on the usual period for pregnancy, conception must have occurred on or around 5 September 1896. The possibility of Wyndham being Anthony's father weakens when an overlooked fact is taken into account: he had left Britain for South Africa on 15 August.

Unhappy at being passed over by Salisbury's government, he had been selected to sit on the newly appointed South African Committee. Its purpose was to investigate the Jameson Raid in the independent Boer Republic of the Transvaal, which, under Paul Kruger, had become the richest state in South Africa. The raid would be a contributory cause of the Second Boer War. Wyndham returned to Britain on 20 November 1896.

Anthony's birth was announced in the newspapers a few days after the event and, a little unusually as it was so often done by the father, formally registered by Sybil in July. The birth certificate gives his name as William Anthony, yet at the christening in September, he was named Robert Anthony. The Edens continued to see Wyndham socially, often without Sibell, both in London and the north-east, where neighbours included the Londonderrys.

Anthony Eden's biographer has said Wyndham was in the South of France in the weeks before going to South Africa, and given that Lady Eden was often there and may have gone to convalesce after her illness, they may have had a rendezvous. Otherwise, for Wyndham to be his father, Anthony's birth date would have to be May, not June, meaning the date would have to be faked to disguise an inconvenient truth. In later life, when she had much-publicised money problems, Anthony would describe his mother as unscrupulous and untruthful. What is clear is that Sybil was infatuated with Wyndham, and given the physical beauty of them both, it is not hard to imagine a passionate liaison. Given the choice of two fathers, it is easy to see why Anthony might favour the poet and politician.

Almost inevitably, Harry has also been suggested as the father (although not by Anthony). Certainly, he and Sybil would have met, and the Greys and his mother's family, the Cooksons, both significant Northumbrian families, knew each other. However, Harry too was away at the relevant time.

By November 1896 Harry was in Rhodesia, from where he wrote features for the *New Review*, although the first time Henley heard from him after he left England was January 1897, noting, 'He is obviously well & as obviously Byronic'.[32] After returning to Britain in April, Harry gave a series of lectures on 'British interests in South Africa', telling his audiences he spoke merely as a traveller who had closely studied the country, where he had enjoyed 'a good intercourse with all kinds of people from Zambesi to Capetown'. He wanted to make the lecture 'both historical and rational' in order to educate people on a complex and controversial subject.[33]

Henley had a chance to catch up socially when he and Anna joined Harry and Nina at Cockayne Hatley to celebrate Queen Victoria's Diamond Jubilee, which Henley said left them both 'horribly the worse for wear'.[34] But however enjoyable their celebration, it would not have dripped with the glitter and gold of the most brilliant party of the Victorian era, the Duke and Duchess of Devonshire's Ball, held at their eponymous London house. Attended by royalty and the cream of society, the dress code was 'allegorical or historical costumes before 1815' and the 700 guests were instructed to style themselves around the theme of royal courts, both mythical and temporal.

The courts of Elizabeth I, Louis XIV and Catherine the Great were understandably popular, giving the perfect excuse for excess, while those Souls who attended typically chose less showy eras. Ettie Grenfell, in green and white, went as a noblewoman of Venice at the time of Romeo and Juliet, with Willie in black embossed velvet. George Wyndham, picking up the Italian mantle, smouldered as Signor di Samare. Violet Granby, choosing a costume similar to her own style, dressed artfully as an earlier marchioness and Balfour looked both sober and dashing as a seventeenth-century Dutch nobleman in black tunic embroidered with jet, black silk cloak and large hat.

Harry and Nina were no doubt excluded from the invitation list, and even for those Souls who went, it was the sort of event that, given the choice, most would eschew in favour of their own, more intimate parties. The ball, which was the last of its kind and the last major event to be held at Devonshire House, might be seen as the pinnacle of aristocratic dominance, both in the political and social scene, although some guests were of origins and occupations that would have seen them barred twenty years earlier. Times were changing.

ACCEPTANCE

When he returned from South Africa in April 1897, Harry had been away from Nina for nine months. It was time to pay her the courtesy of accompanying her as a husband should and presenting to the world some semblance of married life, not only to friends but to family members. After Cockayne Hatley, the Custs and Henleys met up again in Norfolk, with Wyndham and other friends. In September, they stayed at Glen Canisp Lodge in Scotland, albeit Harry arrived a week after Nina, where guests included her cousin, Katherine (née Stuart-Wortley) and her husband, Sir Neville Lyttelton. As he was the brother of Reverend Arthur Lyttelton, whose wife Kathleen was Fawcett's friend, Nina was no doubt keen that he should see her and Harry together.

Harry may have seen himself as the martyred lover when he had to leave Pamela, declaring her his only true wife, but faced with the everyday reality of matrimony with a woman whose life had also been compromised and who, in spite of everything, simply loved him, the question arises as to whether he really punished Nina further (and also denied himself) by not sleeping with her. When it came to basic needs rather than grand passions, it is hard to imagine he would have shunned his loving, and lovely, wife.

That Harry continued to have liaisons with other women is undeniable but whether life with Nina was anything more than respectful coexistence on his part must be surmised. He rarely mentioned her in letters to women friends, except in passing. Her presence at Souls events was intermittent. Perhaps Harry discouraged her from attending, feeling that she cramped his style, or perhaps she still felt she was an outsider.

However, Nina had not been idle while Harry was abroad. She was translating an academic book, and in the spring of 1897, London's New Gallery exhibited her pencil study of a child's head – so poignant, since she would never have her own. Lady Welby still discussed her own work with her daughter, including her latest book, *Grains of Sense*, which looked at the absurdities and anomalies in the use of language.

While Nina marked the jubilee with Harry, her parents were hosting celebration parties for the community at Denton Manor, Lady Welby giving out commemorative medals to the children, assisted by her son. It was a particularly special occasion as Charles, now private secretary to Lord Lansdowne, the Secretary for War, had been awarded the Companion of the Order of the Bath in the Jubilee Honours List.

Her brother's honour surely reminded Nina of the fact that, although she had been married for nearly four years, she had not yet been presented at court in her new status as a married woman, as was the custom. The prohibition on divorcées being presented applied also to any married woman who had lived with her husband before marriage, and as the reason for Nina's marriage was that she was (or thought she was) *enceinte*, she was precluded. While part of her may have been indifferent, caring less now about what some perceived as the reality of her situation, it was nevertheless unreasonable that she should still be punished. It was time for her past to be forgiven and her status formally acknowledged. She must give it her attention.

While Harry and Nina's 'sin' had been to sleep together while they were unmarried, elsewhere behind outwardly respectable marriages, adulterous spouses tiptoed between bedrooms and told stories to conceal their guilt and (those who were kind) to protect their partner's feelings. Sometimes, couples faced the situation and moved on together. After Hermione Leinster died and Mary had Blunt's child, she went on to bear Hugo's 'reconciliation baby', Yvo, in October 1896. Yet Hugo was still pursuing Ettie Grenfell. 'Each time I see you I wonder & worship more,' he told her. 'There is nothing I would not do for you.'[1] Ettie was also determined to make herself more important to Balfour, and so obvious had her flirtations become that he and Mary privately nicknamed her 'Delilah'.

The time was approaching when George Wyndham and Gay Windsor would acknowledge their increasing closeness, leading to a love that would sustain them both. Yet Sibell, however angelic and dull some people found her, was not without passion herself. Lady Paget noticed she 'danced like mad'[2] at a party at Eaton Place, the home of her former father-in-law, the Duke of Westminster, and when Wyndham neglected her, Sibell would turn to Wilfrid Blunt, tempted by his desire for her, although she knew he had other women.

Blunt invited her and Wyndham to Crabbet Park and, although he knew he should not encourage a relationship with his cousin's wife, he spoke to her of his feelings. Sibell was tempted but made it clear she loved George. When they in turn invited Blunt to their home, Saighton Grange, he became miserable when Sibell refused to reply to his request for 'a fulfilment of our love'.[3]

Blunt was popular. In August 1897, Lady Windsor invited him to St Fagans for a week. Now aged 33 and a mother of three, Gay had long enjoyed his poems, which had been confiscated from her as a girl. Blunt arrived typically dressed all in white, in a carriage drawn by four Arabian horses and bearing a tent and spent the time with Gay and her children and Lady Paget, who described him as 'the slightly cracky author of the beautiful *Love Songs of Proteus*'.[4]

All the family were vegetarian, a trend that had gained popularity in Britain on health grounds and from a growing concern for animal rights, although it was favoured mostly by the upper classes, and even then, by a minority. Lady Paget was one of its most prominent advocates. Both mother and daughter were anti-vivisection campaigners, for which they had a high-profile supporter in Lady Paget's friend, Alexandra, Princess of Wales.

Blunt found they embraced healthy living: early to bed, early to rise and lots of fresh air. The countryside was important. Lady Paget, who was also deeply interested in spiritualism, said people did not realise that 'these phenomena are regulated by the most beautiful laws of nature'.

Gay and Blunt went for long walks and she half-promised to join him at Sheykh Obeyd. He was not sure where their new friendship would lead but understood that Wyndham had been an unsuccessful wooer. However, Gay made it clear, to Blunt's disappointment, that on her part, it would not be love. 'I will be a true and faithful friend to you,' she told him, 'but you must not expect more than this, perhaps it is a defect in me that I cannot feel any other way.'[5] This was difficult for Blunt, as 'Friendship plain and simple with a woman is to me an impossibility'.[6]

He wrote a poem for her that he considered his best. They corresponded and made plans to visit the Holy Land together, a destination that interested them both. She accepted an invitation to his London house, for which he arranged a vegetarian meal (spinach, cauliflower and sago pudding), but never went, and her letters petered out. He realised their relationship was not going anywhere and that the obstacle was his cousin. By July 1898, Gay and Wyndham were spending time alone together, aided by Blunt, 'I promised George long ago that I would do my best to further his designs'.[7]

The enigmatic Gay clearly sought something beyond her marriage, but her reasons are elusive, although she was married young. Her husband Robert was not handsome but steadfast and probably a workaholic. He had already served as Paymaster General and as Mayor of Cardiff, he was Lord Lieutenant of Glamorganshire, and now a member of the Privy Council, the advisory body to the monarch which dates back at least six centuries. He held military posts in county regiments and was a director of the *New Review*, while his artistic expertise would soon see him appointed a trustee of the National Gallery.

The Windsors entertained together at their Worcestershire home, Hewell Grange, while public commitments in Wales saw them at St Fagans. No one could accuse Gay of being an indolent aristocratic wife, for she supported Robert in his public duties and used her artistic talents to start a local craft guild. He had other houses too, and perhaps his absences exceeded his presence.

Lady Paget gave a hint when she wrote in her diary from Florence, 'Now I am alone again, as Gay had to return to England to see Windsor, who was too busy and too anxious to come abroad'.[8] Or perhaps passion, if Gay had ever felt it for him, had simply waned.

Loss was something her mother was still getting used to, for Sir Augustus Paget had died suddenly while visiting Lord Salisbury. Some comfort came from the letters she received from around the world and from Queen Victoria, who was a close friend, though twenty years her senior, and one of the few to address her informally as 'Dear Wally'. Her daughter and grandchildren became especially important to her and she liked the fact that eminent men were 'bound together by the kindred feeling of a placid admiration for Gay'.[9]

When Lady Paget attended a séance at a church near St Fagans, where a stone marked the alleged burial place of Guinevere, the medium saw a figure swathed in endless bands of white linen. Gay reminded her mother that Malory said Guinevere was buried swathed in fine Flanders linen. The children were enthralled. From that moment, the legend became real. It was just a matter of time before Gay's knight George Wyndham joined them.

Meanwhile, Nina's wish had also become a reality. Her presentation as a married woman took place on 11 March 1898, a chilly day in London. As she prepared for the event in their elegant house, the unpromising weather did little to lift her apprehension even though, at 31, it was her second presentation. On the first occasion, she had been a fresh, young debutante approaching 18, wide-eyed and serious, waiting for her mother as her sponsor to present her and officially mark her entry into society.

This time, the Drawing Room would be held by the Princess of Wales on Her Majesty's behalf. Nina's sponsor was the Countess Brownlow, who thought it time that her transgressions should be seen to be forgiven. The countess's close relationship with the royal family and Nina's own connections may have helped smooth the way.

Nina dressed carefully in the manner commanded: a pale, low-cut evening dress with train 3 yards long, white gloves and a headdress of three ostrich feathers (one more than she wore as a spinster), with two long lappets of lace flowing from her hair. Such fussiness was not her usual style.

That year she was the subject of a picture painted in exquisitely coloured enamel by Alexander Fisher, its inscription 'Nina Cust the artist' acknowledging her status and its style reflecting her natural elegance. Wearing a softly draped Grecian-style gown, she raises her arms high to hold an extravagant cape, her dark hair gently upswept and braided, her eyes cast down in a pose that, while stylised, suggests the self-effacing persona the world saw.

Unlike Nina, the other women being presented that day to mark their change of status had not been married for long – the Marchioness of Waterford, for instance, for five months, the Lady Francis Godolphin Osborne for sixteen – and if there was a significant delay, it was often because their husbands' occupation kept them abroad. But Nina's marriage had taken place over four years earlier, as society was aware.

The day still grey, Nina and Lady Brownlow departed in good time for Buckingham Palace, but just before 3 p.m., as the Princess of Wales left Marlborough House in a state carriage, a weak sun appeared and rewarded the waiting crowds with a brief sparkle of her diamond tiara and a glitter of her decorations against her black velvet gown. The company over which Her Royal Highness presided, under the protection of two corps of the Queen's Body Guard and two guards of honour, was impressive. As well as members of the royal family, the diplomatic circle was present, dozens of ambassadors and ministers from around the world. The prime minister was unavoidably delayed so was represented by the Marquis of Lansdowne. Lord Brownlow was there too, as a member of the Privy Council and part of the general circle, consisting of military figures and gentlemen attendants on the queen.

Over 100 women were to be presented that afternoon. Aristocrats like Nina had once formed the great majority, but now they were joined by those whose wealthy fathers or husbands had made their money from commerce or the professions. Some fretted that the Drawing Rooms were becoming 'a gathering together of social scum and *nouveaux riches*'[10] but they could not complain about Nina's lineage.

As she waited shivering in the palace's antechamber (no shawls or outer garments allowed), Nina must have reflected ruefully on how, at last, she was judged to be of sufficiently suitable character to be summoned to the Throne Room. She had grown weary of waiting for this acknowledgement of her marital status. A formality, it made no difference to her love for Harry, and she knew their life would still be irregular. But perhaps it signified the start of a new phase in which they would no longer be defined by their sin, especially as they had no child to remind the world of it. Nina knew neither of them was perfect, but the real flaws surely lay in the society in which they lived.

Harry was not overlooked. In May, he was commanded to attend an all-male levee at St James's Palace, held by the Prince of Wales on behalf of the queen. When in December Nina's father died and Harry walked behind his coffin with her brother, it seemed that on the family front too, the past was forgiven. But since his dismissal from the *Pall Mall Gazette* and no longer being in Parliament, what he needed more than anything was meaningful work. He must have grumbled to Henley, who told Charles Whibley he had received a 'lamentable letter from Hamlet in Delahay St'.[11]

Nothing brought his unsatisfactory situation more sharply home to him than the promotion that year of two friends. In September, Curzon achieved his great ambition when Lord Salisbury appointed him Viceroy of India at just 39; he was also created Baron Curzon of Kedleston. Wyndham was appointed Under-Secretary of State for War, a role previously held by Earl Brownlow.

Wyndham had hoped to be made Curzon's successor in the Foreign Office, but Salisbury found him too florid in speech and style – 'I don't like poets,'[12] he once said – and that post went to Hugo Elcho's brother-in-law, St John Brodrick. Nevertheless, as Brodrick pointed out to Sibell, Wyndham should take his new role as a great compliment, for he would be the youngest man in thirty-three years to represent the War Office.

The possibility of war in Europe had increased with the recent military alliance of Russia and France, which saw the Russians raising money to finance factory building, arms programmes and military railroads to the German border. The Kaiser wanted to make Germany's presence abroad commensurate with its new industrial might and believed it should capitalise on the colonial quarrels among France, Britain and Russia. Meanwhile, the unrest in South Africa was not going away, tensions exacerbated by the Jameson raid of 1895–96, Britain's failed attempt to trigger an uprising against the Transvaal by expatriate workers or *uitlanders*.

For Curzon, India was his *raison d'être*. It was, he told Wyndham, 'a vast mystery, a prodigious experiment, a genuine glory'.[13] In December 1898, shortly before he and Lady Kedleston left Britain, the Souls celebrated his success with a grand dinner for seventy at London's Hotel Cecil, 'a most brilliant assemblage of English society', said one of the newspapers permitted to attend.

Although the gathering included luminaries outside the Souls, the press reverted to the teasing of the group with which it liked to amuse itself. 'Naturally the "Order of Souls" would like to take the good things of this life in a rather uncommon way', it smirked, noting that small round tables were used in place of the usual horseshoe arrangement, because 'they dine *en famille*'. There were seven tables, 'oh mystic number!', arranged 'in a kind of Dantesque plan – an outer and an inner circle – and in their fashion were little gardens of real flowers'. The guests resembled 'glorious tulips in their fullest brilliancy', although it was also noted (typical of the Souls' style) that the ladies wore few jewels and not a single tiara, while no ribbons were seen among the gentlemen even though there was a fair smattering of honours among them.

They supped turtle soup, enjoyed sole, whitebait and saddle of lamb, nibbled parmesan pastries and cherries jubilee and quaffed Chateau Lafite (Grand Vin), Vintage 1875, probably from the cellars of Baron Ferdinand de Rothschild, another guest. But the main pleasure was having the opportunity to be together and celebrate Curzon's success, which was the result of determined, even obsessive, hard work, during which he suffered the constant pain of his spinal condition.

Harry attended without Nina, who was in mourning for her father. His old lover, the Marchioness of Londonderry, was there, as was Violet Granby, 'gowned in her usual somewhat pronounced, artistic manner', observed *The Gentlewoman* archly.

The beautiful American socialite Consuelo Vanderbilt, now Duchess of Marlborough, attended with the duke, three years into their unhappy marriage which would see them legally separating nine years later. If she was unable to prove adultery, the main ground for divorce, a wife could obtain a judicial separation on the grounds of matrimonial cruelty, although it carried not much less stigma than divorce and still prohibited presentation at court. As the duchess would write, 'Even a legal separation presented difficulties and made life alone in a great house, with a great name, a complicated problem for a woman still in her twenties.'[14]

Consuelo knew Curzon's wife, Mary, 'a compatriot of mine and a dazzling beauty', whom she noted with surprise was 'wholly absorbed in her husband's career [and] had subordinated her personality to a degree I would have considered beyond an American woman's power of self-abnegation'. Having been a guest at Stanway, Consuelo described the Souls as 'a select group in which a high degree of intelligence was happily allied to aristocratic birth' and whose 'exclusive aura' was resented by those on the outside.[15] Afterwards, Harry, whose humour she enjoyed, would begin paying her close attention, to which she responded positively.

The main distraction of the evening for Harry was surely Pamela. Attending with her husband Eddy Tennant, she was expecting her third child. Her fifth, Stephen, would say his father was so dull, 'I can't even remember what he looked like'. She took lovers and, at that time, it was the architect Detmar Blow.

Her strongest emotions, however, as her great-grandson Simon Blow recalled, were spent on her children. Unusually for her class and era, Pamela 'draped herself' in her children (which her sister-in-law Margot never understood) and devoted herself to making their country home a place of eternal childhood. In a family memoir, Blow said, 'She offered them a demanding love and expected in return their undivided attention. The price of this love was that their worlds must revolve around her.'[16] He became painfully aware of Pamela's emotional legacy, witnessing the effect it would have on his own mother.

George Wyndham attended the dinner alone, as did Gay Windsor. If their closeness took firmer root that evening, it would have to last them for a few weeks, for the next day she and Robert were travelling to Nice and Florence. The reticent Robert was very different from the romantic and exuberant Wyndham, who told Blunt, 'As a rule people do not know how to love; as an exception they love now here, now there; as a rarity, almighty lovers find each other after both are married'.[17]

That night saw the Souls at their best. As Curzon had written a poem for them nearly a decade earlier, now Wyndham composed one for him, with the lines:

> Come back in five years with your sheaves of new Fame:
> You'll find your old Friends; and you'll find them the same.[18]

The words gave reassurance to Curzon on his new path.

Hugo made an amusing toast: Curzon regarded him as the wittiest of his friends. His own speech mused warmly on the pleasant contrast between the recent weeks of heavy talk and 'the wholly frivolous and utterly irresponsible society that is collected round these tables' and acknowledged his loyal friends.[19] He also paid tribute to Mary, with whom he now had two daughters.

His friends' success made Harry determined to get back into Parliament. As 1899 began, he worked on his public profile and was appointed a Deputy Lieutenant of Bedfordshire and a magistrate. In February, he let his London house for the Season and returned to South Africa, for the Second Boer War was brewing.

Harry's views of Prime Minister Lord Salisbury and Cecil Rhodes were not positive. He was at the Granbys' lunch party in May, where they were the main guests. 'I feel,' said Harry, 'as if I were sitting in the company of the two greatest criminals of the age.'[20]

Conscious of her mother's adjustment to life as a widow, Nina divided her time in the first half of 1899 between visiting her in Scotland and seeing friends in Florence. Widowhood brought changes in status. Denton was no longer Lady Welby's legal home, as Charles had succeeded his father as baronet and inherited the estate, where he now lived with Mollie and their children. She would soon look for another residence and meanwhile stayed in Scotland, hosting friends and academic colleagues. Her title, too, belonged to Mollie now, and she became Victoria, Lady Welby.

The subtle change did not bother her, for she never used her title in her writing, seeing it as an irrelevant distraction. Now she was anxious to progress her work and had begun corresponding with the great American philosopher, Charles Sanders Peirce, with whom she shared an intellectual understanding. 'Dear one,' she told Nina, her letter conveying a sense of panic that she was losing her memory, 'I <u>must</u> try and see clearly now such future as I still have, and you must help me'.[21] Nina was busy with her own work too, her art and her writing. She also had the peace of mind of a greater degree of financial independence thanks to her father's will, which gave her an annuity of £500 (around £57,000 today).

Demonstrating his understanding of foreign affairs, Harry wrote 'The Genesis of Germany' for the *New Review*, in which he reflected upon the history of the German people up to the Wars of Liberation against Napoleon and concluded that the modern Germany of Bismarck and the Kaiser compared unfavourably. His feature drew admiration from many, including Lady Welby, who analysed it in her typically forensic way and concluded it was 'brilliant'.[22]

Her letters to Harry and her references to him in her letters to Nina show that, whatever the past, she accepted him as her son-in-law and demonstrate that he did not abandon her daughter, as many have suggested. Nevertheless, wishing others to see him at his best, Nina undoubtedly concealed from her mother the extent of Harry's waywardness which caused their friend W.E. Henley, editing the works of Lord Byron, to exclaim, 'He's Cust, pure and simple Cust! 'Tis the most wonderful reincarnation in all time!'[23]

Beyond the social events that naturally brought them together, Harry and Violet kept up a private correspondence. Professionally, she was still producing portraits, some exhibited at the smartest London galleries, and in late 1899 a collection of them, *Portraits of Men and Women*, was published by Constable. In its review, *Country Life* said her male portraits were more successful than her female ones, with the exception of two: Pamela Plowden and Mrs Henry Cust. Nina's picture appeared last in the book, its position making the portrait more memorable for the reviewer, who found its sense of inexpressible sadness haunting.

Earlier that year, Violet had sat for a photographic feature at Cockayne Hatley, perhaps for publicity purposes, when she and her children were the subject of a two-page spread for *The Sketch*. Two photos show her artfully poised on her own inside the manor house (which the feature pointed out belonged to Mr Harry Cust). In another, she sits in the garden with two of the children, and another charming set shows the children alone. They are named as Lord Roos, aged 12, poignantly stated now to be her only son, Lady Victoria (known as Marjorie), aged 15, and Lady Violet (Letty), 10.

Although 6-year-old Lady Diana appears in a picture with Marjorie, she is misnamed as Letty, with the result that her actual name is not stated. When Violet attended Lord Salisbury's garden party in June for the queen's birthday, one newspaper, on remarking on the number of children present, said Lady Granby was accompanied by 'a lovely little girl', as though Diana's existence was something of a mystery.[24] As Lord Granby had not announced the birth of the child who was not biologically his, and as only the sharp-eyed would have seen a snippet in a handful of papers about her christening, a degree of ignorance was not entirely surprising.

As the nineteenth century charged towards its end, the Second Boer War broke out in October. When Lady Salisbury died in November, Balfour took over from his grieving uncle as acting prime minister at a difficult time for Britain. Harry and Nina soon lost people they knew to the war and in December attended a memorial service at the Guards Chapel for those from the Brigade of Guards who had been killed in three recent battles. As the new century dawned and Harry heard of the death at Ladysmith of his friend G.W. Steevens, he knew it was more important than ever to be in the political front line.

There were those who argued that 1900 was not the first year of a new century but the last year of the old one, the view expressed in the leader article of *The Times* on 1 January. Not that it was the main subject. Politicians and military leaders had overconfidently predicted that the Boer War would be over by Christmas 1899. 'The New Year … is not unlikely to mark a turning point in the history of the British Empire', the article began. 'Two important tasks lie before us, and on the manner in which we fulfil them our future as a ruling people and as a Great Power largely depends.'

Those tasks placed an onerous responsibility on the government. The first was to bring the war to a speedy and successful end; the second was to review the history of the campaign and learn lessons from it, for there were serious concerns that the British Army was ill-equipped to deal with the Boers in terms of numbers of troops and equipment. Balfour had taken a major step in his new role by replacing General Buller, Commander-in-Chief of the British Forces, with Field Marshal Roberts, for Buller's military competence was causing concern.

On the personal front, if an ordinary New Year traditionally saw people making resolutions, the first year of a new century magnified that expectation. Mary Elcho, while keeping up Balfour's spirits in affectionate correspondence – she had missed him at Christmas festivities which he had to bypass altogether, confined to Downing Street – also desperately sought a way to engage Hugo in worthwhile activity. He had lost his Ipswich seat in the last General Election, ending over a decade in Parliament, and after Hermione's death and his 40th birthday, he had become gloomier.

He spent more time with the Marlborough House set, whose leisure pursuits the Souls generally considered philistine and which Mary thought 'common', frittering time and money in yachting and gambling in the South of France and watching bullfighting in Spain. She told Hugo they encouraged 'bad ways & foolish tricks',[25] and she wished he had an interest that would keep him in one place for six months.

His gambling had got worse. In August 1899 he had suffered a spectacular loss on the stock market while he and Mary were in St Moritz, from where she sought solace in Balfour. 'Hugo is undone!' she told him. 'It poisons his whole life and starves his nature this vile and senseless gambling.'[26] And yet 'he keeps his temper well … he's quite a fine loser but oh! A finer fool.' She desperately wanted to stop him.

Although his father, Lord Wemyss, bailed him out, he also carried out his threat to tie up his inheritance and created a trust fund for the Elchos during their lifetime, with Balfour as a trustee, which must have rubbed salt in Hugo's wound. Another General Election was to be held in September 1900, and Mary hoped Hugo might want to stand as candidate for Bristol. She excitedly shared with him her plans for the campaign trail and how she would help him.

Balfour once described Hugo as 'too indulgent to succeed and too clever to be content with failure'.[27] He was defeated by another candidate and upset Mary further by not telling her: she heard it from Balfour instead.

By contrast, Mary's brothers-in-law, Eddy Tennant and Charlie Adeane, husband of Mananai, were approved as Liberal candidates (for Peebles and Huntingdonshire respectively). The Boer War, which was the overwhelming issue of what was dubbed 'the khaki election', had split the Liberal Party between anti-war Radicals and pro-war Imperialists. Liberal supporters of Home Rule saw Irish Nationalists openly championing the Boers. The issue of patriotism and the pressure of the war would see Home Rule assume a political back seat for the next decade.

When it came to canvassing, Pamela, who had never taken any great interest in politics, played her part in supporting Eddy but found that, for all her love of attention, she hated public speaking. George Wyndham thought that his sister was, by birth and inclination, a Conservative and persuaded her to write a series of essays about the world around her for a magazine he had founded called *Outlook*, a successor to the *New Review*. Using the pseudonym 'Clarissa', Pamela wrote eloquently, if sentimentally, about life in the Wiltshire countryside, presenting an idealised picture of the classes coexisting happily in villages where she encountered such curiosities as the belief in the power of the evil eye. In another issue, published alongside Rudyard Kipling, she wrote about her great love of birds.

That summer, as canvassing for the election was in full swing, W. Heinemann published Pamela's *Village Notes* as a book under her own name to mostly positive reviews, although she may have considered some condescending – much as her subjects might have reacted to their portrayal. In promoting her book, Pamela was photographed with her 3-year-old son Edward (known as Bim), for a feature that also included a résumé of the literary achievements and political future of her brother George.[28]

Given the election timing, it was perhaps unsurprising that existing tensions between the Wyndham and Tennant women increased. The Tennants were direct and matter of fact, while Pamela was more ethereal. Margot knew about party struggles for leadership, seen between Asquith, Loulou Harcourt and the successful new leader, Sir Henry Campbell-Bannerman. She lectured Eddy and hoped Pamela would keep such matters quiet, while doubting their sister-in-law's commitment, as did Charty Ribblesdale.

Not that the election made much difference generally to the Souls' friendship. One evening, Balfour dined with the Asquiths and afterwards found himself debating against his host in the House. 'Asquith was the challenger', he told Mary, 'but I felt a mild awkwardness replying to a man in the strength of his own champagne!'[29]

Someone with more experience than Pamela of political campaigning was Nina. In May 1900, she was relieved when Harry was invited to be Conservative candidate for Bermondsey, South London, in place of their retiring MP which, after six years of being out of Parliament, he gratefully accepted.

Harry's selection was due largely to his attitude to the government's handling of the Boer War. Having spent time in South Africa developing his friendship with Paul Kruger, President of the Transvaal, his view was that Britain's handling of the war was crucial. He considered peace to be in the greatest interest of the British Empire, although he recognised that conflict could not always be avoided. 'In the settlement of South Africa,' he told his audience at the Bermondsey Constitutional Club, 'our object must be justice but justice with a minimum of vengeance and a maximum of conciliation.'[30]

Before campaigning got underway, Nina took the chance to escape to Bath, along with Violet Cust and a swathe of society, to take the waters for their health. The town had enjoyed fame since the eighteenth century when it was patronised by royalty, but in the Victorian era a spa was built, and in 1890 alone, 100,000 people flocked to the town seeking cures for a range of problems, from infertility to skin diseases. They would bathe in the hot waters, sweat in the steam rooms and have a range of treatments which, by the time Nina and Violet stayed, had exotic European names and involved complex equipment.

The sisters-in-law stayed at the elegant Georgian Lansdown Grove Hotel, which had been modernised and boasted passenger lifts and electric lighting and was set in picturesque woodland near the Pump Rooms. Of added interest was the ongoing excavation of the original Roman Great Bath, which had been discovered by chance twenty years earlier and in whose vicinity a temple and sacrificial altar had recently been uncovered.

On their return, a visit to the Royal Academy revealed the elegant bust of Nina by the famed sculptor, Alfred Gilbert, made six years earlier and exhibited in that year's show. It is likely Gilbert was at least partly responsible for Nina's burgeoning talent in the craft.

In many ways, 1900 was Nina's year too. In October, her translation of Michel Bréal's book, *Semantics: studies in the science of meaning*, which had first appeared in French in 1897, was published to acclaim by W. Heinemann. Nina's was the first English translation of this complex work, which remains important to academics. Her star was rising.

14

TENSIONS

Whether Harry was too blinded by the book written by his lost love to be properly appreciative of his wife's success can only be surmised, although those in their circle who admired Nina's intellect would have made up for any lack of praise on his part. Lady Welby was naturally delighted, having heard from her daughter-in-law that Nina was not happy. 'At last I have got good news from my darling! I was getting quite anxious after Mollie's report,' she wrote from north London, where Charles was taking her to view houses in the area.

Although Lady Welby would always be welcome at Denton, where she had spent her married life, as a widow it was no longer her home. Instead, she looked forward to the leafy streets and handsome houses of the smart parts of north London, which offered a complete contrast to rural Lincolnshire and were noted for the number of academics and intellectuals who lived there.[1] She thought she might leave her final decision until Nina came to stay that month and asked if Harry would be coming too.

But he was busy canvassing and had secured the support of 25-year-old Winston Churchill, who was standing as Conservative candidate for Oldham after being defeated in a by-election the previous year. Five years earlier, his father Lord Randolph had died, aged just 45, after suffering a debilitating illness which rumour (probably incorrect) said was caused by syphilis. His early death instilled a strong sense of mortality in his son, who was often heard to say that he needed to accomplish his goals before his forties, and gave him a sense of urgency.

Perhaps Churchill was unaware that Harry was (or had been) one of the many lovers his beautiful American mother, Jennie, had enjoyed. Harry never lost his allure for older, married women, although she was only his senior by seven years and was widowed in 1895. However, the timing leads to the unavoidable conclusion that their affair was adulterous for at least one of them.[2]

Despite the men's difference in age (Harry was 39), they had more in common than an appreciation of Lady Churchill. Both had experience as correspondents in South Africa. Churchill was there in 1899 and, while helping to defend an armoured train, was captured and imprisoned. His arguments to be released as a non-combatant were rejected by the Boers, so he escaped and became the object of a manhunt. Once he found safety, he opted to continue covering the war and to fight in it too. On returning to Britain in 1900, he was treated as a hero and was popular with the Souls, particularly Ettie, who became a good friend.

To have Churchill's support gave Harry's campaign a boost. Churchill made a speech supporting Harry at a difficult meeting in Bermondsey, full of hecklers, who Harry joked had been shipped in to cause trouble. Churchill liked his humour, recording that Harry 'suddenly noticed an enormous man advancing on him in a pugilistic attitude. He took off his coat and squared up to him, whispering to his friends behind him, "Hold me back! hold me back!"'[3]

As polling began, Harry received a telegram sent on behalf of his former Lincolnshire constituents, wishing him luck. If Harry had had his way, he never would have left them in the first place.

On the last day of polling, the Conservatives – or more probably, Harry – invited along some interesting female supporters to make an impression, notably Violet Granby and her theatrical friend, Mrs Beerbohm Tree. With their presence, Nina could not remain in the background, and she certainly did not. Accompanying Harry as he drove around to encourage last-minute voters, she was strikingly dressed from head to toe in red, which was then the Conservative Party's colour. (The hues that distinguish the political parties in the twenty-first century were not introduced until later in the twentieth.)

The result was a clear victory for the Unionists, with Lord Salisbury back in his third term as prime minister. Harry beat his Liberal opponent with a majority of 3.8 per cent, and so pleased was one constituent that he made an anonymous donation of £10 to Bermondsey's poor, by way of grateful thanks.

Not everyone was thrilled with Harry's success. His Liberal opponent, John Williams Benn (grandfather of the future Labour politician, Anthony Wedgwood Benn) had been very popular. During one speech, Benn told his large audience that he had a letter in his pocket from Harry's supporter, Churchill, which imputed something unfavourable about Harry's views. Later, in a speech of his own, Churchill revealed Benn to be a liar when he denied ever writing to him. Perhaps by way of retaliation, the Conservatives circulated a pamphlet about Benn, drawing on articles that had appeared in the national press alleging previous political misconduct and exposing his 'true' beliefs, which the pamphlet said were very different to those he publicly espoused.

When the result was announced, Harry went to shake Benn's hand, but he refused, and his supporters subjected the victor to a volley of abuse. One elector was said to have asked Benn, 'Why didn't you circulate to the electors the information about Cust and Stamford? They wouldn't have voted for Cust if they'd known that.'[4] Whoever in the Conservatives had initiated the pamphlet must have failed to consider the potential response, even though it was nearly seven years since Fawcett's campaign had forced Harry to resign as Stamford's MP.

Putting unpleasantness aside, he got on with the job he had been elected to do. As a metropolitan borough and a riverside constituency, Bermondsey had very different issues from rural Stamford, but Harry understood an MP's true function, telling his electorate not to think that, if he was told to vote this way or that, he would do so: he was not going to be their slave but their friend. 'I make no promises of any kind,' he reminded them, 'but so long as we believe in each other, let us stick together and do our utmost to see that the cause we represent is on the winning side.'[5]

The new government would soon be answering to a different monarch. On 22 January 1901, at the age of 81, Queen Victoria died after a reign of sixty-three years. Her friend Lady Paget noted that the shock of the queen's death was such 'that the whole world felt it … Her long reign has driven from the minds of men the recollection of any other state of things.'[6] Her son was now Edward VII (or 'Edward the Caresser', as some nicknamed him).

With his uncle as prime minister once more, Balfour continued as First Lord of the Treasury and Leader of the House and immediately went to Osborne House where the queen had died. He was astonished by the mass of routine work she had to do and how much had built up in her last week, all of which had to be passed on to the king. Gloomily, Balfour could see His Majesty taking up far more of his ministers' time than the queen had done.

Balfour was depressed by the war, he told Mary Elcho, and little wonder. 'A sullen feeling prevails in the country,' said one newspaper, echoing many, for despite promises made by the new government, 'the end of the war is in the dim and distant future'.[7] Furthermore, Lord Salisbury was now 71 and showing signs of slowing down.

The first State Opening of Parliament of the new reign took place on 14 February, the splendour of the event made even more magnificent by the presence of Queen Alexandra, already adored as the pure and wronged wife, while the solemnity of the occasion was emphasised by the emotional words of the king, who spoke of his earnest desire to walk in his mother's footsteps. Among his early appointments was that of Harry's cousin, Lionel Cust (confidant to the king's late son, Prince Eddy), an art expert who was made Surveyor of Pictures in Ordinary to His Majesty and a gentleman usher, while Harry's other cousin, Sir Charles Cust, became First Equerry-in-Ordinary to his longstanding friend, Prince George, now the Prince of Wales.

Harry was also conscious of his friends in high office, where he wanted to be, but at least he was back in the House. At difficult times, love was particularly important to the Souls. Wyndham was now Chief Secretary for Ireland at a still-troubled time. It was a compliment to his political skills, but apart from the challenges he faced, it meant him and Sibell living in Dublin for six months of the year. He liked their house in Phoenix Park and loved the 'green glamour', as he called it, of the countryside, which appealed to his Irish ancestry, but he felt cut off from Westminster and his friends, especially Balfour. At such a time, he needed Gay more than ever.

He did not wish to carry on a deceit, and gradually Sibell began to accept their affair, realising Gay could offer him more than she could. On a visit by Wyndham and Sibell to Hewell Grange, Lady Paget noticed he looked older but still had the same 'violent enthusiasms and a kind of survival of the fittest way about him which may harm him on occasion'. Sibell, on the other hand, looked delicate, 'but her lovely eyes and smile remain. She is like a little saint, quite detached from this world, except for a sort of romantic, unpractical love for the beautiful.'[8] It was a tribute to Gay that she would manage to maintain a friendship with Sibell; they would go on outings together with George.

Churchill, now Conservative MP for Oldham, was also in love, with Pamela Plowden, whom he had met in India in 1896. However, she rejected his proposal and in 1902 married Lord Lytton. Harry wrote an exquisite ode intimating her wistfulness and his friend's heartbreak, although the despair that pierces the verse might well reflect Harry's own feelings.*

But it was perhaps a lucky escape for Churchill. 'She is very sweet and delicious but so busy getting on', said one observer, that she 'would not genuinely like anyone till she was sure they were hallmarked'.[9] Pamela also acquired the reputation of a vamp, who made men unhappy, echoed in Harry's poem. Later, her affair with Julian Grenfell, fourteen years younger, would upset his mother Ettie, who mistrusted her as a protégée of Violet Granby. However, Ettie herself would come to discover the allure of younger men.

In July 1902, Lord Salisbury resigned due to failing health and Balfour became his unchallenged successor. The first bachelor prime minister since Pitt the Younger, Balfour's new power made him a greater magnet to Ettie, who tried even harder to impress him, leaving Mary Elcho feeling inadequate, as she always did where politics were concerned. But for Balfour it was a burden, at least at the beginning, for his Chancellor of the Exchequer resigned, leaving him with a Cabinet reshuffle to deal with. 'Why was I born to do this kind of work?' he groaned to Mary, 'What have I done that it should be thrust upon me?'[10]

Stanway became more of a retreat than ever in that first year of premiership. There, he met the socialists Beatrice Webb, founder of the Fabian Society, and her husband, Sidney, who were holidaying locally. They found the Gloucestershire countryside beautiful and thought Lady Elcho 'a fascinating and kindly woman, married to a card-playing and cynical aristocrat, living in the most delightful old house'.[11] If Balfour

* See Appendix 2.

could retire from public life, he would 'stay at Stanway as long as you and Hugo allowed me, and start another book'.[12]

One perk, however, was driving to Downing Street in his Daimler. Balfour was an enthusiastic motorist, and the first prime minister to have his own car.

In May that year, Mary gave birth to Irene ('Bibs'), believed by some, probably wrongly, to be Balfour's. How far their relationship was sexual is uncertain, but hints are found in correspondence and in Mary's diaries. In one letter, Balfour told her that, among the few interesting books he could find in Germany, were:

> ... manuals of instruction in Latin on the best way to become a wife without also becoming a mother! I bought one of these last as a curiosity – I hope you are not going to allow all the blood to be sucked out of you by that Vampire Balfour ...

This was followed by six lines scratched out by Mary.[13]

After her affair with Blunt, she had become freer and more relaxed, caring less about Hugo's mistresses and was less in thrall to Balfour, even teasing him. She wrote from Germany:

> I do look very pretty in my bath, thousands of nestling bubbles that show off the modelling – breasts supported by water, of perfect shape with rosy tips! limbs of a ghostly whiteness – Really like a Venus or a Rhine maiden ... Yesterday, while reading George's Introduction [to the poems of Shakespeare] I slipped into Venus and Adonis – my dear!! *You* may consider yourself lucky – that's all I say!!! Write to me freely – I will destroy your letters.[14]

Such images surely sustained the prime minister as he grappled with the problems of the day. The Boer War had finally ended in May, but the current big issue was tariff reform, propounded by his Secretary of State for the Colonies, Joseph Chamberlain.

Once an ardent free trader, Chamberlain now wanted to impose a system of protective tariffs, 'Imperial Preference', on trade from outside the Empire, with the aim of strengthening unity within it and protecting Britain's economy from the increased threats of cheap imports from Germany and the USA. A political hot potato, as divisive for the Conservative Party as Home Rule had been for the Liberals, it was strongly opposed by free trade supporters, and although Harry had been one of them, he now favoured Chamberlain's proposals. Free trade might be the ideal, but he had come to realise that it made no economic sense for the country.

However, just as Harry's political life was taking off again, his health became worse, and he became prone to bouts of influenza. He and Nina employed a nurse at their London house, perhaps for both of them, along with permanent staff comprising a butler, lady's maid, cook and two housemaids; a relatively modest number given the size of the house and the entertaining they did. Nevertheless, the overall cost, together with the fact that the Granbys had bought a house in Bruton Street and ceased renting Cockayne Hatley, probably contributed to Harry's decision to sell his estate.[15] It cannot have been easy, for Cockayne Hatley had been in his family for three centuries.

In the summer of 1902, the Custs holidayed in the Scottish Highlands, and Harry wanted to visit Gosford on the way back but told Mary Elcho, 'Nina's health makes exact dates a little uncertain but we shall go to N. Berwick for a week anyway'.[16]

Notwithstanding his own health, Harry worked hard for Bermondsey and involved himself in local events, from the Primrose League to opening factories. For all his apparent confidence, he still suffered from self-doubt. After hearing Margot speak publicly, he told Mary, 'I would gladly give the half of my kingdom for the quarter of her self-confidence – for however bumptious I seem, I am always convinced that all my "*pensées et propos*" are the stale ones of an idiot & so produce nothing but litters of the dead'.[17]

In 1903 the press, describing him as 'an airy, bright figure' who had shown 'independence', noted Harry was 'less conspicuous in the present Parliament, but as he is able and ambitious … he may yet find an appropriate opportunity'.[18] In fact, he was desperate for a central role in government, ill health or not, and was becoming depressed, not helped by the death in July of his friend, W.E. Henley, whose ashes would join those of his little daughter at Cockayne Hatley.

In September, Harry reluctantly took the step of asking Balfour for work, urged to do so, he told him, by friends and family. His timing was deliberate, for a major political crisis had just occurred. Balfour could not support Chamberlain's proposals for tariff reform, favouring instead the use of retaliatory tariffs rather than full-blown protectionism. His policy rejected, Chamberlain resigned to pursue his campaign with greater vehemence, and other ministers followed. Another Cabinet shuffle lay ahead.

Harry's letter to Balfour verged on the desperate. He pointed out that, although he had differed in opinion on some departmental issues, he was:

> … entirely in agreement with your views in all essential political questions, and especially in your distinction between Preferential Tariffs with the Colonies & Retaliation … But the gist of the matter is this. I want work very badly. When I have work to do, I think I can do it adequately. So, if you can find it possible to give me work in the service of the present Government & of the country, I would ask you to remember me, & I think you will find me a not contemptible subordinate.[19]

But the vacated posts were filled without Harry, who saw Alfred Lyttelton step into Chamberlain's role as Colonial Secretary, despite the king's doubts about his lack of experience.

If Balfour replied to Harry's letter, the content is unknown. While he was fond of Harry and appreciated his abilities, he knew his flaws, and he knew his politics were becoming increasingly independent. A maverick, however brilliant, was not what he needed right now. Balfour may also have been sensitive to gossip during the last election that Harry had influence over him and would 'hang on to him like a leech'. Lord George Hamilton, then Secretary of State for India, thought Balfour too involved with the Souls and his closeness to Harry could 'damage him in the eyes of the House'.[20] Later, the Souls' friend, Richard (by then Viscount) Haldane, who admired their gifts generally, would nevertheless muse 'whether their influence was on balance good'.[21]

There was also the conversation Harry allegedly had in late 1902 with a backbencher, Herbert Maxwell, who reported it to Balfour: 'Harry Cust sounded me out about my willingness to join a movement to upset the present administration in favour of one with Rosebery at the head'.[22] Harry reportedly said that 'the country is sick of the present people. There is no man in the Cabinet except Arthur Balfour and Joe Chamberlain and we want something else.' Although Maxwell said Harry acknowledged 'that the great obstacle to his project was the affection our people had for you [Balfour]', it hardly indicated the loyalty Balfour needed.

By contrast, George Wyndham was having his golden hour. He remained Chief Secretary for Ireland, and his great legacy was the revolutionary Land Purchase (Ireland) Act, also known as the Wyndham Act, which became law in the summer of 1903. At a time when Home Rule was still an issue, the Act was said to 'kill Home Rule by kindness', by allowing the transfer of land ownership from landlord to tenant.

His success was achieved partly with the unlikely help of Wilfrid Blunt – unlikely because of their very different political stances on Ireland in relation to Home Rule – and was prompted by Gay Windsor. In March 1903, she visited Blunt with a message from Wyndham asking if he could help with the Irish members on the proposed bill. In fact, it was probably Gay's idea to ask him. The incongruity of Blunt, once the jailed, helping the jailer may have made Wyndham think that his cousin's assistance was too unlikely to merit consideration.

In July, as the bill was going through its third reading and was assured victory, Wyndham hosted the king on his state visit to Ireland, travelling with him on the royal yacht and joining Sibell in Dublin. In a letter to Pamela, he described how, as he rode in the carriage with Their Majesties, the reception was (as an old hand told him) unprecedented for a royal visit even in the poorest parts of the city, while the cheering in Phoenix Park was so loud that the horses almost bolted.

While the sight of a new monarch after Victoria's long reign was bound to arouse interest, Wyndham's anticipated Act was doubtless the main cause of excitement and was hailed as one of the most important pieces of social legislation since the Act of Union 200 years earlier. He would need to hold close to him the memory of that adulation, for his personal glory would be unexpectedly short-lived.

Soul member Alfred Lyttelton, as Secretary of State for the Colonies, led a debate in early 1904 over the highly controversial issue of whether workers from China should be allowed into South Africa to work in the goldmines. One February afternoon, Wyndham and Harry escorted their wives to the public gallery to watch the debate, before joining their colleagues on the benches below.

Sibell and Nina watched the men argue (perhaps it was the day Harry was criticised for talking too long and fiddling with an ill-fitting collar) about issues which they, as women, were powerless to affect, as another observer was acutely aware. Balfour's sister-in-law, Lady Frances Balfour, a regular attendee, was there too. She was now part of the Executive Committee of the National Union of Women's Suffrage Societies (NUWSS), whose president was Millicent Garrett Fawcett. Clearly, they had reached some sort of truce after their disagreement over the Harry Cust debacle. Frances was also President of the London Society of Women's Suffrage, the largest single suffrage group in Britain.

The women's presence in the gallery was noted in the ladies' column of a newspaper. At a time when a woman's looks still tended to be her defining attribute, Lady Frances, not a noted beauty, was described as an intellectual who was devoted to politics. By contrast, Sibell, mother of the 25-year-old Duke of Westminster, was said (at 49) to look 'wonderfully young and pretty', while Nina, now 37, was 'one of the most fascinatingly lovely young women I have ever seen, with ivory pale, clear-cut features, soft wavy hair and the gentlest, sweetest looking eyes imaginable'.[23] Flattering it may have been, but no doubt she would have preferred to be described in terms of her work.

Although Harry was disappointed at being overlooked for a Cabinet role, he contributed to the *entente cordiale* and remained active in the Primrose League and, as was the Souls' way, tried not to let politics spoil his friendship with Balfour, although self-interest doubtless played a part. In the summer of 1904, the pair were guests at the Granbys' dinner party for Rudyard Kipling. Harry already knew Kipling, whose portrait Violet had drawn three years earlier, but it was James Rennell Rodd's first time of meeting the famed author. Rodd thought he was rather contemplative but put it down to the 'gifted hostess, whose beauty was unsurpassed by any of my generation'.[24]

At 48, Violet was indeed still lovely and remained a popular subject for artists. Two years earlier, she had sat for the sculptor George Frampton, whose marble bust of her secured his membership of the Royal Academy. He reflected her aesthetic style in the medallions on the lapels of her bolero bearing a peacock design, in her earrings and in her curious medieval-style headdress that fastened under her chin. She still loved Harry and such occasions affirmed their relationship, especially as Nina was taking the waters at Bad Schwalbach in Germany.

A translation of Machiavelli's work was published in September with Harry's introduction, elegant and erudite. It had caused Henley to fret while he waited to hear whether Harry would do it; his aversion to committing to deadlines could be infuriating. 'I've heard nothing of Cust,' he had raged to Charles Whibley. 'What he wants, what's his game, what he's up to – all this, so far as I'm concerned, is so much a muddle. Do he mean to do the *Machiavel*? I know not. Do you?' He wanted Whibley to tell Harry 'that he's shaping more like the Abstract Shit than anyone I've known since RLS [Robert Louis Stevenson]'.[25] A year later, Henley was waiting for Harry to produce something else. 'I can get nothing out of HC,' he fumed.[26]

Harry fulfilled his promises, but everyone was left exhausted in his wake. As usual, he was forgiven, his work more than justifying the agonising wait, but this trait of what was seen less as the unpredictability of genius and more as unreliability could mitigate against him.

The clever and literary Whibley would forgive Harry most things. A short, funny-looking man was how Mary's daughter, 18-year-old Cynthia Charteris, saw Whibley when she met him at Lord and Lady Windsor's Hewell Grange in 1905 but she soon fell under the spell of his humour.

Harry was there too, showing he had lost none of his willingness to lark about. They played a typically rumbustious game where Cynthia was the Lorelei and, lying on a sofa, had to lure drowning sailors towards the rocks while everyone sang. Harry and Whibley were among the doomed men 'propelling themselves along an immense length of parquet floor in a frantic and very close race to the fatal rocks'.[27] Whibley won, but as she stretched out her hand towards him, Cynthia accidentally knocked his spectacles off, and they were 'ground to powder under the knees of Harry', the runner-up. Whibley's good-natured reaction so impressed Cynthia that she became a lifelong friend.

As an Apostle, Harry attended the lavish annual dinners of the Cambridge Conversazione Society, now under the presidency of his friend, Henry Babington Smith, and he continued to embrace and be embraced by literary circles, dining with J.M. Barrie and Jerome K. Jerome, the writer and humourist, who was enjoying fame for his comic travelogue, *Three Men in a Boat*. *The Sphere* regretted Harry did not have a paper:

> He is wasted in Parliament. Anyone who really wishes to can sit in Parliament but how few men are born editors. Mr Cust is a born editor. He can inspire young men. But the gods when they gave him this gift gave him also a sense of mocking humour and sealed his doom.

No paper in England wanted such an editor, it said, however well connected he was.[28]

As 1905 progressed, Balfour faced increasing dissension in his party and recognised the growing unpopularity of some of its key issues. He believed he sensed emerging Liberal disunity and thought that if the Liberals formed an administration under Sir Henry Campbell-Bannerman, the chasm would grow, strengthening the Conservatives' position at the next General Election. In order to achieve this, on 4 December, Balfour resigned as prime minister. The next day, Campbell-Bannerman duly formed a Liberal government but decided to capitalise on the opposition's unpopularity by immediately calling a General Election. It was not what Balfour had intended.

In what was expected to be a very tough campaign, canvassing was more crucial than ever. Nina played her part as an MP's wife in being seen to support Harry, for however irregular their marital situation might be, a united front was what the electorate expected to see. Putting aside her natural reticence, she got involved in ventures in Bermondsey and appeared on public platforms. As Harry was the Ruling Councillor of the local Primrose League Habitation, Nina was appointed its Dame President. She distributed prizes at charity dances and smiled when she was cheered. 'Hope you won't overwork at Bermondsey,' Lady Welby wrote anxiously, conscious always of her daughter's health.[29]

There was one invitation she no doubt accepted reluctantly. Her relation, the Reverend Edward Talbot, who had been a thorn in their side after their marriage, was now Bishop of Southwark, within whose borough Bermondsey lay, and when he gave his first garden party that summer, Nina dared not refuse the invitation.

Harry scored popularity points when he made a generous contribution to the refurbishment of Bermondsey's concert hall, for which he was thanked at a lively meeting with musical interludes and comic sketches. It was a tribute to the ease with which he dealt with his constituents in a working-class area that the chairman referred not only to his political work having made a mark but to their luck in having a member 'who represented others of the highest and best educated class in the House and out of it'.[30]

He drew laughter when he joked that he noticed his portrait had been moved to a remote corner and replaced by a stuffed perch. But he also had to acknowledge two charges levelled against him: absence from his constituency and ill health. The former was due to the latter, he said, and could not be helped. Earlier that year, for instance, a severe bout of influenza had felled him for weeks. He surmised that the election would be in early 1906 and leave only a few weeks to prepare for what he warned would be a tough fight this time, and he sought their support once more. Loyal optimism flourished. The local papers crowed that Harry's Radical opponent was 'cordially disliked in many quarters', whereas 'Mr Cust has a charm of manner that is irresistible'.[31]

Even Wyndham had been having a tough time. His stressful work in Ireland had exhausted him, and he was worn down by 'pettiness, malice and ignorance', he told Sibell.[32]

Alcohol was making it worse. A breakdown loomed, as witnessed by a young man who visited him in Dublin in 1903 with a view to becoming his assistant. He found 'Melancholy, Humour, false Hilarity, elemental passions … nobility of soul blending into a wailing dirge'.[33]

In August 1904, doctors recommended a complete rest. He began a long holiday, starting with a visit to Hewell Grange with Sibell to join Gay and her children. Sibell left first, enabling her husband to spend time with his mistress. 'George stayed longer and was excellent company,' Lady Paget noted, 'the boys hung on his lips and he himself was supremely happy in this sympathetic circle and unable to tear himself away.'[34]

The combined perils of political fame and good looks inspired fantasists. That summer, a woman called Beatrice de Lysle was prosecuted for obtaining a loan on false pretences by telling the lender she was a countess and the wife of the Rt Hon. George Wyndham, whom she said she had married in Italy in May 1897. The gullible lender was led to believe that Wyndham had committed bigamy, although he admitted he did not really think he was that kind of man.

If only that were the sole cloud in his life. He spent part of his break in Germany, leaving his under-secretary, Sir Antony MacDonnell, in charge in Ireland. Balfour had expressed his misgivings about Wyndham's choice in MacDonnell, for although he had proved to be an excellent administrator in India, he was an Irishman, sympathetic to Home Rule and known for his fiery temper. Before accepting the post, MacDonnell had demanded and obtained from Wyndham an assurance that certain conditions would be met, which in effect gave him greater latitude than a civil servant would normally have.

In Wyndham's absence, a plan for devolution was published by Lord Dunraven, founder of the Irish Reform Association. Although it was not Home Rule, it was seen as a significant step towards self-governing. The plan excited the Opposition and was made worse when it emerged that MacDonnell himself was helping to draft it, born of a misunderstanding. In September, McDonnell had written to Wyndham telling him he was helping with the proposed scheme but received no reply, so pressed ahead. Dunraven's impression was that Wyndham had approved it, and on 25 September 1904 it was published.

Wyndham was horrified: he immediately returned from Germany, wrote to *The Times* and denied he knew about the project, but the more extreme Irish Unionists would not accept it. MacDonnell's action was condemned, although he was exonerated of disloyalty. Nevertheless, determined to clear his name, he produced passages from the letters he had sent Wyndham. But Wyndham had no recollection of ever seeing them. Years later, he would find a crucial letter between the pages of a book he had taken on holiday.

Gay Windsor provided balm, and Wyndham also enjoyed diversion in correspondence with the sculptor Auguste Rodin, who had recently completed a bronze bust of him. Wyndham had sat for Rodin in Paris for several days, for up to five hours a time, and developed a fondness for the great man, with whom he talked art and nature and met beautiful women. After Wyndham returned home, they discussed the work in progress in letters. He was delighted with the result, and they stayed in touch.

Wyndham's health worsened. In January 1905, Balfour told Sibell he was seriously alarmed. Wyndham's appearance before Parliament in February to explain himself was disastrous, his statement almost incoherent. The Irish Unionists would not subside, and his mental state deteriorated further. He joined his parents at Clouds where, on 4 March, Balfour's private secretary arrived to obtain his resignation in the interests of the party and his health.

Churchill would say that Balfour had repeatedly refused Wyndham's resignation, accepting it only when he broke down completely. Others saw it as an example of Balfour's cold-bloodedness in sacrificing his devoted protégé to the 'Ulster pack'. Mary Elcho discussed her brother with Balfour and felt that, although he said he was in a state of wretchedness and indecision, deep down he had really decided that George should go.

He and Sibell left for Italy, where she promptly fell ill. He nursed her, telling his mother they were 'like acrobats, who alternately support each other'.[35] This consideration for his wife, now 50 to his 42, born out of respect and affection, was maintained alongside his love for Gay. As Sibell recovered, Gay joined the pair at her mother's villa.

Lady Paget felt sorry for Wyndham and was 'deeply touched by the nobility, generosity and strength' of his character. He had been badly let down by those who ought to have stood by him, and yet 'not a word of blame escaped his lips'.[36] In other circumstances, she would have been a devoted mother-in-law. Her view of Wyndham's noble spirit suggests she considered him worthy of being her daughter's lover.

His wife, meanwhile, was increasingly withdrawing into religion. When Lady Paget stayed with them afterwards at Saighton, she wondered when Sibell's household found time for eating and sleeping, for she was dressed by 7.30 a.m. ready for the first of four services, all conducted by a priest who was very High Church.

Perhaps Mary tried to amuse her brother by relating the king's visit to Stanway in July, for which her children diligently practised their bows and curtseys, although on the day, Yvo ended up doing a curtsey, much to his mortification. The king was kind to him, though, and enjoyed himself so much, playing bridge under the tulip tree, that he stayed two hours longer than expected.

Curzon, too, was having difficulties, personally and professionally. India was physically a challenging place to live. His wife, Mary, suffered bouts of ill health, and the role of viceroy was extremely demanding. Nevertheless, in 1903, as he entered the last year of his five-year tenure, he asked to be considered for a further term, and Balfour agreed.

Curzon requested six months' leave in England first, and in March 1904, Mary gave birth to their third child, another daughter. That summer, Lord and Lady Kedleston were welcomed by the Souls and feted by the country, but a further pregnancy resulted in a miscarriage, after which Mary nearly died. Against all odds, she recovered and rejoined Curzon in India in early 1905.

However, news of the viceroy's conflict with General Lord Kitchener, Britain's Commander-in-Chief in India, was coming to Balfour's attention, largely via the ambitious Kitchener himself. He had the ear of the new Lady Salisbury, whose husband, James, Balfour's cousin, had succeeded as marquess in 1903. Originally Curzon had lobbied for Kitchener's appointment, but the commander-in-chief found that some of Curzon's actions had alienated the army and he embarked on a course of action that would undermine the viceroy's supremacy.

Balfour's Cabinet increasingly sided with Kitchener, aided and abetted by the mishandling of the affair by the now Secretary of State for India, St John Brodrick. Eventually, in August 1905, Balfour told the king that Curzon's judgement made him unfit to be viceroy. Later, Balfour would say that he regretted his decision to let Curzon stay on more than almost any other in his premiership. Curzon tendered his resignation, which Balfour accepted with alacrity and almost immediately announced his successor.

Feeling crushed, Lord and Lady Kedleston arrived back in England in December and anticipated the usual official welcome given to a returning viceroy and vicereine. The king asked Balfour and Brodrick to meet them at the station, a positive gesture in the circumstances, but neither of them went. After years of friendship, a deep rift opened between Curzon and Balfour.

No other Souls were there to meet them either, despite the sentiments of Wyndham's poem on the eve of the couple's departure, for they were at Stanway for the week. All they managed was a telegram. Loyalties were weakening. At a difficult time, Souls' friendships were less certain.

15

The Young Ones

As 1906 began and the General Election loomed, Wyndham and Curzon contemplated their futures after the enforced changes to their careers. For Ettie Grenfell, however, the year began in celebratory mode, for not only had she recently inherited the Panshanger estate in Hertfordshire from her uncle, Lord Cowper, but the king elevated Willie, sportsman, politician and conservator, to the peerage.

The confirmation of Lord Cowper's will assured the king of the prosperity he required of new peers, and Balfour had included Willie's name in his last honour's list. Lady Desborough (the title chosen by Willie) thanked her dear Balfour warmly: 'No words will express the gratitude that I do feel for all your goodness about it', and Willie was 'walking on air'.[1]

Together with Taplow Court, where they had entertained over 100 VIPs from India and the colonies for the coronation, the Desboroughs now had two country seats. For the 1906 Season, they also rented a house in Grosvenor Square, where in February Ettie hosted the first London dinner party that was all her own, mixing Souls and other friends (including the still-adoring Evan Charteris) with theatrical figures and diplomats – a favourite was the Portuguese envoy to London, the Marquess de Soveral, who thought Ettie, now 38 and the mother of five, the only woman who could look stately and voluptuous at the same time.

The General Election took place in January 1906, as Harry had predicted. Balfour's tactic had misfired, and he summarised the result in a telegram to Mary at Gosford, 'Lost by a large majority hope to be at Whittingehame tomorrow night but cannot be sure'.[2] After nearly twenty years of his party being in office, the Liberal Party won a landslide victory. This triumph was their only one, however, for it was the last election in which they would hold an absolute majority in the House of Commons and in which they would win the popular vote.

Balfour was worn out but felt surprisingly optimistic about a new political era. He became Leader of the Opposition, and although he lost his seat, along with over half his party, he was soon offered another, thanks to his uncle.

Lord Salisbury and others put pressure on the MP for the City of London to retire. Salisbury considered him useless, and besides, once his ailing father in the House of Lords died, he would take his seat there. Balfour was adopted as the City's candidate and won a by-election in February.

George Wyndham also remained in Parliament, retaining his seat at Dover, but Harry was less fortunate. He had tried hard in a campaign where the opposition was much more aggressive than before.

Harry's meetings were not the only ones disrupted by planned heckling. In the week before polling began, eighteen meetings around the country, including Balfour's and Lloyd George's, were severely disturbed in an attempt to silence the speakers, and several had to be abandoned altogether.

Harry's cool composure in the face of hostile interruption from supporters of his opponent, Dr George Cooper, was praised. At one Bermondsey meeting, Harry was on the platform for over an hour but was able to speak for only a quarter of it. However, although he was insulted frequently, he never exhibited 'a symptom of temper, or even irritation, [nor was he] induced to make the obviously scathing retorts to which the obstructers laid themselves open'. Harry faced his opponents 'with the pluck of the public school-bred English gentleman, and by the end of the evening even they had ceased to exhibit personal animosity'.[3]

Hecklers or not, Harry must have realised the writing was on the wall when the Bermondsey Free Church Council, after approaching both him and Cooper, decided to give their support to the latter. It was hardly surprising, for the Free Churchmen – Methodists, Quakers and other Nonconformists, of which there was an established community in Bermondsey – traditionally looked to the Liberal Party for removal of their civil and religious disabilities.

The nail in the Conservatives' coffin in this election was the complex and controversial 1902 Education Act, or 'Balfour's Act,' which established

Local Education Authorities (LEAs) in place of elected school boards. After enjoying control over local schools, the Nonconformists saw it handed to the LEAs, which they resented, for it meant they would have to contribute to the upkeep of Anglican schools. Harry's dinner guests one evening had been surprised when Balfour, without any embarrassment, asked a legal expert to explain the draft bill to him, in front of members of the opposition.[4]

Harry's disappointment was surely deepened by others' sentiments. 'Journalists of both parties will be sorry that that very clever member of their craft, Mr Harry Cust, will no longer be in the House', wrote *The Sphere*, and named two prominent authors who had been elected in what were the dying days of the 'gentleman politicians' – Hilaire Belloc and C.F.G. Masterman, both Liberals.[5] Fun was poked at the 'fallen gods of society', among them Harry. 'Old Parliamentarians will look in vain for the associate graces of literature and yachting so effectually embodied in Mr H Cust', said the *Daily Express*.[6]

Harry was undeterred. Two weeks later, his supporters welcomed him at the Bermondsey Club, where his unconcealed contempt for the way in which the Liberal Party, one of 'parasites and hangers-on [with] no common bond of adhesion', had conducted itself in the campaign drew cheers, as did his announcement that he intended to stand again if Bermondsey would have him.[7]

A member proposed a toast to the absent Nina. In response, Harry paid public tribute to her. If there was one person more than another who had worked really hard in the recent contest, he said, that person was his devoted wife. Without her, he did not know what he would have done: a crowd-pleasing gesture, perhaps, but Harry knew how important her part was.

Nina's health continued to be fragile, like her mother's, although it did not stop either of them working. That year, Nina had the honour of being exhibited at the Royal Academy in its prestigious Summer Exhibition, with a sculpture of her niece, Joan.

Lady Welby was delighted to find her own work being increasingly feted by eminent philosophers and scientists, who were encouraging her to contribute to another book, but her life was frequently disrupted by attacks of what she called 'internal gout', which affected her kidneys and for which she constantly sought a cure. Although she thought Nina was essentially 'sound as a campanile', she nevertheless worried about her 'terrible thin paleness', which resulted from her own 'nervous shocks & long trial that cost me the three most precious years of my life & fatally broke the intellectual thread'.[8]

Although Nina had no children, Charles and Mollie had five to whom Lady Welby was, as her letters indicated, an adoring grandmother. If Nina had given birth, Harry's attitude to children might have been different, although the knowledge that childbirth had killed his mother must have had a deep impact. As it was, 'Harry never pretended an interest in children or boys, even when closely related to him', recalled his nephew, Sir Ronald Storrs, who hardly saw him until around 1902, when he was 21 – just as well, for children were often discomforted by Harry's sardonic way of talking to them – 'but his kindness grew until he treated me almost as a son'.[9]

Visiting Harry at St James's Lodge, Storrs would be 'exalted by the suddenly extended intellectual horizons he opened'. Sitting around the table, Storrs delighted in 'a variety of social experience, ranging from the presence together of Ras Makonnen of Abyssinia and the Archbishop of Armagh' to discussions between political opponents Balfour and Asquith. Harry's extraordinary range of interests and accomplishments were a dazzling inspiration to the young man.

Some of the Souls' children were now young adults, although their parents' romantic lives often remained unsettled. For Pamela, the sudden death in 1906 of Dorothy, wife of Sir Edward Grey, the Foreign Secretary, in a road accident, changed her life, albeit subtly at first.

Eddy Tennant and the handsome, intellectual Grey were good friends, and their wives shared a mutual respect. Pamela thought Dorothy beautiful and interesting, and after the Greys stayed with the Tennants at their country house, Wilsford Manor, Dorothy told Pamela admiringly, 'You do so supremely know how to live; and I don't believe even politics can interfere or make your life dusty'.[10] Grey was godfather to the Tennants' third child, Christopher, born in 1899. He and Dorothy had no children of their own: she had requested that their marriage be sexless.

Grey and Pamela were very good friends and shared, he said, nearly every taste and interest in common, especially books and birds. After Dorothy's death, they became more intimate. However, despite Grey's reputation for integrity, Pamela's great-grandson, Simon Blow, has said that her son David, born in 1902, believed Grey to be his real father.[11]

Eddy was aware of the closeness between his wife and Grey, although he upset Pamela by saying he did not know what jealousy was. Occupied with business and politics, and soon to be made Lord Glenconner, he was often in Scotland, where he eventually found comfort with a mistress.

In 1906, Pamela had her fifth child, Stephen, and devoted herself to making Wilsford a place of eternal childhood. But her love for her children was not equal. Pamela openly disliked her eldest child and only daughter, Clarissa (Clare), which, according to Blow, she made clear in her book, *Sayings of the Children.* She found Clare's temperament difficult. Her eyes were 'as cold as Scotch pebbles', she would say.[12]

Mainly, however, Pamela's grievance was that Clare was growing up to be as beautiful as she was. 'A disturbing threat,' said Blow. 'Whenever she could, therefore, she would put her daughter down.'

As though compensating for her disappointment in Clare, she raised young Stephen to believe he would have been happier as a girl, dressing him until he was 6 in flowing robes and giving him a taste for women's clothes and make-up. Beautiful, sensitive and talented, Stephen Tennant would become one of the Bright Young Things of the 1920s, beloved of the artistic world and, famously, by Siegfried Sassoon.

The Souls' romantic lives were sometimes an embarrassment to the next generation, dubbed 'the Coterie', who could be less understanding of what they saw as their parents' double standards and indulgences. Ettie Desborough was feeling the depressing effect of creeping age, complaining to Mary Elcho that she was getting tired of spending hours with her middle-aged face in front of the mirror. She had a horror of losing the passion and vitality she had always enjoyed and encouraged in others, so it was not surprising that she turned to 'the mounting joy & hope of the young generation',[13] cultivating friendships with those of her children's age, especially men.

Since 1904, Ettie had been enjoying a relationship with Archie Gordon, son of Lord Aberdeen, who at 20 was only four years older than her son, Julian. Archie had been visiting Taplow for years and was an undergraduate at Willie's old college, Balliol. At the time, close friendships between wealthy older married women and well-bred young men at the start of their professional lives were not uncommon and, to avoid any suggestion of scandal, there could be nothing clandestine about them.

Inevitably, sometimes things went further. Archie's energetic enjoyment of life echoed Ettie's, and his charm and humour greatly appealed to the older woman. Her younger son, Billy, and daughter, Monica, liked him too, as did Ettie's friends, although Julian was less enamoured of his mother's relationship, while her cousin, Bron Herbert, wanted her to promise never to have Archie in the house.

'My beloved E,' gushed Archie in a letter from Italy, 'I can't begin to speak of all the joy of seeing you, & seeing you *often* & *much* … I have the whole universe waiting to be talked about & all my life to be submitted to you'.[14] A love of older women clearly ran in his family, for in August 1906, Archie's eldest brother, Lord Haddo, aged 27, horrified the family by marrying a draper's widow, aged 49. But just a week later, Ettie's relationship with Archie became the source of unpleasantness and potential scandal.

Archie was also fond of Violet Asquith, the 19-year-old daughter of Henry Asquith (now Chancellor of the Exchequer). Her stepmother, Margot, had earmarked Archie for Violet, who reciprocated his feelings. After all, it was the young people's turn to experience the Season, to make friends and to fall in love.

Violet and Archie had agreed to go to a party given by Frances Horner, but Ettie persuaded Archie to take her to a play instead. Archie did not tell Violet of his arrangement with Ettie and when Lady Horner angrily rang Violet the next day, the young woman discovered the truth and was bitter and hurt. Her reproaches 'drove Archie into a paroxysm of anguished remorse',[15] while her brother Raymond, Margot and others made unpleasant remarks about Ettie and her young admirer.

Violet was shocked and humiliated and felt betrayed. Ettie tried to make amends, telling Violet (and asking her not to tell anyone) that she had wanted *her* to know the real truth because 'it is the greatest thing in the world'. Ettie deeply regretted that Violet had heard a story that seemed full of 'lies and petty treachery' and that the episode had caused Archie such distress.

Ettie's letter helped to restore Violet's faith in Archie, but it took much longer before Violet felt she could face the older woman. Margot made matters worse, for she was furious that Ettie had taught Archie to tell lies. 'There has been any amount of fuss between Ettie and Margot over Archie Gordon – too absurd', Mary Elcho told Balfour. 'I am so dreadfully afraid that M, if she gets the chance, will say things that may make Ettie never forgive her, or at any rate hate her for a time.' Ettie was 'humble and frightened apologetic and has been on more than one occasion reduced to tears!'[16] It was a tribute to Ettie's persuasive and epistolary skills that she and young Violet would become great friends.

In October, Julian Grenfell went up to Balliol and brought friends home to Taplow and Panshanger with whom Ettie is also thought to have had affairs. The strict moral standards she expected from her children were at odds with her own behaviour, and Julian, in particular, resented this.

Their elders' digressions aside, Violet Asquith said she and her siblings were constantly told by their stepmother 'how lamentably we fell short of [the Souls'] standards – in wit, in intellectual ambition, in conversational skill and social competence'.[17] In that sense, at least, their parents had set an impressive example.

That year, 1906, saw several Souls suffer emotional upheavals. George Curzon's beloved wife, Mary, died in his arms at their London home, aged 36, leaving him with three small girls. Wilfrid Blunt's wife, Lady Anne, no longer prepared to tolerate his infidelities, left him, the final straw being when his mistress moved into their home.[18]

While Harry suffered no such trauma, the year was not the easiest on that front. His knowledge of Pamela's closeness to Grey must have made him dwell on what might have been. In August, Violet Granby had a change of status when the Duke of Rutland died, raising the marquis to 8th Duke and Violet to duchess. Press coverage highlighted sensitive issues, such as the blondness (like Harry) of 14-year-old Lady Diana, whose photo appeared (correctly named this time) in the *Daily Mirror.*

Her mother's portrait sketch of Diana enacting Joan of Arc captured the nascent allure of the young woman, who would grow up to be another acclaimed beauty. With her mother's love of theatre and Harry's natural inclination to the dramatic, little wonder Diana would embrace the stage. Even at the age of 3, she was reciting poetry 'with an accuracy which is simply marvellous', enthused Violet's cousin, David Lindsay, although it was necessary to follow in a book because her diction was 'quite impossible to understand'.[19] Harry would have been amused by his daughter's precocity, so like his own.

He would have been less happy when a scandal threatened to expose his identity as her father in May 1908. A pamphlet about Violet was sent to David Lindsay's mother by a German governess who had been previously employed by the Granbys, concerning wages she claimed she had been cheated out of. 'It is most scurrilous', wrote David, although he thought the monetary claim possible given the 'haphazard ways of the Granby family'. But more serious was its 'specific accusations of immorality' against Violet. Although the manuscript was hard to read, 'the upshot is pretty clear and in more than one place it is directly stated that Harry Cust is the father of the girl Diana. I haven't seen the latter for years but I have always heard that her likeness to her reputed father is quite striking'.[20]

This governess, when Diana's sister, Letty, kept crying, used to tie up her chin with ribbon to stop the corners of her mouth drooping, and perhaps such conduct, along with other irregularities, had got her sacked, resulting in the vengeful pamphlet. How far she disseminated it before she was (almost inevitably) paid off cannot be ascertained, but it must have caused damage in the interim.

Whatever was known or suspected by others about her paternity, Diana herself would not discover the truth for a few more years. For now, the young woman delighted in being in Harry's company, sometimes at parties at Hackwood, an estate in Hampshire where George Curzon had lived since his wife died. Among his guests were Souls and Cabinet ministers 'with their wives or the women they loved', Diana recalled. 'They strolled, high heeled, with parasols on the lawn, through the aisles of beeches' while she mingled with other young people of the Coterie, and during one after-dinner guessing game found herself shouting excitedly at the Leader of the Opposition, 'Use your brain, Mr Balfour; use your *brain*'.[21]

Diana only discovered later that they were called the Souls, for her mother loathed the term, and while Diana enjoyed their company generally, Harry was 'a man I loved with all my heart … I clung to him at Hackwood and walked through the beech groves and capped quotations and giggled over our fellow guests'. Since the days when they were living at Cockayne Hatley, he was her 'rock'. There is poignancy in her affection for the man who could never reveal to her their real relationship:

> He was our 'familiar', an evergreen olive tree, classic, fresh, tender and funny, easily convulsed by silent laughter. Very beautiful, I thought him, with noble hands and impeccable filbert-shaped nails. He wore a coat such as I never saw another man wear – dark blue cloth, flaring full, short with a flat sable Eton collar. It was like Holborn's *Ambassadors*.[22]

It has been said that Harry did nothing worthwhile after losing his seat in 1906, drinking himself into obscurity. But although he did drink, the rest of the charge could not be further from the truth. He may not have become prime minister as predicted in his youth, but he knew the Liberals' day would not be long-lived and he wanted to get back into the House.

While his health continued to impose random restrictions upon him, making him more dependent on Nina, he remained involved in current affairs and community projects. He continued to promote the Conservatives in Lincolnshire where Earl Brownlow, once so politically active, was suffering ill health. In the world of journalism, he was named, along with Lord Northcliffe and Lord Burnham, owner of the *Daily Telegraph*, as one who maintained the 'dignity and recognition' of journalism 'over the mere money making concerns of commercialism'.[23]

Nina, whose creative star continued in the ascendant, completed two splendid busts of the earl at Belton that year, one in marble, the other in bronze mounted on wood veined to resemble marble.

While out of Parliament, Harry's friendship remained unaltered with those who were still in it. In March 1908, his dinner guests included Balfour and Asquith, then acting prime minister for the ailing Henry Campbell-Bannerman (who resigned a week later, making Asquith prime minister). Also present were H.G. Wells, Alfred Lyttelton, George Leveson Gower, Winston Churchill and his friend, Frederick Smith (later Lord Birkenhead), a brilliant young barrister and budding Conservative politician. Nina was out dining with friends. It was the usual mixed bag politically, culturally and also class wise, for Smith and Wells were from very ordinary families, but their company was what mattered to their host.

What a memorable evening it turned out to be, one that Wells would immortalise in his book, *The New Machiavelli* and that demonstrated much about Harry. Leveson Gower recalled that in the middle of dinner:

> … a servant announced, 'If you please sir, the room is on fire'.
>
> 'We are not finished dinner,' remarked our imperturbable host, 'bring in the next course and ring up the fire brigade.'
>
> When six engines arrived, the firemen naturally said the guests should leave:
>
> 'Not a bit of it,' said Harry. 'What! Send my guests away before dinner is over! I never heard of such a thing! You get on with your job and we'll get on with ours. It's quite safe, we're on the ground floor, with a window opening on to the terrace.'

The firemen reluctantly withdrew and continued to fight the flames but soon water started trickling through the ceiling. Leveson Gower was wearing a brand-new suit:

> … and presently an enormous discharge of dirty water descended upon me, to Churchill's intense delight. I was soon revenged by an even larger and dirtier downpour upon his devoted head.
>
> 'This is getting intolerable!' cried Harry, who rang the bell and ordered 'foot baths and bath towels.' The foot baths were placed to catch the heaviest cascades, and the company continued their dinner swathed in bath towels.[24]

An amusing night was had by all, even Asquith who, as one guest publicly revealed, gamely wrapped a towel around his neck, 'for although of the severe, rather than the genial variety, the acting Premier is not, at moments of extreme inspiration, free from happy impulses'.[25]

Indeed, Asquith was often in high spirits, for he was usually to be found 'filling his skin with champagne'.[26] David Lindsay saw him 'quite drunk on several occasions' and thought him more reliant on alcohol than any other public figure of the time. Perhaps that partly explained why, as a female guest at another party discovered, Asquith could be 'most delightfully daring in his gallantry, and acts with a naively delicious disregard of such possible punishments as black looks, crimson cheeks and astonished audiences'.[27] Lady Ottoline Morrell was more direct, protesting that he would take a lady's hand as she sat next to him and place it on his erection.

In short, Asquith was a sexual menace. If Harry knew his daughter had to defend her face from 'his fumbly hands and mouth',[28] perhaps he would have regarded his friend less tolerantly. Margot was finding that marriage was not plain sailing. Her initial instinct after his first wife, Helen, died had been 'To be a stepwife and a stepmother was unthinkable'.[29] Of his five children, she only met Violet on their engagement, and he took her to see the others, who were living with their governess in the country, only once before they married. Violet was extremely close to her father and had a stormy relationship with Margot, although later she would say she admired her devotion to him.

Since their marriage, Margot had been vital in furthering Asquith's ambition and getting him to Downing Street by introducing him to the world of the Souls and other influential individuals, which he had not experienced in his first marriage. Emotionally, though, they were worlds apart. If the Tennants 'believed in appealing to the hearts of men', said Margot, the Asquiths 'believed in the free application of intellect to every human emotion … We were as zealous and vital as they were detached, and as cocky and passionate as they were modest and emotionless.'

Yet such detachment did not preclude Asquith's enjoyment of young women. Their marriage was affected by the fact that Margot had lost three babies, the last in 1906, and doctors said she should not have any more beyond the two who had survived, Elizabeth born in 1897 and Anthony in 1902. Essentially that meant the end of marital relations, which caused her much guilt. If her brother Eddy had never felt jealous, Margot too 'thought you had no right to claim one man', said Diana. 'But I didn't either. I mean, jealousy was common; the awful word was common.'[30]

Diana was one of the 'little harem' of young women whose admiration Asquith craved (although not enough to support women's suffrage). He would become obsessed with Venetia Stanley, a friend of his daughter, Violet.

Meanwhile, despite the Souls' greater age and responsibilities, their gatherings retained much of their spirit and spontaneity, the difference for Harry being that these days Nina was more likely to be with him. Fun, 'fast and furious', was had at Stanway in April 1908, as they joined Mary, George Wyndham, Balfour and others in being 'the rats' to Arty Paget's Pied Piper of Hamelin as he played his guitar.[31] Hugo was absent from the throng, probably to be found in the arms of his latest mistress, Lady Angela Forbes.

But politically, things were changing. The Liberal Party now contained Radicals whose stance leaned further to the left than most of the party, Home Rule was unresolved, and the young Labour Party had won seats at the last election. Harry was driven to get involved with Frederick Smith and R.D. Blumenfeld, 'Blum', the genial American editor of the *Daily Express*, in starting the Anti-Socialist Union in 1908, which aimed to counteract 'the fallacious statements put about by Socialist writers and speakers, particularly those who speak in parks and open spaces'.[32] The glue that bound the Souls together – that civilised discourse was possible between those of different views – would dissolve.

16

New Horizons

Even the German Ambassador, Prince Lichnowsky, noted that Asquith was 'fond of the ladies, especially the young and pretty ones'.[1] Yet in 1909, while the prime minister got away with sexual harassment and Loulou Harcourt, a paedophile who preyed on both sexes, continued in the Cabinet post to which Campbell-Bannerman had appointed him, the Custs' past still pursued them.

In March, Nina's history book was published, to glowing reviews. *Gentlemen Errant* narrated the adventures of four noblemen as they travelled through Europe in the fifteenth and sixteenth centuries. 'In the skilled hands of Mrs Henry Cust', enthused one newspaper, it was 'one of the most entertaining books imaginable'.[2] *The Scotsman* praised 'the vigour and brilliancy' of her style. Her mother was thrilled: 'I am swelling with pride in you (but then I always have been from the day of your arrival!)'.[3] But when Virginia Woolf – Miss Stephen, as she still was – received a copy to review, she determined that she was not going to be complimentary. She told her intimate friend Violet Dickinson that the author 'is a woman who had a child before she was married … and atones for it by studying medieval Germany. My review,' she sniffed piously, 'is going to deal with the subject of the illicit passions in a masterly way and to suggest better means of penitence'.[4] However, she too would be captivated.

As Miss Dickinson was also a friend of Violet Cust's and probably aware of Nina's childless state, perhaps she took the opportunity to correct the misapprehension Miss Stephen was under. On the other hand, she was also a great friend of Kathleen Lyttelton, Fawcett's supporter during the Cust crisis. It seems unlikely, though, that anything she might have said in Nina's favour would have altered Miss Stephen's view of her conduct.

For Harry, the spectre of Millicent Garrett Fawcett still loomed. 'Can you imagine a life less "fortunate" than mine,' he complained bitterly to Margot. 'Every time I am offered a constituency 1893 is, in two days, flung in my face, AJB [Balfour] notwithstanding.'

He was melancholic, for, as the negative aspects of his past still haunted him, the pleasurable parts were being swept away. St James's Lodge was about to be demolished, along with the rest of Delahay Street, to make way for new Treasury buildings. In packing up his home, he came across old papers which made him nostalgic, for they were 'all beautiful and clean and dewy and delicious', he told her, 'and to me, breathing a second spring'. He wanted Margot to keep them safe while he moved. She might enjoy reading 'the tiny archives of my little home which your government insists on pulling down tomorrow [because] I think you love the old tethers of affectionate days as much as I do'. Margot would probably see such documents as 'merely moorings but to me they are my only anchorage'.[5]

Her friendship was still important to him, the 'bad married dog', as he called himself. 'I know that you entirely disapprove of me but I know too that you are the most darling, loyalist friend I have ever had, bar one.' Few people saw the darkness that Harry's natural exuberance disguised. When it manifested itself as self-pity, they dismissed it as mere indulgence, and while an element of that undoubtedly affected him, his demons went deeper.

The 'second spring' would come, but for now, the past seemed a better place than the present. At 47, he wanted to be back in the beating heart of the political world and he was aware of the rise of others, especially Churchill who, angered by the Conservatives' stance on tariff reform and their drift towards protectionism, had dramatically 'crossed the floor' of the House of Commons in 1904 to join the Liberal Party, where he would remain until 1925. In 1908, the year he married Clementine, he was appointed President of the Board of Trade at just 33.

In October 1909, Churchill and Harry were guests at Blunt's party. Blunt thought Harry was 'quite outclassed by Winston' in political discussion, for Churchill had 'studied all these problems thoroughly and is wonderfully quick in defending his position'. Harry, on the other hand, was 'wonderfully well equipped for talk, having a far greater knowledge of history and literature and a real poetic side, which Churchill is wanting … Both have wit and quickness of repartee and the power of epigram. It is first-class sword-play between them.'[6] The champagne flowed, and Churchill's erudition was unimpaired by having drunk seven glasses of his host's best Madeira, although 'Harry was more affected and when we were on our way to bed talked rather incoherently about the moon and forgot which floor of the house we were on'.[7]

Inevitably since Harry began his political career, society had been changing. The women's movement had gathered momentum. Under Millicent Garrett Fawcett's presidency of the National Union of Women's Suffrage Societies, the suffragists were less militant than the suffragettes in the Women's Social and Political Union, whose violent tactics Fawcett privately condemned.

Security for prime ministers was non-existent, making them easy targets. In September, Harry was one of several friends who witnessed suffragette attacks on Asquith while they stayed at Lympne Castle in Kent, owned by Margot's brother. On leaving church, he was molested by three women, one of whom was dressed as a nurse and another who hit him repeatedly.

That evening, after Asquith's party had finished playing golf, the same women appeared and began striking him in the face with their fists. Herbert Gladstone, the Home Secretary, and Asquith's son Raymond managed to get them outside, and Harry pretended to be the golf club's secretary, politely telling the women that whatever their dispute with the prime minister, club rules prevented them from walking on the grass. They were so surprised they stopped.

However, that night, as the Asquiths and their guests sat in the dining room of Lympne Castle, the women scaled the medieval walls and hurled two large stones through the window, shouting before they vanished into the night. As the press continued to report the glittering balls held during the Season, stories ran alongside of soirées in London houses where actresses provided entertainment as a warm-up to speeches by Christabel Pankhurst.

Changes were noticeable elsewhere, too, leading to a reduction of the power and wealth of the ruling classes and the decline of the aristocracy. In 1905, Robert Windsor-Clive had been created Earl of Plymouth when the king re-established his family's defunct earldom, which had died with the 8th Earl for want of an heir. His honour was partly due to his accomplishments as First Commissioner of Works, which included changing the Mall, opposite Buckingham Palace, from a general thoroughfare to a processional route, and being instrumental in the erection of Queen Victoria's statue.

Lord Windsor's reaction was muted, and Lady Paget wondered why she could not get an answer from her son-in-law or from Gay, now Countess of Plymouth, as to whether he would be the 1st Earl or the 9th. There was also a viscountcy that the king wanted him to take as a second title, which he needed to think about.

It was left to their daughter Phyllis to reply to her grandmother, saying that neither she nor her mother had 'the vaguest notion' as to what number earl he would be. Gay, deeply involved with charitable causes and animal welfare, and whose life was about to get busier, told her mother that Windsor 'knows very little and cares still less about it … Windsor is so hunted just now that really he can't manage to give it *very* much attention'.[8]

Lady Paget thought their reaction was 'amusing, considering what importance people generally attach to such things'. By contrast, her own delight reflected both the views of the old nobility and a widely held prejudice of the time, 'We are these days accustomed to see honours bestowed only upon Jews, brewers, bankers, and manufacturers'.[9]

Wyndham, expressing congratulations for his old friend who also happened to be his mistress's husband, told Lady Paget he was 'delighted, because it is right to restore ancient dignities to old families'.[10]

But such 'old families' were under threat, his father, Percy, noting, 'The truth probably is that the reign of the Upper and middle class is over … If it has any future it can only be realised by fighting for its remaining convictions and not by concessions.'[11]

In 1909, the Chancellor Lloyd George's 'People's Budget' proposed an unprecedented taxation on the income and lands of the wealthy. Its aim was to fund social welfare programmes, but it was seen as an attack on the property classes. Although it would become law the following year, its rejection by the House of Lords led to a constitutional crisis and a curtailing of the Lords' power by the House of Commons. Wyndham told his friend, the sculptor John Tweed:

> The 'Gentry' of England – as a type – are interesting; probably we have done what we are here to do. We are a survival. By 'we' I mean the countryside English gentry … Let the coming world, of oriental finance, & of Colonial Britons, know what the old people were like, who were nurtured for centuries on English acres.[12]

Although the 'old order' was on the way out, few could imagine just how much Britain would change in the next ten years.

Within the Souls, while romantic love still surprised and took many guises, love for their children would sometimes prove to be the most painful. As Lord and Lady Plymouth gave a ball in July 1908 to mark the end of the Season, they could not know that five months later their eldest son and heir Oti would die, aged 24. He was in India as aide-de-camp to the Viceroy Earl Minto, Curzon's successor, when he caught enteric fever. Wyndham, who had come to know him well, grieved too. 'It has been such anxiety for [the Plymouths] and now this great sorrow,' he told his mother. 'But he was given to the Empire as much as if he had died in battle.'[13] His words were tragically prescient.

Gay may have sought solace from the world of spiritualism with whose theories she was familiar, as was her mother, and in which interest had been increasing, with paranormal claims and mediums claiming contact with the dead. Challenging the old religious world view, the Society for Psychical Research (SPR) was in its third decade of research into whether alleged phenomena could be explained in naturalistic terms or pointed to aspects of consciousness not yet known to science. Its council members comprised eminent scientists, psychologists, mathematicians and philosophers. Arthur and Gerald Balfour had each been president, and now it was the turn of their sister, Eleanor Sidgwick, Principal of Newnham College, Cambridge.

Lady Paget had been a member of the SPR since 1890. Members among the Souls included Lady Brownlow who, when her sister Gity Pembroke became obsessed with her dead husband, invited the physicist and parapsychologist Sir Oliver Lodge to Ashridge to talk to her. Pamela Tennant joined in 1909 and later exposed a fake medium at Wilsford, and Mary Elcho hosted the American medium Mrs Herbine at Stanway, where a spirit called Sidney addressed them, much to the contempt of Mary's son, Ego, who wrote of his mother's 'dotty or potty friends who infest Stanway'.[14] Such sittings were often regarded as entertainment, but the Great War would see séances become a vital, even obsessive part of people's lives.

For the first time, experiments in 'cross correspondence' were undertaken by the SPR to see if the dead could communicate through messages sent to selected mediums. The written results were compared and analysed for all possible explanations. Apparently random and meaningless in isolation, the SPR found the fragments interlocked meaningfully when the scripts were collected and compared. The impression was of an organising intelligence, not easily attributed to the mediums themselves.

One of the SPR's most trusted mediums was Kipling's sister, Alice 'Trix' Fleming, whom Lady Paget encouraged to develop her psychic abilities and who was invited to Clouds by the Wyndhams. One 'sender' was Balfour's late sweetheart, May Lyttelton, whose apparently accurate communications to a medium called Mrs Willett would excite speculation. She would continue to receive messages from May over the next decade, sometimes with Balfour present – but while fascinated, he was never convinced.

Ettie Desborough needed her religious strength in 1909 when her young lover, Archie Gordon, now 25, was seriously injured in a car crash and died three weeks later. She was at his hospital bedside with his parents and Violet Asquith, who had agreed to marry him. Feeling it her Christian duty always to find the positive, even when looking at death, Ettie longed for those who loved him to think of his death only 'with thankfulness and joy [for] it would have hurt him so to bring *sadness* to life'.[15] Her attitude would be sorely tested in the coming years.

Mary Elcho, in a sentiment from a contemporary poem, told Balfour she feared Archie was 'one of those who will take their impression fresh back to the Mint, one of those who die in their glory. The lads who never grow old.'[16] Such words would come to represent a lost generation.

Ettie's son Billy told her the things she wanted to hear – that her love for Archie was great, that he had adored her and would not have wanted anyone to be unhappy. Julian, however, became severely depressed and suffered a nervous breakdown. He was also aware of his mother's relationship with Patrick Shaw-Stewart, whom he hated. He was Julian's age and four years younger than Archie.

For Nina and Harry, with no children over whom to fret, the demolition of Delahay Street pushed them in a new direction and into a lovely house near Kensington Gardens. Lady Welby saw it as a positive move. 'I feel you are making a fresh start & home!' she told her daughter. 'I am much looking forward to seeing you in it'.[17]

Chancellor's House, at 17 Hyde Park Gate, had eleven bedrooms, several reception rooms, a dining room, library and billiard room, with electric light and bells throughout. There was stabling for four horses and four carriages and a large private garden, always a bonus for central London.

Their 'fresh start' in fact began in February 1910 when, as polling for yet another General Election drew to a close, whose results Harry followed with interest,[18] they left for Egypt and were away for nearly three months. Such a long trip taken together may not have happened before, but Harry's erratic health made him more dependent on Nina, and after seventeen years of marriage, an equilibrium had surely been reached. The trip was driven partly by health issues for both of them – Egypt's heat made it an attractive winter resort – and by the chance to witness Britain's role on the world's stage, at an interesting time when nationalists were agitating for independence.

They stayed in Cairo with Harry's nephew, Ronald Storrs, who was now Britain's Oriental Secretary. Storrs clearly shared the Cust genes: his friend T.E. Lawrence said he was 'the most brilliant Englishman in the Near East and subtly efficient, despite his diversion of energy in love of music and letters … of whatever was beautiful in the world's fruit'.[19]

Another trait that uncle and nephew shared was a total lack of card-playing instinct, needing to be reminded every night of the rules of the game. To Storrs, Harry was a 'fountain of joy' who, like Lawrence, made him feel close to the source of life. When Storrs returned to Egypt and Palestine in the 1930s, he would find 'Englishmen, Frenchmen, Egyptians and Armenians whose memories of [Harry] were as fresh as if he had been with them but the year before'.[20]

Harry's desire to be near the heart of action was fulfilled shortly after their arrival. Storrs worked under the consul general, Sir Eldon Gorst, whom Harry had known at Eton and who arranged for them to have an excursion into the desert. As they returned, Gorst riding an Arab pony and everyone else on donkeys, the station master met them with a telegram for Gorst. Immediately, he galloped away to the station, where a special train took him to Cairo. The news he had received was the assassination of Egypt's prime minister, Boutros Ghali Pasha, whose appointment Gorst had supported. The assassin, a young Egyptian nationalist, confessed to the murder, the first of a senior statesman in Egypt for over a century and the first of a series of assassinations until 1915.

Storrs also accompanied the Custs to Jerusalem. As they stood on the Mount of Olives watching the sun set beyond the city, Harry, with his knack of turning the dramatic into the unforgettable, recited verses from Tennyson's 'In Memoriam', timing the lines to coincide with the last rays: 'A solemn radiance even crowned/ The purple brows of Olivet'.[21]

Nina kept her mother updated on their experiences, which reminded Lady Welby of her own extraordinary travels as a young woman with her mother, Emmeline Stuart-Wortley, in what already seemed, as she read her old diary, like a lost world. 'I must say I am glad to have been in Palestine before it was vulgarised,' she told Nina, 'when one could realise the great ones of old as they were, & the villages & cities were still sacred from the profaning touch of the "Cook" tribe.'[22]

A publisher wanted Lady Welby to write a book of reminiscences which would also help to sell the academic book she was collaborating on. She was unsure, yet she told Nina, 'I can't deny there have been many dramatic incidents & experiences in my life … I could do it if you would help me, my darling & you would be my very best advisor'.[23] She regretted that she had not asked her late Uncle Johnny, 6th Duke of Rutland, about her mother's early life, when she was engaged to marry the widowed Prince Leopold of Saxe-Coburg after his wife Charlotte died in childbirth, leaving Victoria the crown. Her brother had burnt all the royal letters.

In their absence, Lady Welby was receiving interesting visitors, such as the philosopher Bertrand Russell and others whom Harry had introduced, including H.G. Wells, whose recent 'New Woman' novel, *Ann Veronica*, was causing a sensation. Its storyline, about a young woman whose reputation is compromised by an older man, becomes a suffragette, is imprisoned and falls in love with a married man with whom she has children and lives happily, caused *The Spectator* to condemn it as 'capable of poisoning the minds of those who read it'. When libraries in Hull banned it as 'making a mockery of marriage', a local clergyman said he would rather send any daughter of his into a house infected with typhoid or diphtheria than give her the book.[24] Lady Welby would have none of it. 'I utterly refuse to believe that a man with those paunchy candid eyes is a bad man,' she told Nina. 'Apparently *The Spectator* has a personal grudge. Well, I can imagine that.'[25]

Lady Welby and Wells shared beliefs about women rooted in eugenics, a form of social Darwinism founded by Francis Galton, whom Lady Welby knew, which 'dealt with all influences that improve the inborn qualities of a race and with those that develop them to the utmost advantage'.[26] Wells and Welby believed in the elevation of motherhood beyond that of the traditional definition. Like other eugenic socialists, Wells argued for a system of state support for mothers, 'the endowment of motherhood'. Lady Welby wrote about the importance of the 'race mother' as an empowering force for female self-definition and social regeneration, a view that female modernists found hard to accept.

Wells was attracting censure for his personal life and free love doctrine. When he visited Lady Welby, he was married, but his mistress had recently given birth to his daughter. Married twice to women he loved, but neither of whom satisfied him sexually, he had several long-term relationships, as well as many briefer affairs, mostly condoned by his second wife. His relationships with three young women half his age caused a scandal.

His friendship with Harry was founded on mutual admiration and, for Wells, gratitude for the opportunities Harry had given him. He would write on the flyleaf of his book, *The World Set Free*:

To the Honourable
H.C. Cust,
Noblest and Best of
Editors,
Inventor of Authors,
Friend of Letters
from his affectionate contributor
H.G. Wells[27]

On 6 May, shortly before the Custs arrived home, Edward VII died, aged 69, following a series of heart attacks and a lifetime of erratic health. His last words, typically, were an expression of pleasure that his horse had won at Kempton Park that afternoon. His son became George V who, with his consort Queen Mary, provided a more virtuous example of marriage without the often-scandalous material associated with the late king.

As one of his aides-de-camp, Earl Brownlow was commanded to walk with the coffin as it processed from Buckingham Palace to Westminster Hall, then to Windsor Castle, and to attend the internment itself at St George's Chapel. At 66, whatever ill health he was suffering, he would have to put it aside in his final duties to his king. The countess, the same age, was bidden to attend the funeral but declined as it would be too fatiguing, and she made her apologies to her friend, now the Dowager Queen Alexandra.

The coronation took place the following year. Ettie Desborough was greatly honoured when Queen Mary appointed her a Lady of the Bedchamber, the highest level of lady-in-waiting before Mistress of the Robes. Ettie was required several times a year, for two-week periods, to accompany the queen on royal visits and other occasions, and to live in when the Court was at Windsor.

Health, as always, was on Lady Welby's mind and she was worried that Nina was in pain. She wanted her and Harry to see Doctor Strode, a surgeon whose speciality seemed to be massage and vibration and who the novelist Arnold Bennett said had 'almost cured' him of 'intestinal failure'.[28] Lady Welby thought him a man of 'genius and insight, & I believe might do you both real good'.[29] 'I am counting the days now until you come, darling', she told Nina. 'I do hope you won't suffer afterwards from all this exertion. I have been <u>achingly</u> anxious for

I know you are that about Harry & you don't spare yourself enough. You know you're not a dray horse!'[30]

Their adventures did take a toll. On their return, Harry wrote to Mary Elcho – he had written to her from Galilee but received no answer – and sent his best wishes for her daughter Cynthia's engagement to Asquith's younger son, Herbert 'Beb'. He had missed Mary's call inviting him to an event, probably a celebration. 'We go to Belton tomorrow,' he told her, 'but back very soon and I so want to see you. Poor Nina is [having] a rest cure for a month or more – perhaps you will ask me to Stanway – do.'[31]

An invitation duly arrived. 'You sweet, I always love being with you,' he replied. He had given up other commitments, including Hackwood, not for the party but for Mary, 'with whom, as you know so well, my relations have been ever non-marital but I've loved her none the less … & the world is yet young'. She seemed to have organised it especially for him. 'I hate to have given you so much trouble and wish – oh, a world of things,' he sighed. 'Maybe age improves dreams. Bless you for your sweet kindness.'[32]

The uncertainty of his own health prompted Harry to execute a hastily written will at Belton in March 1911, witnessed by Lord Brownlow and his butler. There were no frills. He left the London house and all other property and belongings to Nina, with the proviso that on her death any items that had come from Cockayne Hatley or were associated with the Brownlow Cust or Cockayne families should go to his brother or his heirs.

If it was a specific episode of illness that prompted him to write it, he recovered quickly, for a week later he was a dinner guest of the Earl and Countess of Warwick at the Ritz Hotel in the company of Prince Alexander of Teck, Queen Mary's brother and a prominent soldier, and the Rumanian minister, whose country would soon be involved in the Balkan Wars. Preparation for conflict, always near to Harry's heart, was a common theme, although there was also a racier element to the evening with the presence of the sculptor John Tweed and Miss Eve Fairfax, Rodin's intimate friend and the model for his marble sculpture, *La Nature*. The evening was followed by an invitation to dine with Count Mensdorff, the Austro-Hungarian Ambassador, and other European nobility, a reminder to Harry that although he was not in Parliament his presence was still valued.

As spring bloomed, so the Souls were reminded of mortality when, in May, Charty Ribblesdale died after a long struggle with tuberculosis, leaving three daughters and a son; her eldest son, Thomas, had predeceased her, dying in Somaliland seven years earlier. She had been too ill even to attend the wedding the previous year of her 18-year-old daughter, Laura, to Lord Lovat, the 40-year-old chief of Clan Fraser and a distinguished soldier – their engagement had caused something of a rumpus, as he was Roman Catholic.

Charty had only heard from others the details of Laura's wedding, which required police to control the crowds. The bride's Aunt Margot had helped organise the occasion, which saw Laura leave for the church from 10 Downing Street, where the reception was held. Harry gave as a gift a copy of the works of Alfred de Musset, in brown calf with gilt lettering and marbled endpapers, housed in a mahogany and walnut case. It bore two inscriptions: one read, 'L. Lovat, H. Cust', the other was written by Harry in French, '*A mon ami, le mari de mon amie*', presumably referring to her husband. Charty gave her daughter two volumes of the works of Molière produced in the same way as Harry's gift and in an identical case, in which she wrote, 'L. Lovat from her Mother, Given to her by H. Cust'. In a third volume, Harry's own inscription from earlier days reads, 'To Lady Chartie, with very much love, Wells, December [?] 1877. H.J.C.C.'[33]

If 1877 is a correct reading, it suggests Harry and Charty knew each other longer than had been thought. On 7 April 1877, 20-year-old Charty got married and spent her six-week honeymoon in northern Italy, where Harry visited that same year, aged 16, bringing back an album of local scenes in which was found his portrait sketch annotated with demons.[34]

Perhaps there was something more significant than close friendship and familial love in such gifting. Laura was born on 12 January 1892, although, unusually for the times, not christened until much later, in July 1893, together with her younger sister, born in May. Laura must have been conceived in April 1891. It was a month for racing, in which Harry spent part of the first week at Croxton Park races with the Belvoir Castle party, followed by a few days at Belton; he left around 9 April. Charty spent at least one day, 14 April, in Wiltshire at the Beaufort Hunt without her husband. If she and Harry sought it, the opportunity was there.

By the time of Laura's wedding, Charty knew she was not going to recover. Giving her daughter the books would have been a discreet way of letting her know of her long friendship with Harry and, by inference, of any other truths she had kept to herself.

Laura's honeymoon was spent at Easton Grey, lent to the couple by her other aunt, Lucy Graham Smith, who had been widowed in 1908 and whose artistic talent saw her exhibited at the National Portrait Gallery. However, after her early fertility problems, she developed arthritis and suffered terribly. While her condition may have restricted her artistic output, she was happy to help others, including her niece Elizabeth, Margot's socially precocious and talented daughter.

Asquith attended his sister-in-law's funeral, as did Lucy and their brother Eddy, now Lord Glenconner. Margot went to Charty's memorial service. Lord Ribblesdale was absent from both occasions, still recovering from the effects of a riding accident five months earlier, in which he broke a leg. For some time, he had been staying at the Cavendish Hotel in London and now moved in permanently. When his 'Angel Queen', as he called Charty, deteriorated, he had turned for comfort to Lady Angela Forbes, who had become Hugo's mistress.

Others in the Coterie were marrying too. In August 1912, the Custs were guests when the Rutlands' daughter, Lady Marjorie Manners, married the Marquess of Anglesey, the wedding attended by royalty and the service conducted by the Archbishop of Canterbury. Harry could admire his daughter, Lady Diana, who at 20 was the eldest bridesmaid, her already dazzling beauty enhanced by her dress in shades of shell pink, embroidered with crystals. Adored by many, seven years later she would marry Alfred Duff Cooper.

Earlier that year, Lady Welby had died at the age of 75, her obituary in *The Times* describing her philanthropic and intellectually rich life, and Nina began the weighty task of curating her vast correspondence. Harry still sought time away, staying that autumn in Littlehampton, a genteel seaside town, golfing, yachting and reading. Replying on behalf of them both to an invitation from Mary Elcho, he told her they should love to come, 'but will you write to Nina as if you had <u>not</u> written to me, as I think she would like it, and I will watch engagements'. Contrary to social etiquette, it seemed invitations addressed to his wife for both of them were rare, and while his words showed consideration, it was also clear that the emotional life of 'the bad married dog' still included others:

> I loved your letter, dearest Mary, as I love you. You are one of the only blessing & peace-distributing (tornado-touches here & there, of course) in the storm-tost teacup of my life & I think I have more than once expressed my open regret that I am not your legal spouse.

Mary might roll her eyes at his melodramatic words, but he also sought her sympathy, allowing himself the indulgence of self-pity. 'I've not had a very good time & think I am going in for a change of life … I love your letter, & you … for you are in it, and have done me lots of good.'[35] Before long, though, events would put his self-pity into proportion and give him a new purpose.

Love and War

According to Mrs Willett, the medium who received messages from Balfour's dead love, she knew he was going to resign as Leader of the Opposition on 8 November 1911 because, the night before, she had a vivid dream, in which she felt she had seen into his very soul.

Balfour had indeed been considering resigning for a while, telling only Mary Elcho and three others he trusted in October. The constitutional crisis that resulted from the House of Lords' rejection of the People's Budget led to the Parliament Act of 1911, which would limit the power of the Lords and have a profound effect on parliamentary politics. Exhausted by the acrimonious fighting over the Act, which had divided his party and severely tested his friendships, especially with Curzon and Asquith, and after twenty-five years of being in Parliament without a break, Balfour resigned.

'George and I both feel the sadness one cannot help feeling but which has to come to all fair things,' Mary told him sadly after he visited her the night before and she had watched him drive away for the last time as leader. 'But I shall feel more cheerful when I see you at Stanway and Pina [the chow chow] will not mind at all whether you are leader or not – nor more shall I!'[1]

Balfour's departure came at the end of a mixed year for Mary and her siblings, which saw Pamela become Lady Glenconner when Eddy was created baron, but in which their father, Percy, died. At the age of 47, George Wyndham inherited Clouds and in 1912 commissioned Pamela's former lover, Detmar Blow, to make alterations, which included building a chapel for Sibell, partly in gratitude for her understanding of his relationship with Gay.

He would not enjoy his inheritance for long, although he did not know it when, in April 1913, he attended the wedding of his son, Percy, 'Perf', aged 26, an officer in the Coldstream Guards. He was marrying Diana Lister, the Ribblesdales' daughter.

The wedding was another glamorous occasion where the newlyweds' friends from the Coterie mingled with their parents' friends from the Souls, who looked with pride and hope upon the next generation. As mother of the groom and his half-brother, Hugh, Duke of Westminster, Sibell commanded as much press interest for her religious life: 'She is to the manor born of such ceremonial as is half ecclesiastic and half social … Her very rings have an Episcopal rather than worldly aspect'.[2] Wyndham surely smiled at his own portrait as a long-winded man of letters and a poet who wrote odes about rooks and enjoyed bibulous trips with his friend Hilaire Belloc.

Two months later, Wyndham was in Paris with Gay and her 27-year-old daughter, Lady Phyllis. It is little known that the reason for the women's presence was that Phyllis, petite and delicately beautiful, had fallen pregnant by the sculptor John Tweed, aged 44 and married, and was seeking an abortion.[3] Like her parents, Phyllis moved in artistic circles, and Wyndham's friend was very attractive and very successful.

Wyndham and the women stayed in the elegant new Hotel Lotti, built by his stepson, the Duke of Westminster, who kept a permanent suite there. On 4 June, Wyndham dined alone on a heavy meal, the details of which he recounted to Hilaire Belloc in what would be his last letter. Four days later, he suffered a fatal heart attack.

Officially, it happened after he experienced chest pains and was receiving morphine injections from a nurse. In fact, he died in the arms of a prostitute.[4] His body had to be returned to the hotel with some difficulty, as rigor mortis had set in.

Sibell heard the news of her husband's death while she was at Clouds. Perf had the difficult task of bringing his father's body back to England, telling Sibell he looked 'very peaceful and very beautiful'.[5] Of the death of her adored son, Madeline Wyndham, now 78, wrote little in her diaries, unlike the lengthy tributes she usually gave to her beloved pets. 'George died in Paris. Was buried' was the extent of her entry.[6]

The Arthurian Knight could scarcely have imagined a less romantic death for himself. Why he had succumbed to such temptation might be explained by his increased depression. 'Politics broke his heart,' noted Sybil Eden, to whom he had written in January explaining why he had not seen her recently. 'Even a scolding from you is better than nothing!' he had told her. 'What I want is a sight of your face.' He had been so busy in the House – 'We are over-driven and I am tired' – and he hoped she would soon be in London; if not, perhaps she could see him at Clouds between 20 February and 12 March? 'It is the worst of politics that I cannot see the people I love or do the things best worth doing.'[7] Hopelessness and nostalgia imbued a poem about Easter that he wrote in March, which began, 'I have forgotten how to sing'.

Anthony Eden, who had just passed his 16th birthday, wrote to his 'Darling Little Mummie' from Eton. 'I was afraid George Wyndham's death would be a dreadful shock to you. It certainly does seem a great shame. There is a good notice about him in the *Chronicle* which I will send to you.'[8] Although he was aware of their friendship, it is not certain when Eden first became aware of the possibility of being Wyndham's son, but references to him in diaries and letters suggest it was later. Their physical resemblance was said to be particularly noticeable in Rodin's bust of Wyndham.[9]

Balfour delivered a eulogy to a silent House of Commons. A shocked Wilfrid Blunt dedicated his poem 'To a Happy Warrior' to him. Elusive as ever, Gay's response to his death can only be imagined.

Harry was one of the many Souls who attended the funeral. Wyndham, a year younger, was barely 50 when he died. The year gave Harry further opportunity to reflect on mortality, for in February his niece Elizabeth, his brother's daughter, had died at just 16. In July, Alfred Lyttelton, whose brief time as Colonial Secretary under Balfour's premiership was, as predicted by Edward VII, not very successful, was hit in the stomach by a cricket ball and died days later, a particularly cruel fate for the brilliant cricketer.

For Harry, the year had begun promisingly, in a manner that demonstrated the Custs' continued presence in influential circles and gave him the opportunity to assess the global situation at an increasingly sensitive time. He was a dinner guest of Lord Beresford of the Admiralty, along with his old friend, the Russian Ambassador, Count von Benckendorff (whose wife had once said of Harry, 'I find his hair vulgar but his face seduces me'), and the Ambassadors of France, Austria-Hungary and Spain. At Downing Street, he and Nina caught up with Sir Edward Grey, now Foreign Secretary, and Viscount Haldane, Secretary of State for War. Souls such as Curzon (now involved with the novelist Elinor Glyn), the Horners and Plymouths joined with the Churchills and other prominent figures.

At the Rutlands' house party at Belvoir Castle, where Harry joined Balfour and Mary Elcho and other close friends, such as the Duchess of Marlborough, it felt almost like old times. What made it different was the presence of Balfour's successor as Leader of the Conservative Party, Andrew Bonar Law. He had introduced a new style of speaking in the House, a harsh, pugnacious style of rhetoric that was very different from the elegant discourse of Balfour's, but the party felt they needed someone who was less philosopher, more warrior. The nature of political debate was changing forever.

In September, Harry and Nina joined the Asquiths and their daughter Elizabeth in Venice, as guests of society hostess, Emerald Cunard. The presence of Violet and Lady Diana, now 21 –'dazzling, disconcerting', said Mrs Keppel, mistress of the late king – was something Nina had become accustomed to.

Ronald Storrs and the artist Philip Burne-Jones, son of the late Edward, were guests too. Harry's nephew was impressed by the prime minister's retention of cultural information while they were sightseeing, while Diana was reminded of his other interests – 'Mr Asquith was interested in his daughter's friends and I was one' – and she noted how he liked her to hold his arm while they climbed the stairs of a church. 'A lot of my passion for Venice came from him and his *Baedeker*,' she wrote, 'and the gruelling questioning of an evening on the day's learning … Hand in hand we would gaze up at Colleoni … and buy presents for Margot.'[10]

As always when in good company, Harry hid his darker thoughts and shone. After visiting a church, he amused them all by persuading Burne-Jones that St Tryphonius had a basilisk as his familiar and on the spot composed a classical-style poem, which the artist illustrated with a cartoon of the beast. But inside, he howled. On returning from Venice, he wrote to Pamela, who had spent every New Year's Eve since 1893 re-reading his letters and crying:

> I've been dreaming of you insistently which must mean something, and also spurs my constant desire sometimes to see you & brings back memories of former & better days, all very dear and asking for renewal. So do tell me when & where you shall be soon, with not too much brood about your knee & let me see you as of old, if you will. I have autumned & wintered here [at Ashridge], bar some visits, since I came from Italy, *ça n'est pas précisement la noce*. Bless you always.[11]

It was not mere self-indulgence. Harry's poignant letter to Ettie Desborough in January 1914 acknowledged his faults and the realisation of his end. He thanked her for a book about her late uncle, Lord Cowper, 'For I loved him with all my heart. He stood first for a dozen qualities I care the most for, perhaps because they are so far from myself.'

He was particularly low: 'I hope I may meet you before I die but feel no confidence.' As if in preparation, for the last three months he had been 'quite brazenly godly, righteous and sober', such that she would not know him 'by sight or soul'. He quoted, morbidly, from Thomas Nashe's poem *In Time of Pestilence.*[12]

In dying early, his friend Wyndham had at least been spared the rest of the political crisis that now divided friends. Asquith had introduced the Third Home Rule Bill in 1912, opposed by Ulster's Protestants who formed the majority. The Conservatives supported Ulster's move towards armed revolt.

After all Curzon's years of friendship with Margot, he did not invite the Asquiths to his ball in May 1914. She sent him an angry letter and received an icy reply, saying it was unthinkable they should be received, given the government's Ulster policy. Such a response would not have been in Curzon's contemplation twenty years earlier. By the time Margot next saw him, at Hackwood in September, she felt less angry, more pitying. His suggestion that if she met his guests, it might provoke a scene was 'ridiculous'. 'Poor old boy', she wrote in her diary, 'but I never turn a hair if I'm really fond of someone.'[13]

Meanwhile, Asquith was writing obsessively to his daughter's friend, the clever and beautiful Venetia Stanley, even as war approached. They had started corresponding in 1910, although she was not his only young female correspondent, but by 1914, when he was 62 to her 27, flirtation had turned into an obsession, at least on his part. She was his confidante on all matters, and sometimes he wrote to her several times a day, even during Cabinet meetings. When Margot realised it was becoming serious, she wrote miserably to Ettie, 'She is even teaching Henry to avoid telling me things … I'm far too fond of H. to show him how ill and miserable it makes me.'[14]

Marital issues arose elsewhere. In June that year, Hugo Elcho's father died, elevating him to 11th Earl of Wemyss and 7th Earl of March and Mary to countess, but their change of status brought 'trouble & the sense of fresh responsibilities & burdens & less freedom', she told Blunt. She also hated her new name: 'I feel that Romance & Poetry have fled with my old *pretty* name!'[15]

It should all have been a welcome change, but much of the late earl's property was tied up in trust because of Hugo's gambling. The only asset he received outright was his father's London house, which he promptly sold. Although their annual income increased, death duties imposed a massive financial burden, and Mary was filled with dread when Hugo said he wanted to let Stanway and move into Gosford.

Eventually, he decided against it. Mary remained at Stanway and Hugo lived mostly at Gosford with his mistress and gambling companion, Lady Angela Forbes, who had divorced her husband in 1907. Mary had tolerantly hosted Angela and her daughters at Stanway, telling Balfour she was 'a very hard nut'.

She still loved to entertain. By now, Nina had been initiated into the joys of Stanway. 'How can I ever tell you how much I enjoyed your delicious party,' she enthused to Mary. 'I wake in the night to think about it and laugh – "Insanity in isolation" grows pale beside the crowded madness of Stanway.'[16]

Meanwhile, events were unfolding that would eclipse the threat of civil war in Ireland and give Harry a renewed *raison d'être*. In June, he met Lord Kitchener when Storrs, who had worked under him in Egypt after Gorst's death, took him to lunch at Harry's house. Kitchener was known (perhaps surprisingly, given his fierce reputation) as an avid collector of porcelain, and Harry caught him eyeing up a valuable Chinese teapot. In a nervous but bold attempt to divert him, Harry said how much the family were looking forward to his forthcoming visit to Ashridge, with 'one of the finest collections of china in England, Field-Marshal – and no inventory'.[17]

The Ashridge visit was another where Harry was present as events unfolded. Kitchener was staying nearby and drove over with his sister. The Brownlows' other guests included Harry's niece, Pearl Wheatley, who recalled how, as they sat and talked, a telegram arrived for Kitchener, who read it in silence. He said nothing of its contents but apologised to Lady Brownlow and said he must leave. She would know the reason the next day, he said, and he would take care of her.[18]

He had received news of the assassination of Archduke Franz Ferdinand of Austria, who only seven months earlier, with his wife, had been Their Majesties' guests at Windsor Castle. His assassin was a Serbian student.

The unsettled situation in the Balkans rapidly deteriorated. As the European powers declared their allegiances, the likelihood of war increased. Sir Edward Grey appealed for peace in Germany through its Ambassador, Prince Lichnowsky, the only German diplomat who raised objections to his country's efforts to provoke an Austro–Serbian war. The prince did everything he could, but on 3 August was obliged to tell the House of Commons that the peace of Europe could not be preserved.

Lichnowsky and his wife were friends of Harry's. The princess liked to spend afternoons in his long library at Chancellor's Gate reading *Madame Bovary* aloud. That evening, Storrs went to see the couple in the German Embassy to say goodbye and found them in tears, defeated. When Harry visited them for the same purpose, the prince repeated bitterly, in a rebuke of his country, '*Sie sind verrückt in Berlin, sie sind verrückt*' ('They are crazy in Berlin, they are crazy').[19]

When Lord Grey told the Commons, 'The lamps are going out all over Europe', the Souls' sons swiftly joined up. Within weeks, Gay's son, Archer Windsor-Clive, aged 23, was dead, as was Perf Wyndham, 27. Balfour told Mary he was glad George had died before his only son, for 'he was spared the worst pain of increasing years – the pain of seeing death spare the old and seize the young'.[20] Nina's nephew, 26-year-old Richard Welby, also died. A lieutenant in the Grenadier Guards, he was killed on 16 September, his family's grief compounded by the fact that initially they were told he had been slightly wounded but in fact he was already dead. And so it continued.

Harry may have been unencumbered by children and ignorant of the fierce love they instilled, but he understood his friends' grief; in war he found new purpose. By September 1914, he had founded the Central Committee for National Patriotic Organisations (CCNPO), whose purpose was to unify and co-ordinate the work of other leagues 'in educating and arousing the country as to the reason, justice and necessity of the war'.[21] From its headquarters near Charing Cross in London, the CCNPO endeavoured to boost morale and encourage enlistment by publishing posters and pamphlets, supplying articles to the press, and organising public meetings and lectures. To spread its message countrywide, the committee also organised a series of tours using specially equipped caravans, called 'War Vans'. It also sought to encourage enlistment and promote the Allied cause in neutral countries.

Asquith agreed to be honorary president, with Balfour and Lord Rosebery as vice presidents under Harry's chairmanship. Harry could not do the work without Nina's help. They wrote tirelessly to their many friends and contacts asking them to help in ways most suited to their experience. Responses varied widely, from the supportive to the sceptical, even hostile, which got short shrift from Harry.

Among the supporters was H.G. Wells, who told Nina from his Essex home, Easton Glebe, that he was writing a series of articles for English and American papers called 'What's Coming?' on the effects of the war and his predictions for the aftermath. He would be happy to give a historian friend the translation rights in Spanish for his articles.[22]

A writer from Kent offered her services as a local honorary secretary, 'or for any newspaper propaganda to be carried on in neutral countries. As the author of the *Scarlet Pimpernel* my name Baroness Orczy is known in practically every country in Europe but I am *de facto* Mrs Montagu Barstow'.[23]

The author Algernon Blackwood, living in neutral Switzerland, thought Germany's conduct in Belgium had caused people to view the Allies more favourably and asked for pamphlets to be sent to him.

When it came to dissenters, George Bernard Shaw's letter to Nina must have been one of his earliest expressions of contempt for Britain's reaction to the war and the misuse of propaganda. While he thought there was 'a very strong case for the war', the official case presented by the government (and by association, the CCNPO) was 'transparent humbug'.

In any event, it was 'not going to be won by pamphlets: what we want are recruits – in short, blood and iron'. Even then, all those who had accepted the 'official' case had already been recruited 'and we are now going on atrocities and scares and forged German diaries'. Instead, he opined, the terms of service needed to be improved, such as better pay 'and abolition of useless oaths of allegiance which keep off Irish troops'. Shaw wanted to be left to help in his own way and said that if his name should crop up, Nina should assure the committee that she regarded him 'as a monster'.[24]

In 1915, Asquith's devoted daughter Violet married his private secretary, Maurice Bonham Carter, and Venetia Stanley married her old suitor, Edwin Montagu. When Asquith had heard of their engagement in May, he was heartbroken.

Days later, facing hostility after press exposure of a critical shortage in the supply of munitions, he took the decision to form a coalition government with the Conservatives. In the new Cabinet, Balfour replaced Churchill as First Lord of the Admiralty and Curzon was appointed Lord Privy Seal. Lord Beresford, champion of the Royal Navy, refused his friend Harry's request to give a talk, as he did from others, for he was angry that neither before nor since the coalition had the government approached him: 'If my advice had been taken, there would have been no war, and if my proposals had been accepted, from six to eight thousand officers and men would not have been murdered in the Fleet'.[25]

'War strips bare and illuminates what peace disguises and huddles away', wrote Harry in the preface for a short book he had persuaded the distinguished Russian journalist, G. de Wesselitsky, to write, called *Russia & Democracy: the German Canker in Russia*, published in July 1915.[26] Both the book and preface were widely praised and the Custs received expressions of gratitude from the Russians for Harry's support and initiative. Wesselitsky himself was effusive. 'What a clever organiser he is', he enthused to Nina, 'and how powerful is the influence for good he is exercising through the Central Committee. I hope before the war is over, the Government will ask him to join the Cabinet.'[27]

While that may have been Harry's wish, and certainly was in the past, he must have known it was unlikely to happen now. At least by doing the work of the CCNPO he could, as Wesselitsky recognised, be a force for good, which was a reasonable, if unsatisfactory, substitute for being in political office.

Besides, differences emerged between Harry's view of the work of the organisation and Asquith's. In 1915, Asquith said he wanted the CCNPO to give up its work in neutral countries and restrict its overseas work to the Empire. When the inevitable move towards compulsory military service began, it was no longer necessary to encourage recruitment, and a government department began to encroach on the CCNPO's propaganda work. Instead, it began to focus more on the home front, with campaigns to promote thrift and the growing of medicinal herbs, on which they consulted prominent experts.

Pamphlets such as 'The Family Laundry' and 'Poultry Without Capital' encouraged everyone to practise good husbandry. No one was deemed too noble. The Archbishop of Canterbury told Harry that the Archbishop of York had appointed a committee of bishops to consider the scheme and contact him (possibly helped by the fact that Harry's relation was the Dean of York). From Buckingham Palace, Sir Frederick Ponsonby told him that 'The King and Queen, I believe at your instigation, have been filled with an unholy desire to grow medicinal plants at Windsor ... The Queen thinks that if Their Majesties' example would be of any use, it would be well worth while making the experiment at Windsor' and invited Harry to go and see him.[28]

Some chose to scorn. The ever-spiteful Sybil Cust, joining Nina at Belton in 1915, wrote (before actually seeing her), 'She's more ill than usual, having tired herself with sending thousands of letters in all languages to every country in Europe, with a statement on the Mind of England about the War. It is pathetic, for I really don't think half of them will be read, or do any good if they are.'[29]

In 1916, Harry changed the focus of the CCNPO towards helping Britain emerge from the war as a great trading nation, concerned that British companies had been losing overseas orders to their German competitors. He believed radical change was required in Britain's approach to business training and the CCNPO launched a Training for Business scheme, asking educational institutions and businesses to identify problems with the existing system. Now the Custs' correspondents included youth leaders such as Robert Baden-Powell.

By December, a lack of confidence in Asquith's leadership saw the Conservatives withdraw and form a coalition government with a minority of Liberals under David Lloyd George, who became prime minister. After decades of friendship, the bond between Balfour and Margot would be severely tested.

Not everyone was patriotic, as Harry discovered early on. Terrified of losing another child, the Duchess of Rutland sought to keep her son, John, the Marquis of Granby, out of the war and asked her former lover for help. Violet's idea was to go straight to the top. The Secretary of State for War was now Lord Kitchener. 'Of course, Kitchener of Khartoum is absolute and could put John on his own Staff – or anywhere', Harry told her. 'Or on Sir John French's staff, which they say is safe. But I know you will be brave, my sweet, and understand that John's own future has to be considered. That's the awful difficulty of it, the two reasons of State.'[30]

Yet, even though Kitchener had stayed at Belvoir, Violet was nervous of approaching him directly, not least because of his notorious dislike of women. She considered other ways of reaching him, thinking Field Marshall Lord Grenfell might be her best hope. Harry agreed it might be a solution, but otherwise, 'If John must go to the Front, a big Staff … is much the safer'.[31] Meanwhile, he would go on 'thinking and thinking'. Ultimately, however, Violet followed her own agenda, as John would discover to his shame.

At least Harry's daughter was playing her part. Although she received 'nothing but discouragement and tears'[32] from her mother, Diana won her own battle by being allowed to train as a VAD nurse at Guy's Hospital.

As the death toll rose, Harry wrote a poignant piece that spoke of their souls forming a 'sort of national Golden Treasury, sacred and serene'.* In 1915, those souls were augmented by Ettie's sons – first Julian, who had received the DSO for bravery and whose poem 'Into Battle' was published in *The Times*, and weeks later, Billy – and Yvo Charteris, Hugo and Mary's youngest boy, killed after just five weeks at the Front. Hugo was 'most piteous – heartbroken and like a child … and so *naively astonished*.'[33] Yvo's sister Cynthia, having also lost a close friend, asked despairingly, 'Oh why was I born for this time? Before one is thirty, to have known more dead than living people is really hard. Stanway – Clouds – Gosford – *all* the settings of one's life given up to ghosts.'[34]

---

* See Appendix 2.

Balfour was there for Mary as always. His letters were a mixture of philosophical thoughts and simple sympathy, 'The world just now is full of sadness and you have more than your share'.[35]

On the first anniversary of the war, Balfour, as First Lord of the Admiralty, together with the Canadian Prime Minister, addressed a huge meeting Harry had organised at London's Opera House to affirm the Empire's commitment to the war. It was held in parallel with a service at St Paul's Cathedral attended by the king and queen and at services throughout the country.

Edward Fitzgerald, aged 23 in 1915, was also fighting, although his biological father Hugo was unlikely to be aware of it. 'My naughty but dear brother has gone to the Dardanelles', Lord Desmond Fitzgerald, a major in the Irish Guards, told Ettie.[36] Desmond, clever and sporty, and heir to their eldest brother Maurice, Duke of Leinster, was a friend of Ettie's daughter, Monica, and Ettie hoped they might marry. She had already received Desmond's condolences. Now she channelled her grief into recording her sons' lives in her book, *Pages from a Family Journal*, which inaugurated the legend of the lost generation, while also supporting Mary in her grief. Hugo, writing now in pain, no longer in lust, told Ettie, 'I was fonder of Yvo than anything else in the world … He never gave one any excuse to feel anything other than pride'.[37]

It would have been harder to say that of Edward, who, although he fought proudly, had led a chaotic life so far. Good-looking, charming and reckless, his short marriage, made at 21, was nearly at an end and had caused a scandal, for his wife was a Gaiety Girl, in a profession still considered disreputable. Edward had also inherited Hugo's love of gambling and was already approaching his second bankruptcy. Desmond was the great hope for the family and the title, for Maurice, an epileptic and a depressive like their mother, Hermione, had been committed to an asylum after a suicide attempt at 21. An uncle kept the Duke of Leinster's condition from the public, and the estate remained in the hands of trustees. But in March 1916, Desmond was killed, aged 28, and the dukedom faced a grim future.

That year, Hugo and Mary lost another son, Ego, heir to the earldom. *The Times* commemorated him as one who best 'embodied the heroic spirit of the young generation'. Ettie, whose insistence on seeing the positive had been pushed to the limits of even her extraordinary endurance but sustained by her Christian faith, did not disappoint her friends in her response to their grief. 'Thank you so much,' wrote Hugo, 'you have a genius for sympathy that no-one else has.'[38]

As Ettie soothed others, so others helped her, in a way that reflected the deepest elements of friendship that had blossomed between the Souls. After Julian's death, Gay Plymouth, who had lost two sons, told her, 'With such as he was, one feels there can be no real parting. He will always be there on the horizon, visible to all who knew him or heard of him, giving courage or inspiration.'[39]

For the Custs and other Souls, the start of 1916 had served as a reminder of life continuing in the midst of destruction when they came together at the wedding of the Marquis of Granby, who (having avoided active service) married Margot's niece, Kathleen 'Kakoo' Tennant. At a large wedding for wartime, the khaki dullness of the groom and other male guests was offset by splashes of colour in the women's outfits amid a swathe of black which, while fashionable, also served as a sober nod to those who were absent. The younger members were less restrained. The groom's sister, Lady Diana, with their mother's artistic talent, designed the medieval-style bridesmaids' dresses, while the flamboyant page's costume worn by Pamela's son, 10-year-old Stephen Tennant, gave him the opportunity for dressing up that he would always enjoy.

In difficult times, love was more important than ever, although the Souls' children, whatever their age, might still be caught in the slipstream. In his stressful role, Sir Edward Grey increasingly found solace at Wilsford with Pamela, whose 'uncontrolled emotional impulses'[40] her daughter Clare escaped in 1915, aged 19, by marrying a cavalry officer, Adrian Bethell. The following year, Clare gave birth to Diana, Simon Blow's mother, but soon left both her daughter and husband for Lord Tennyson's grandson and sought a divorce. In the ensuing scandal, Clare lost custody. Diana would not see her mother again for fifteen years, until she was 17, when Clare showed her little interest or affection; the emotional fallout reverberates still.[41]

In May 1916, at the age of 45, Pamela also had a baby, Hester, conceived the month Clare married, but who died hours later. While Pamela grieved, her son, Bim, was killed at the Somme. By 1918, Madeline Wyndham would lose five grandsons.

In August 1916, Harry told Margot he was 'suddenly very blind, which frightens me', although he was excited about the meeting for wounded soldiers the following day at the Royal Albert Hall, which the CCNPO had organised on the second anniversary of the declaration of war. He thought it would be 'a great success',[42] and it was. Queen Mary placed the royal box at the committee's disposal, at an emotional event attended by over 3,000 wounded soldiers, to whom Field Marshal Lord Haig sent a moving telegram from the Western Front, read out by Harry.

He also wanted Margot to tell Asquith that he had received confirmation of the organisation's first meeting with China, which would come to supply much-needed labour to Britain. With the training scheme he and Nina were working on, and a conference to address in December, life was busy. But in February 1917, he went down with a severe attack of influenza and announced that he would have to cancel his engagements and would be unable to answer correspondence for some weeks.

He never would again. On 2 March, aged 55, Harry died at Chancellor's House with Nina by his side. His doctor certified the cause as two-fold: thirteen days of influenza, together with exhaustion and his lifelong curse, syncope. By then, he was 'a frail and delicate man', said his private secretary, noting that Harry's unceasing devotion to the work 'so patriotically given was, in the opinion of many the cause of his early decease'.[43]

Through her poetry, Nina mourned:

O God, my God, where'er Thou art,
Keep my beloved in Thy Heart;
Fold in Thy Heart that heart so bright,
Heal him with Thy most gentle light.
And since Thou mad'st forgetfulness,
Forget what'er Thou find'st amiss;
And since Thou mad'st remembering,
Remember every lovely thing.
And then, my God, lean down and see …
And, pitying, remember me.[44]

Epilogue

Brighter than the Sun

Harry's self-deprecating humour had saved him from arrogance, his self-knowledge from delusion, but neither could save him from death. A family group joined Nina at the funeral at Belton, the estate to which he had expected to succeed but which he had exchanged for another, more enduring inheritance.[1] After a cremation at Golders Green, his ashes were removed from their overnight resting place in Belton's private chapel and placed in the doorway of the church, the casket covered with a 200-year-old family pall. At the end of the service, conducted by a clergyman relation, the casket was placed in an oak-lined niche in the west wall and sprinkled with earth by Lord Brownlow, followed by the singing of a verse of the national anthem.

That day, a memorial service was also held at St Margaret's in Westminster, attended by the cream of Britain's political and literary world, by the titled and the untitled, and by those who hugged close to themselves their intimate memories of Harry in his heyday. Many Souls were among the congregation, some still feeling the keen sharpness of grief closer to home from the loss of cherished children. Pamela, writing a memoir of her son, Bim, and now obsessed with spiritualism, did not attend, but Eddy went – three years later he would die, leaving her free to marry Lord Grey.

George Curzon, now Leader of the House of Lords, attended with his second wife, Grace, also widowed, whom he had recently married. There was no allocation of seats according to status. The Curzons sat near the back with Balfour, now Foreign Secretary, while the Asquiths slotted themselves in wherever they could. As Curzon had known Harry for much of their lives, it was fitting that he should write an appreciation for *The Times*, which began mournfully with a quotation from Milton's 'Lycidas':

> But O the heavy change now thou art gone
> Now thou art gone and never must return.

Everyone who knew Harry would have recognised the person Curzon eulogised and those who did not would surely have been intrigued by this man, 'who created a stir everywhere he moved, and lit in others the vital spark which his own nature so easily generated'. He had 'travelled widely, seen most things, known everybody, been everybody's friend'. His astonishing intellect and love of scholarship made him 'the unchallenged and licensed leader of the press room and the dinner table. Quip, retort, repartee, allusion, epigram, jest, all flew with lightning speed from the active workshop of his brain.'

In the affectionate piece, it may have seemed there was no end to Harry's talents or his apparently golden existence. And yet, said Curzon, his abruptly severed life 'seemed to all of his friends to fall short of that achievement which such gifts might have led both them and himself to expect. Fate ever seemed to be stalking him with uplifted dagger.' His friend mused on what had prevented him soaring higher. Perhaps it was 'circumstance or ill-health, or the weakness of some link in the chain of his moral and intellectual being, or the buffets of fortune'.

The answer, as Curzon knew, lay in all of those. He knew, for he was one of those who had tried to avert a scandal, that Harry's actions meant he was obliged to compromise his life in a marriage he had not chosen. He knew that he suffered poor health and his nerves were 'habitually at high tension', and he knew of Harry's predicament in being pilloried by those who wanted changes that only suffrage might bring. But no one could know exactly what went on within that quick and complex mind, what nightmares he had suffered as a child when he called out for his mother and she did not come, what visions of mortality haunted him even as a young man and made him live life as though each day were his last.

Shortly after he died, someone offered their commiserations to Lady Diana Manners on the death of her father, believing she knew it was

Harry. Shocked, she thought they meant the Duke of Rutland. Thus, she discovered the truth, and once she had digested it, she was happy.

That he was loved by many was not in doubt. James Rennell Rodd wrote of his lifelong friend, 'He left a greater blank in the hearts of his associates than any other man that I have known … To be with him was a privilege, and his gift to life was the constant pleasure which radiated from his presence.'[2] Margot considered Harry 'in some ways the rarest and the most brilliant of them all. He might have done anything in life' but he was also 'fatally self-indulgent'.[3]

The *Daily Telegraph* described him as 'one of the most brilliant and one of the most attractive men of his epoch … also very wayward, and destined by his waywardness to spoil what might have been a great life and a brilliant career'.[4] His widow, familiar with his flaws, may not have called it waywardness, for he had stayed with her in a marriage of sorts for twenty-three years. 'Some day I should like you to come if you will – but not yet', Nina told a friend. 'I still have to learn *how* to live without him … I have been the happiest conceivable woman on earth.'[5]

That happiness had depended, at least in part, on self-abnegation, without which their marriage, entered into in such circumstances, could not have survived. At their London house, a visitor noted that his sunny presence seemed to linger and to brighten the gloom of her shadowed life: 'I who the radiance of your days have seen, Thank God'.[6]

Nina would immortalise her flawed but beloved husband in an exquisite marble effigy, his tomb bearing the words, 'Of all sorts, enchantingly beloved', and in her poignant poetry collection. Giving a copy of *Not All the Suns* to a trusted colleague of Harry's, Nina wrote inside the words of the Blessed Lady Julian of Norwich, 'He said not, thou shalt not be tempested, thou shalt not be travailed, thou shalt not be afflicted; but he said thou shalt not be overcome'.[7]

With Sir Ronald Storrs, she collaborated on a collection of Harry's poems, published in Jerusalem when Storrs was governor. She continued their work in the CCNPO and when the training scheme he sought was launched in 1918, it was named after him. His work was acknowledged in Parliament and Nottingham University endowed a series of talks called the Cust Foundation Lectures, on a topic relating to the British Empire, the first of which was delivered by Balfour.[8]

Nina continued to write and to sculpt, and her work is still exhibited today.[9] Her love for Harry fuelled her creativity and made her soul sing.

Two weeks after Harry's death, Lord Brownlow suffered another bereavement when his wife Adelaide died. Upon the earl's own death in 1921, the baronetcy and the estates that should have been Harry's passed to his brother, Adelbert, who became 5th Baron Brownlow. Yet, although Belton eluded Harry in life, he has a place there in death. Nina's marble bust of him sits in the house, where portraits of each of them hang. Despite her own frail health, she outlived him by thirty-eight years. Her ashes lie with his at Belton Church, of which he used to quip, 'Belton Church is dedicated to the memory of God and the glory of the Cust family'.

Reflecting upon the Souls, Sir James Rennell Rodd recalled the 'beautiful and clever women, the complement to a group of brilliant men, whose unconstrained relations had broken down many of the barriers of mid-Victorian convention'. In all the countries he visited as a diplomat, he had never met any section of a society 'more interesting or more charming'.

Balfour told Margot Asquith, by then the Countess of Oxford, that 'no history of society in the nineteenth century can fail to write of the influence which you and your friends have had in the social and political life of the country. Till the 'Souls' emerged into London, Tories and Liberals of distinction never met.'[10]

In 1928, as he recuperated at Stanway after a stroke, Balfour 'commanded' Mary and Ettie 'emphatically and categorically to write about the Souls'.[11] Mary saw them:

> … as they were long ago, beloved spirits of the glamorous past, bright and glowing … They were not poseurs, they were real and very much alive, keen and strenuous in work and play, 'not idle singers of an empty day,' just a group of intimate friends who lived and loved a long time ago.[12]

Appendix 1

The Margaret Thatcher Theory

The eyes have it, those large, steely blue orbs, unmistakably similar in shape, giving Britain's former prime minister Margaret Thatcher and Harry Cust a common physicality. The rumours that she had aristocratic, even royal blood have circulated for years, particularly in grand Tory circles, although largely based on the wrong premises and thus often dismissed. Inevitably, certain facts and circumstances which give some credibility to the theory that Harry was her real grandfather have been overlooked.

Lady Diana Cooper told the author Michael Thornton in an interview in 1979 that Thatcher was her niece, because her biological father, Harry Cust, had had an affair with Thatcher's grandmother, Phoebe Stephenson, making their daughter, Beatrice, and Lady Diana half-sisters. According to her, Phoebe briefly worked as a housemaid at Belton House near Grantham, owned by Harry's cousin, Earl Brownlow.[1] The child born of the alleged liaison was Thatcher's mother, Beatrice Ethel Stephenson (later Roberts).

The theory was embraced enthusiastically by Lady Diana's son, Viscount Norwich,[2] who was keen to investigate whether he and Thatcher really were first cousins. He told Thornton that the prime minister's daughter, Carol Thatcher, said she was aware of the story, and he wanted to request from her a sample for DNA analysis.

Commentators have sneered that Margaret Thatcher, a grocer's daughter from Grantham, would have liked to think she had blue blood.

Thatcher herself, whose demeanour during her premiership developed a marked regality, did not comment directly on the rumour, although when her biographer put the theory to her, 'she answered with a certain pride, "Blue eyes aren't the preserve of the aristocracy".'[3]

Certainly, there was friendship with the Brownlow family through politics, in which Thatcher's father, Alfred Roberts, was involved. In her memoirs, a photograph shows him standing next to the 6th Baron Brownlow (Harry's nephew, Peregrine, a close friend of Edward VIII), and another shows her aged about 10 next to Lady Brownlow at a children's Christmas party.[4] The Brownlows' daughter Caroline believed the theory, although, in her view, Thatcher was Harry's daughter rather than his granddaughter, which is impossible.[5]

As Thatcher began to rise up the political ladder, the Brownlows looked upon her favourably, and after she became prime minister in 1979, she arranged with Peregrine's son, Edward, by then 7th Baron Brownlow, to borrow silver from Belton to improve the cutlery at Downing Street.[6] She also borrowed a green enamel box painted with views of Grantham, which had been presented to Lord Brownlow when he had completed his year of office as mayor of the borough.[7]

As major landowners in the area with a reputation for benevolence and a long history as Tory grandees, the Brownlows' kindness towards Thatcher as 'local girl makes good' in the harsh world of politics is not particularly remarkable in itself. If their generosity was because she was part of the family, albeit on 'the wrong side of the blankets', then one might assume that somewhere along the way that fact would have been communicated to her.

The reality of the matter, especially where Harry Cust was concerned, is most likely that no one knew for sure: Lord Brownlow (Edward) did not.[8] Equally, the fact that speculation about her origins seems to have been started by snobbish members of the Conservative Party, who found it hard to believe that a woman from humble beginnings, with brains and good looks, could become prime minister and therefore sought to find a link between those qualities and the aristocracy, should not prevent the theory being examined.

Thatcher's grandmother Phoebe was born at Fishtoft, in Lincolnshire, in 1849 and married Daniel Stephenson on 25 May 1876. (Her maiden name was Crust, whose proximity to Cust is merely coincidental.)

Thatcher said that Phoebe was a factory machinist before she married and worked in domestic service afterwards because they were so poor. In 1881, Daniel was working as a railway porter at Burgh le Marsh, a small market town near Lincolnshire's coast, and he and Phoebe had two children, a girl and a boy. By 1891 they were living at 10 South Parade, Grantham, and Daniel had become a railway guard. They also had another child, Beatrice, born on 24 August 1888, who would be Phoebe's last.

There was a nine-year gap between their previous child, Arthur, born in 1879, and Beatrice, born when Phoebe was 39. A large gap between the penultimate child and the final one has never been unusual, not least when the mother is approaching the end of her fertile years – a sort of 'last chance' baby, although as the average life expectancy of a woman of Phoebe's generation was around 42, it was a risky decision to take, if indeed they did. Such babies might be conceived accidentally if it was assumed that the woman was 'safe'. Assuming a full term of pregnancy, Beatrice must have been conceived around 25 November 1887, although if she was born even a week prematurely, which was more likely than late for an older mother, that would change the conception date to early December.

The year Margaret Thatcher's mother was conceived was also the year of Queen Victoria's Golden Jubilee, when celebrations were held over all the country, including at Belton. While no evidence has come to light that Phoebe worked there – the National Trust says there are no remaining records of staff, and it was not a year for the national census – it is possible that she did so, nonetheless, and temporary staff were also required for events hosted there.

Belton was not the only grand house in the vicinity owned by the Cust family or their friends, which Harry visited and at which Phoebe may have worked. In the centre of Grantham, a Mrs Musson ran a 'First Class General Registry Office for Servants. Patronised by the Nobility' and had a permanent advertisement in the local press which suggested that demand was particularly high during 1887.

There were opportunities for Harry and Phoebe to be in the same place at the same time that year. Harry was finishing his legal studies and was musing on a political career. As his father had been MP for Grantham, and his cousin Earl Brownlow owned Belton, he increasingly stayed there. That summer, Belton's gardens were opened to the public on Sundays. Events hosted there included a concert in the coach house and the Primrose League party in September for 200 members, with a huge tea provided by Thomas Lenton of Grantham. His business was just a mile from the Stephensons' home and employed workers for such occasions.

One of the Brownlows' favoured caterers was Thomas Watson, whose Dysart Café in Grantham was even nearer. Harry was certainly at Belton in early January 1888, to help the Brownlows entertain the Prince of Wales, and he was in Grantham again days later, to greet the prime minister as he stopped at the station: perhaps Daniel Stephenson was on guard duty that day. However, unless Beatrice was born several weeks early, that particular timing does not fit with her conception.

Even if the opportunity presented itself to Harry, the likelihood of his taking it seems remote. Phoebe was eleven years his senior and while he was accustomed to being pursued by older, married women, those with whom he slept were usually beautiful and high born. Phoebe was not only working class, she was also, by at least one account, plain. Of course, she may also have been witty and engaging. If they met at a social event open to all, such as the Primrose League, he might have been sufficiently amused to seduce her, but really it was not his style. On the other hand, he liked to drink, and he had his demons. If they encountered each other while she was working in service, even if temporarily, he would have had little opportunity to enjoy the frisson of flirtation beforehand and anyway, as a young man with the advantages he possessed, he did not need to sleep with the servants.

As for Phoebe, married for eleven years with two children, she may have found Harry devastatingly handsome and a world apart from her railwayman husband but unless she made it a habit to sleep with rich young men, it seems unlikely she would make an exception, even for Harry. According to Thatcher's description of her grandmother in later years, it would seem she was definitely not that sort of woman. She was 'very, very Victorian and very very strict',[9] a believer in austerity and duty and improving proverbs, such as 'Cleanliness is next to godliness'. With that portrait, the image of her romping with Harry, however briefly, rapidly recedes.

Thatcher's mother Beatrice was pretty and dark-haired, and her husband Alfred a tall, good-looking chap with blonde hair and light blue eyes – very like Harry. Thus, the theory, however interesting, becomes less plausible. And yet sometimes, in television clips of Thatcher and in certain photographs, the similarity to Harry is striking. After all, no one can really know what happened in 1887.

Appendix 2

Miscellany by Harry Cust and Nina Cust

'*Non Nobis*' – Harry Cust:

NOT unto us, O Lord,
Not unto us the rapture of the day,
The peace of night, or love's divine surprise,
High heart, high speech, high deeds 'mid honouring eyes;
For at Thy word
All these are taken away.

Not unto us, O Lord:
To us thou givest the scorn, the scourge, the scar,
The ache of life, the loneliness of death,
The insufferable sufficiency of breath;
And with Thy sword
Thou piercest very far.

Not unto us, O Lord:
Nay, Lord, but unto her be all things given—
May light and life and earth and sky be blasted—
But let not all that wealth of love be wasted:
Let Hell afford
The pavement of her Heaven!

By Harry Cust, thought to be written for Pamela Plowden, later Countess of Lytton:

Beautiful Face!
Is your heart broken that you look so sad?
Is there no heart on earth that once made glad
Your heart, to hearten yet your flower of grace?
Is God untender towards you? Or can Man,
Loving such dear eyes,
Or, save despairing,
Far too much caring,
Grudge his uncrownedness in the race he ran,
And squandered life and lived and lost the prize?
They pay the worthiest cost
Whose lives for you were lost.

(The two pieces below are courtesy of Lord Brownlow.)

Harry Cust's tribute (*c.*1915) to those killed in the war:

Everywhere and every day there will be amongst the living the others of their generation – a fellowship of presences, some dim, some shining, but presences never to be wholly put away … plucking at their hearts, flooding sometimes their memories, seeming sometimes to touch their hands, masterful sometimes to govern and to save their souls. There will be a sort of national Golden Treasury, sacred and serene, in which men and women will enter at their need to find new faith, new courage and unfathomed inexhausted consolation.

Untitled poem by Nina Cust:

By silvered fields where cowslips throng,
Over the dawn-dark hills,
Up from the coppice, clear and strong,
Ceaseless a bird projects his song –
Sad earth with music fills.

Up from one small orchestral throat,
One small hot pulsing breast,
Speeds to the sun each golden note –
Hangs on the air, afire, afloat –
Glorious, sweet, possessed.

ACKNOWLEDGEMENTS

I should like to give warm thanks to the following people who have very generously given me their time and assistance in various invaluable ways, including access to family papers and permission to quote from them, providing information and contacts and permitting use of their family pictures:

The late Lord Brownlow (7th Baron); the Earl of Wemyss and March; Artemis Cooper; Lord Crathorne; the Duchess of Rutland; Lord Egremont; the late Countess of Avon; Simon Blow; Lord Gage; Ivo Mosley; Jason Cooper; Hugo Vickers; Jo Loder; Mick Thompson; Morten Davidsen; Andrew Wallis and Roger Bolton.

Many thanks also to my husband for his unfailing support and encouragement.

BIBLIOGRAPHY

Manuscripts

Asquith Papers (AP) (Bodleian Library, Oxford)
Avon Collection (AC) (Birmingham University)
Wilfrid Scawen Blunt Papers (Fitzwilliam Museum, Cambridge)
Elizabeth Barrett Browning Letters (The Carl H. Pforzheimer Collection of Shelley and His Circle, New York Public Library)
Oscar Browning Papers (King's College, Cambridge)
Brownlow Papers (BP) (Lincolnshire Archives)
Lord Crathorne Collection (LC)
Desborough Papers (DP) (Hertfordshire Archives and Local Studies, Hertford)
Millicent Garrett Fawcett Papers (MGF) (Women's Library, London School of Economics)
Duke of Rutland Private Archives (RA)
Henry Babington Smith Papers (HBS) (King's College, Cambridge)
Stanway Papers (SP) (Earl of Wemyss and March, private collection)
Clara Thomas Archives and Special Collections (CT) (York University Libraries, Canada)
Whittingehame Papers (WP) (National Records of Scotland)

Books

Abdy, Jane, and Charlotte Gere, *The Souls* (London: Sidgwick and Jackson, 1984).
Asquith, Cynthia, *Remember and be Glad* (London: Barrie, 1952).
Asquith, Cynthia, *Diaries, 1915–1918* (London: Pimlico, 1987).
Asquith, Margot, *Off the Record* (London: Frederick Muller, 1943).

Asquith, Margot, *Autobiography* (London: Eyre & Spottiswoode Ltd, 1962).

Asquith, Margot, *Great War Diary 1914–1916* (Oxford University Press, 2014).

Atkinson, Damian (ed.), *The Letters of W.E. Henley to Charles Whibley* (Aldershot: Taylor & Francis, 2000).

Bailey, Catherine, *The Secret Rooms* (London: Penguin, 2013).

Balsan, Consuelo Vanderbilt, *The Glitter & the Gold* (Maidstone: George Mann, 1973).

Baring, Maurice, *The Puppet Show of Memory* (Boston: Little, Brown & Co., 1922).

Beauman, Nicola, *Cynthia Asquith* (London: Hamish Hamilton, 1987).

Blow, Simon, *Broken Blood* (London: Faber & Faber, 1987).

Blumenfeld, R.D., *In the Days of Bicycles and Bustles* (New York: Brewer & Warren, 1931).

Bolton, Roger, *The Witch, Poet & Spy and Other Little Gaddesden Lives* (Surrey: Grosvenor Publishing, 2014).

Bolton, Roger and Julia, *A Family at War: The Talbots of Little Gaddesden* (Surrey: Grosvenor Publishing, 2013).

Browning, Robert and Elizabeth, *The Brownings' Correspondence* (Wedgestone Press, 2017).

Campbell, John, *Margaret Thatcher: Volume One, The Grocer's Daughter* (London: Vintage, 2007).

Cannadine, David, *The Decline & Fall of the British Aristocracy* (London: Penguin, 2005).

Charteris, Mary, *A Family Record* (London: The Curwen Press, 1932 – privately printed).

Chipchase, Paul, 'Some account of the literary production of Lady Welby and her family' pub. in *Essays on Significs: Papers presented on the occasion of the 150th anniversary of the birth of Victoria, Lady Welby*, H. Walter Schmitz (ed.) (Amsterdam & Philadelphia: John Benjamins, 1990).

Connell, John, *W.E. Henley* (London: Constable, 1949).

Cooper, Lady Diana, *The Rainbow Comes and Goes* (London: Random House, 2018).

Coult, Douglas, *A Prospect of Ashridge* (London: Phillimore, 1980).

Crathorne, Nancy, *Tennant's Stalk: The Story of the Tennants of the Glen* (London: Macmillan, 1973).

Cust, Nina, *Not All the Suns* (London: Nicholson & Watson, 1944).

Dakers, Caroline, *Clouds: The Biography of a Country House* (New Haven and London: Yale University Press, 1993).

Davenport-Hines, Richard, *Ettie: The Intimate Life and Dauntless Spirit of Lady Desborough* (London: Weidenfeld & Nicolson, 2008).

Dooley, Terence, *The Decline and Fall of the Dukes of Leinster, 1872–1948* (Dublin: Four Courts Press, 2014).
Douglas, Alfred, *Oscar Wilde and Myself* (London: Duffield, 1914).
Egremont, Max, *The Cousins* (London: Collins, 1977).
Egremont, Max, *Balfour* (London: Collins, 1980).
Ellenberger, Nancy Waters, *The Souls: High Society and Politics in Late Victorian Britain* (Eugene: University of Oregon, 1982).
Ellenberger, Nancy Waters, *Balfour's World: Aristocracy and Political Culture at the Fin de Siecle* (Woodbridge: The Boydell Press, 2015).
Fane, Lady Augusta, *Chit-Chat* (London: Thornton Butterworth, 1926).
Fingall, Elizabeth, Countess of, *Seventy Years Young* (Lilliput Press Ltd, new edition, 1991).
Gladstone, Mary (Mrs Drew), *Her Diaries and Letters* (London: Methuen, 1930).
Hamilton, Trevor, *Arthur Balfour's Ghosts* (Exeter: Imprint Academic, 2017).
Harris, Frank, *Oscar Wilde: His Life and Confessions* (London: Wordsworth Editions, 2007).
Horner, Frances, *Time Remembered* (London: W. Heinemann, 1933).
Hosmer, Harriet, *Letters and Memories* (New York: Moffat, Yard & Co., 1912).
James, M.R., *Eton and King's: Recollections, Mostly Trivial, 1875–1925* (Cambridge: Cambridge University Press, 2011).
Lambert, Angela, *Unquiet Souls: The Indian Summer of the British Aristocracy* (London: Papermac, 1984).
Lawrence, T.E., *Seven Pillars of Wisdom* (Ware: Wordsworth Editions, 1997).
Leach, T.R., *Belton House, the Brownlows and the Custs* (unfinished manuscript, *c.*1993, Brownlow papers, Lincolnshire Archives).
Leslie, Anita, *Edwardians in Love* (London: Hutchinson, 1972).
Leveson Gower, George, *Years of Content 1858–1886* (London: John Murray, 1940).
Leveson Gower, George, *Years of Endeavour 1886–1907* (London: John Murray, 1942).
Lichnowsky, Prince, *My Mission to London 1912–1914* (New York: George H. Doran, 1918).
Lindsay, David, *The Crawford Papers* (Manchester: Manchester University Press, 1986).
Longford, Elizabeth, *A Pilgrimage of Passion: The Life of Wilfrid Scawen Blunt* (London: Tauris Parke, 2007).
McDonald, Deborah, *The Prince, His Tutor and the Ripper* (North Carolina: McFarland, 2007).
Mackail, J.W., and Guy Wyndham (eds), *Life and Letters of George Wyndham* (London: Hutchinson, 1925).

Mallet, Victor (ed.), *Life with Queen Victoria: Marie Mallet's letters from Court, 1887–1901* (London: John Murray, 1968).
Manchester, William, *The Last Lion, Vol. I* (London: Little Brown, 1983).
Montgomery Hyde, H., *The Londonderrys* (London: Hamish Hamilton, 1979).
Moore, Charles, *Margaret Thatcher, The Authorised Biography, Vol. 1: Not for Turning* (London: Allen Lane, 2013).
Paget, Lady, *In My Tower* (London: Hutchinson & Co., 1924).
Popplewell, Sir Oliver, *The Prime Minister and His Mistress* (Lulu Pub., 2014).
Raverat, Gwen, *Period Piece* (London: Faber & Faber, 1952).
Rennell Rodd, James, *Social and Diplomatic Memories, 1884–1893* (London: E. Arnold, 1922).
Renton, Claudia, *Those Wild Wyndhams* (London: William Collins, 2014).
Ridley, Jane and Clayre Percy (eds), *The Letters of Arthur Balfour & Lady Elcho, 1885–1917* (London: Hamish Hamilton, 1992).
Robertson Scott, J.W., *The Life and Death of a Newspaper* (London: Methuen, 1952).
Ronaldshay, Earl of, *The Life of Lord Curzon, Vol. 1* (London: Ernest Benn, 1928).
Sanecki, Kay N., *Ashridge: A Living History* (Chichester: Phillimore, 1996).
Storrs, Sir Ronald, *The Memoirs of Sir Ronald Storrs* (New York: G.P. Putnam Sons, 1937).
Storrs, Sir Ronald, *Orientations* (London: Nicholson & Watson, 1945).
Sturgis, Matthew, *Oscar: A Life* (London: Apollo, 2018).
Thatcher, Margaret, *The Path to Power* (London: Harper Collins, 1995).
Trevelyan, Janet Penrose, *The Life of Mrs Humphry Ward* (New York: Dodd Mead & Co., 1923).
Tweedsmuir, Susan, *The Lilac and the Rose* (London: Duckworth & Co., 1952).
Tynan, Katharine, *The Middle Years* (London: Constable, 1916).
Vansittart, Lord, *The Mist Procession* (London: Hutchinson, 1958).
Waterhouse, Michael, *Edwardian Requiem: A Life of Sir Edward Grey* (London: Biteback Publishing, 2013).
Wells, H.G., *Experiment in Autobiography* (London: Victor Gollancz, 1934).
West, John D., *Maidenhood and Motherhood, or Ten Phases of Woman's Life* (Chicago: King & Law, 1887).
Wharton, Edith, *A Backward Glance* (Project Gutenberg, accessed online, originally published 1934).
Wilson, A.N., *Victoria: A Life* (London: Atlantic, 2014).
Wyndham, Joan, *Dawn Chorus* (London: Virago, 2004).
Ziegler, Philip, *The Biography of Lady Diana Cooper* (London: eBook, Faber and Faber, 2011).

Notes

Prelude: Precipice

1 Today, the grounds of the Ashridge estate are managed by the National Trust. The house and gardens belong to a business college but retain features enjoyed by the Souls.
2 Ettie Grenfell would become Lady Desborough.
3 Susan Tweedsmuir (née Grosvenor), *The Lilac and the Rose.*
4 *Ibid.*
5 Sir Ronald Storrs, *The Memoirs of Sir Ronald Storrs.* Storrs was Harry's nephew, the son of his eldest sister, Lucy.
6 Maurice Baring, *The Puppet Show of Memory.*
7 Letter from Harry Cust to the Marchioness of Granby (Violet), 8 September 1890, Duke of Rutland's private collection.
8 Frances Horner (née Graham), *Time Remembered.*
9 Letter Arthur Balfour to Lady Elcho, 16 August 1893, Stanway Papers (SP).
10 Storrs, *Memoirs.*
11 From 'A Thanksgiving' by Nina Cust, in her collection *Not All the Suns.*
12 From 'The Harvest Moon' by Nina Cust.
13 Lady Paget, *In My Tower.*
14 Letter from Violet Granby to Ettie Grenfell, 31 October 1890, Desborough Papers (DP), Hertfordshire Archives and Local Studies (HALS).
15 By marriage to politician Duff Cooper, 1st Viscount Norwich, she would become Lady Diana Cooper, famed beauty, writer and actress.
16 Letter from Balfour to Lady Elcho, 16 August 1893 (SP). 'Matthews' was Henry Matthews, former Home Secretary.

17 Letter from Pamela Wyndham to her sister, Mary (by marriage Lady Elcho), 3 February 1891 (SP).
18 John D. West, *Maidenhood and Motherhood or, Ten Phases of Woman's Life.*
19 *Ibid.*
20 Letter from Nina Welby-Gregory to Hon. Arthur J. Balfour, undated but from subsequent events, probably mid to late September 1893. Whittingehame documents, GD433/2/482, National Records of Scotland.
21 From *The Importance of Being Earnest.*

Chapter 1: All the Gifts

1 A daughter, Emily Gertrude, born in Sara Jane's first marriage to Major Sidney Robert Streatfeild, died in 1846 before her second birthday.
2 Isaac Cookson of Co. Durham.
3 Letter 3019, Robert and Elizabeth Browning, *The Brownings' Correspondence.*
4 Letter 3031, *ibid.*
5 Letter 3053, *ibid.*
6 Storrs, *Memoirs.*
7 Her real name was Sara Marie.
8 Francis's father (Harry's grandfather) was the Reverend and Hon. Henry Cockayne Cust. He was a Canon of the Royal Chapel at Windsor Castle until his death in May 1861.
9 Letter 3092, Robert and Elizabeth Browning, *The Brownings' Correspondence.*
10 Storrs, *Memoirs.*
11 Quoted in the church leaflet of St John the Baptist, Cockayne Hatley, 2006 edition.
12 When Sir Brownlow Cust died (1807), his son John, Henry's older brother, inherited Belton. John also became 1st Earl and 2nd Baron Brownlow.
13 Harry's full name was Henry John Cockayne Cust.
14 *Shrewsbury Chronicle*, 25 October 1861.
15 *Eddowes Journal*, 8 January 1862.
16 *Ibid.*
17 The future King Edward VII.
18 *Oswestry Advertiser*, 26 December 1866.
19 Letter from Robert Browning in France to Francis Cust, 22 September 1867 (Carl H. Pforzheimer Collection of Shelley and His Circle, New York Public Library).
20 *Wrexham Advertiser*, 21 September 1867.
21 In 1852, Elizabeth gave Sara Jane a copy of Robert's poems of 1850, inscribed 'With Elizabeth Barrett Browning's affectionate regards to Mrs. Streatfeild – Paris – 1852', now in the archives of Eton College.
22 After Emma's death, Robert retired from his distinguished career in the Indian Civil Service and returned to England, becoming an orientalist and missionary strategist.
23 Storrs, *Memoirs.*
24 *Ibid.*

Chapter 2: Friends and Lovers

1 M.R. James, *Eton and King's: Recollections, Mostly Trivial, 1875–1925.*
2 Harry Cust to Oscar Browning, 29 June 1879, Oscar Browning Papers, King's College Cambridge, OB/1/450/A.
3 He was a sportsman, poet and tutor to HRH Prince Albert Victor of Wales. He died in 1892, aged 32.
4 James, *Eton and King's.*
5 Sir James Rennell Rodd, *Social and Diplomatic Memories 1884–1919.*
6 James, *Eton and King's.*
7 Harry Cust to Oscar Browning, undated but on Pitt Club notepaper and must be between 1881 and 1882, OB/1/450/A.
8 Oscar Browning was lauded as a major educational reformer.
9 From 1890 he was HRH the Duke of Clarence and Avondale.
10 Lionel Cust became a prominent art historian, museum director and courtier, later knighted.
11 She was the great-aunt of artist Gwen Raverat, a granddaughter of Charles Darwin.
12 R.C. Jebb's sister, Eglantyne Jebb, was married to their cousin, Arthur Jebb; their daughter, also Eglantyne, was the founder of Save the Children.
13 Mother of Gwen, by her marriage to George Darwin.
14 Gwen Raverat, *Period Piece.*
15 *Shrewsbury Chronicle*, 20 October 1882.
16 *Ibid.*
17 Harry Cust to Henry Babington Smith, 23 June 1883, Henry Babington Smith Papers (HBS), Trinity College, Cambridge, HBS 70.
18 Tweedsmuir, *The Lilac and the Rose.*
19 Harry Cust to Henry Babington Smith, 5 July 1883 (HBS).
20 *Ibid.*
21 Harry Cust to Henry Babington Smith, 10 July 1883 (HBS).
22 *Ibid.*
23 Harry Cust to Henry Babington Smith, 1 August 1883 (HBS).
24 Harry Cust to Henry Babington Smith, 18 August 1883 (HBS).
25 Harry Cust to Oscar Browning, 3 March 1884, Oscar Browning Papers.
26 Harry Cust to Henry Babington Smith, 6 April 1884 (HBS).
27 Harry Cust to Henry Babington Smith, 30 July 1884 (HBS 70, 118 (1)).
28 *Ibid.*
29 Matthew Arnold, contemporary poet.
30 Recorded for June 1884 by Mary Gladstone (Mrs Drew) in *Her Diaries and Letters.*
31 Horner, *Time Remembered.*
32 Mary Elcho in her essay on the Souls (SP).
33 Quoted in Nancy Crathorne, *Tennant's Stalk: The Story of the Tennants of the Glen*, p.177.
34 Simon Blow, *Broken Blood.*
35 Quoted by David Cannadine in *The Decline & Fall of the British Aristocracy.*
36 Margot Asquith (née Tennant), *Autobiography.*

37 Quoted in Angela Lambert, *Unquiet Souls: The Indian Summer of the British Aristocracy*, p.23.
38 Lady Emily Lutyens, 'A Blessed Girl', quoted in Max Egremont, *Balfour.* Emily was sister to Betty Balfour, wife of Arthur's brother, Gerald.
39 Quoted in Margot Asquith, *Autobiography*, p.24.
40 *Ibid.*
41 Curzon's note, quoted in Earl of Ronaldshay, *The Life of Lord Curzon, Vol.1.*
42 He died in 1881.
43 E.F. Benson, 'As We Were', quoted in H. Montgomery Hyde, *The Londonderrys.*
44 The Earl of Pembroke and Harry also shared a connection through Pembroke's wife, Gertrude (known as Gity), who was Adelaide Brownlow's sister.
45 Margot Asquith, *Autobiography.*
46 Hyde (who worked for the 7th Marquess) said the family papers make it clear that 'there is absolutely no evidence that he never spoke to her again in private, each going their separate ways'.
47 Harry Cust to Henry Babington Smith, 8 September 1884 (HBS 70, 119).
48 Harry Cust to Henry Babington Smith, 1 December 1884 (HBS 120 (1)).
49 Sir George Leveson Gower, *Years of Content 1858–1886.*
50 *Cheltenham Looker-On*, 18 April 1885.
51 'Apostles' derives from the original membership of twelve.
52 Harry Cust to Henry Babington Smith, 3 May 1885 (HBS 65(1)).
53 Harry Cust to Henry Babington Smith, 12 January 1886 and 7 March 1886, (HBS 121 (1) and (2)).

Chapter 3: Coming Together

1 Named Alfred Christopher, he would die of meningitis, aged 2.
2 Quoted in Crathorne, *Tennant's Stalk*, p.184.
3 Alfred Lyttelton, quoted in Nancy Waters Ellenberger, *The Souls: High Society and Politics in late Victorian Britain.*
4 Mrs Courtney, quoted in J.W. Robertson Scott, *The Life and Death of a Newspaper.*
5 Leveson Gower, *Years of Content 1858–1886.*
6 *St James's Gazette*, 23 November 1886.
7 Lady Augusta Fane, *Chit-Chat.* The place was probably the Devil's Punch Bowl in Surrey.
8 Cynthia Asquith (née Charteris), quoted in Nicola Beauman, *Cynthia Asquith*, p.41.
9 Ettie Grenfell, quoted in Lambert, *Unquiet Souls*, p.88.
10 *Ibid.*, p.99.
11 Margot Asquith, *Autobiography.*
12 Lady Angela Forbes, quoted in Lambert, *Unquiet Souls*, p.93.
13 Margot Asquith, *Autobiography.*
14 In 1875, Sir William Welby assumed the additional surname (and arms) of Gregory. Nina's surname became Welby-Gregory but Lady Victoria remained Welby.
15 Paul Chipchase, 'Some account of the literary production of Lady Welby and her family', pub. in *Essays on Significs*, p.46.

16 Nina Cust, from 'A Thanksgiving'.
17 H.G. Wells, quoted in Beauman, *Cynthia Asquith*, p.15.
18 Mary Elcho to Balfour, quoted in Claudia Renton, *Those Wild Wyndhams*, p.39.
19 Margot Asquith, *Autobiography*.
20 Alice Comyns Carr, quoted in Renton, *Those Wild Wyndhams*, p.7.
21 Mary Charteris, *A Family Record*.
22 *Ibid*.
23 Mrs Ward to Mrs A.H. Johnson, 21 October 1888, quoted in Janet Penrose Trevelyan, *The Life of Mrs Humphry Ward*.
24 Balfour to Mary Elcho, 29 April 1890, quoted in Jane Ridley and Clayre Percy (eds), *The Letters of Arthur Balfour & Lady Elcho, 1885–1917*.
25 *Ibid.*, p.16.
26 *Manchester Evening News*, 5 January 1887. Lord Randolph had proposed a radical budget with which the Cabinet disagreed and had boxed himself into a corner, giving him little alternative but to resign.
27 Horner, *Time Remembered*.
28 *Ibid*.
29 Harry Cust to Mary Elcho, 4 January 1887 (SP).
30 From Clouds, the Wyndham family home, 12 January 1887 (SP).
31 Laura Tennant, quoted in Renton, *Those Wild Wyndhams*, p.59.
32 Wheatley was a widower. His first wife was Wilfrid Blunt's sister.
33 Elizabeth Barrett Browning, quoted in Harriet Hosmer, *Letters and Memories*, p.154.
34 Mary Elcho, essay on the Souls (SP).
35 Lord Haldane, *Memoirs*, from an extract published in *The Times*, 1929.
36 Rennell Rodd, *Social and Diplomatic Memories, 1884–1893*,

Chapter 4: Flirtations

1 Wilfrid Blunt Papers, Fitzwilliam Museum, Cambridge.
2 Balfour to Mary Elcho, 1–3 January 1887, quoted in Ridley and Percy (eds), *Letters of Arthur Balfour & Lady Elcho*.
3 Quoted in Richard Davenport-Hines, *Ettie: The Intimate Life and Dauntless Spirit of Lady Desborough*.
4 Margot Asquith, *Autobiography*.
5 Cynthia Asquith, *Remember and be Glad*.
6 Margot to Harry, 26 September 1887, Asquith Papers (AP), Bodleian Library.
7 Margot Asquith, *Autobiography*.
8 Margot to Harry, undated except for 'The last day of the Queen's Hotel, Harrogate', so likely October 1887, (AP).
9 Margot to Harry undated, probably November 1887 (AP).
10 Margot to Harry from Queen's Hotel, Harrogate, undated except 'Saturday', likely October 1887 (AP).
11 Margot to Harry, 19 October 1887 (AP).
12 Margot to Harry undated, from 35 Grosvenor Square, probably October/early November 1887 (AP).

13 Margot to Harry, 19 October 1887 (AP).
14 Harry to Margot 20 October 1887, Margot Asquith, *Autobiography.*
15 Margot Asquith, *Autobiography.*
16 Margot to Harry, 2 November 1887 (AP).
17 Margot to Harry undated except 'Thursday night', from The Glen (AP).
18 *Ibid.*
19 Rennell Rodd, *Social and Diplomatic Memories.*
20 In 1887, the Third Reform Act gave the vote to all working men, which meant those who owned land valued at more than £10 or who paid annual rent of £10, but it still left 40 per cent of all adult men unable to vote.
21 The great-great grandfather of Britain's former prime minister David Cameron was speaking in October 1887.
22 Harry to Mary Elcho, January 1888 (SP).
23 Harry to Mary, 10 March 1888 (SP).
24 Harry to Mary, 25 March 1888 (SP).
25 Harry to Mary, 12 September 1888 (SP).
26 Quoted in Beauman, *Cynthia Asquith*, p.15.
27 Balfour to Mary, quoted in Egremont, *Balfour*, p.70.
28 Margot to Harry, 21 November 1888 (AP).

Chapter 5: Ambitions

1 *Grantham Journal*, 24 November 1888.
2 *Stamford Mercury*, 6 April 1888.
3 *Stamford Mercury*, 20 July 1888.
4 *Stamford Mercury*, 30 November 1888.
5 George Wyndham to Lady Grosvenor (Sibell), 12–13 January 1888, quoted in Terence Dooley, *The Decline and Fall of the Dukes of Leinster 1872–1948*, p.84.
6 Charty to Harry from Stanway, undated but must be pre-1890, for she refers to Harry still lodging in Paris, no. 137/139 (AP).
7 Hermione to Evelyn, quoted in Dooley, *The Decline and Fall*, p.81.
8 Hermione to Lord Houghton, 29 January 1891, quoted in Dooley, *The Decline and Fall*, p.80.
9 Hermione to Evelyn, quoted in Dooley, *The Decline and Fall*, p.85.
10 Lord Wemyss to the author at Stanway, March 2018.
11 Mary to Ettie, 26 December 1888 (DP).
12 Doll Liddell to Lady Wenlock, 16 December 1888, quoted in Davenport-Hines, *Ettie: The Intimate Life*, p.49.
13 Hugo to Ettie, 6 May 1889 (DP).
14 Ettie's first child (of five) was Julian, born 30 March 1888, followed by Gerald ('Billy') on 29 March 1890.
15 Hugo to Ettie, 23 August 1889 (DP).
16 Cynthia Asquith, *Diaries, 1915–1918.*
17 Lady Frances Balfour to Betty Balfour, June 1889, quoted in Renton, *Those Wild Wyndhams*, p.125.
18 *Irish Society* (Dublin), 1 June 1889.

19 Hermione to 'Darling', quoted in Dooley, *The Decline and Fall*, p.89.
20 Hermione to Evelyn, quoted in Dooley, *The Decline and Fall*, p.87.
21 Margot Asquith, *Autobiography*.
22 Charty to Harry, from 35 Grosvenor Square, undated except 'Friday' but probably 1889 (No. 193, AP).
23 Charty to Harry, 15 September 1888 (No. 104, AP).
24 Charty to Harry, undated but probably 1889, as written before Curzon left Britain (No. 112, AP).
25 Charty to Harry, 3 January 1889 (No. 105, AP).
26 Charty to Harry, undated, from 35 Grosvenor Square (AP).
27 Charty to Harry, undated except 'Friday, from Hotel Royal', Dieppe (AP 129/130).
28 Charty to Harry from Stanway, undated but must be pre-1890, as she refers to Harry still lodging in Paris (No. 137/139, AP).
29 Charty to Harry from Gisburne, undated but probably 1889 (No. 141, AP).
30 *Ibid*.
31 Margot to George Curzon, Christmas Day 1890, collection of Lord Crathorne (LC).
32 Margot to Ettie Grenfell, 26 October 1889 (DP, C71/5).
33 Charty to Harry, undated but probably 1889, as written before Curzon left Britain (No. 115, AP).
34 Jane Abdy and Charlotte Gere, *The Souls*, p.17.
35 *Buckinghamshire Herald*, 13 July 1889.
36 *Links and Clues*.
37 Margot to Ettie Grenfell, 26 October 1889 (DP).

Chapter 6: A Kind of Fame

1 Harry to Lady Granby (Violet), 19 January 1890, from the Duke of Rutland's archives (RA).
2 Sent to Violet on 21 January 1890 (RA).
3 Harry to Violet, 22–23 January 1890 (RA).
4 *Ibid*.
5 *Ibid*.
6 Harry to Violet, 24 January 1890 (RA).
7 Harry to Violet, from Belton, undated but 'Friday', probably the same week in January 1890 (RA).
8 Harry to Violet, 25 January 1890 (RA).
9 Harry to Violet, 9 February 1890 (RA).
10 Harry to Violet, 2 March 1890 (RA).
11 Harry to Violet, 5 March 1890 (RA).
12 Balfour to Mary Elcho, 5 March 1890 (SP).
13 *Stamford Mercury*, 14 March 1890.
14 *Ibid*.
15 Harry to Violet, 16 April 1890 (RA).
16 Lady Welby to Nina, 11 April 1890, Welby correspondence, Clara Thomas Archives and Special Collections (CT).
17 Harry to Violet, 28 May 1890 (RA).

18 *Ibid.*
19 Harry to Violet, 29 May 1890 (RA).
20 Harry to Violet, 7 July 1890 (RA).
21 Mrs Humphry Ward, quoted in Earl of Ronaldshay, *The Life Of Lord Curzon, Vol.1.*
22 *Derby Mercury*, 16 July 1890.
23 Quoted in A.N. Wilson, *Victoria: A Life*, p.513.
24 Harry to Violet, 17 July 1890 (RA).
25 Harry to Violet, 8 September 1890 (RA).
26 Maud Tree was the actress wife of actor and theatre manager, Herbert (later Sir) Beerbohm Tree. She often provided cover for Violet's trysts with Harry.
27 'Venice', James's essay published in 1882, his longest in a series on the city.
28 Violet to Ettie, 27 October 1890 (DP, C1764/1).
29 Violet to Ettie, 31 October 1890 (DP, C630/2).
30 Harry to Ettie, Christmas 1890 (DP, C630/3).
31 Margot Asquith, *Autobiography*.
32 Hugo (Lord Elcho) to Ettie, 7 December 1890 (DP).
33 Hugo to Ettie,12 December 1890 (DP).
34 Hermione to Evelyn, quoted in Dooley, *The Decline and Fall*, p.89.

Chapter 7: Temptations

1 *Stamford Mercury*, 9 January 1891.
2 Hon. Percy Wyndham to Mary Elcho, 14 September 1888 (SP).
3 Pamela Wyndham to Mary Elcho, 3 February 1891 (SP).
4 Harry to Ettie Grenfell, 21 March 1891 (DP, C630/5).
5 *Pall Mall Gazette*, quoted in *Grantham Journal*, 14 March 1891.
6 Balfour to Mary Elcho, 16 July 1891, Ridley and Percy (eds), *Letters of Arthur Balfour & Lady Elcho.*
7 *The Times*, 14 July 1891.
8 Rennell Rodd, *Social and Diplomatic Memories*.
9 Balfour to Mary Elcho, 16 July 1891, Ridley and Percy (eds), *Letters of Arthur Balfour & Lady Elcho.*
10 He is known particularly as the composer of 'Jerusalem'.
11 Quoted in Nancy Waters Ellenberger, *The Souls: High Society and Politics in Late Victorian Britain*, p.132.
12 Balfour to Mary Elcho, 5 August 1891, Ridley and Percy (eds), *Letters of Arthur Balfour & Lady Elcho.*
13 Quoted in Davenport-Hines, *Ettie*, pp.57–58.
14 Quoted in Matthew Sturgis, *Oscar: A Life*.
15 As a result of the 1891 Congress, the International Peace Bureau (IPB) was founded.
16 *Grantham Journal*, 9 January 1892.
17 Diary of Wilfrid Blunt, S.M.Vol. XVI, Fitzwilliam Museum, Cambridge.
18 Robertson Scott, *The Life and Death of a Newspaper.*
19 Deborah McDonald, *The Prince, His Tutor and the Ripper.*
20 Wilfrid Blunt and Hon. Percy Wyndham were first cousins.

21 Alfred Douglas, *Oscar Wilde and Myself.*
22 Wilfrid Blunt, quoted in Max Egremont, *The Cousins*, p.156.
23 Wilde quoted in Frank Harris, *Oscar Wilde: His Life and Confessions.*
24 Blunt, quoted in Egremont, *The Cousins*, p.157.
25 Blunt diary, S.M.Vol. XVI, Fitzwilliam Museum, Cambridge.
26 Charles Whibley, literary journalist and author.
27 Edward Cook, quoted in Robertson Scott, *The Life and Death of a Newspaper.*
28 Interview with Harry in *The Sketch*, 10 May 1893. The interview was probably given earlier that year.
29 Robertson Scott, *The Life and Death of a Newspaper.*
30 *Grantham Journal*, 2 July 1892.
31 *Ibid.*
32 *Stamford Mercury*, 8 July 1892.
33 Three seats were also won by the Independent Labour Party.
34 Violet Granby to Ettie Grenfell, 22 April 1892 (DP).
35 Letter from George Leveson Gower to Lady Wenlock, 12 May 1892, *Years of Endeavour 1886–1907.*
36 Philip Ziegler, *The Biography of Lady Diana Cooper.*
37 *Yorkshire Evening Post*, 23 November 1892.
38 Hugo Charteris (Lord Elcho) lost his seat as MP for Haddington in 1885 but in 1886 was elected as one of the two MPs for Ipswich.

Chapter 8: Suffer the Little Children

1 Hermione, Duchess of Leinster, to Evelyn de Vesci, undated, quoted in Dooley, *The Decline and Fall*, pp.89–90.
2 Quoted in a feature by Ryle Dwyer for the *Irish Examiner*, posted online 6 October 2016.
3 *Yorkshire Evening Post*, 21 May 1892.
4 Hermione, Duchess of Leinster to Evelyn de Vesci, undated, quoted in Dooley, *The Decline and Fall*, p. 91.
5 Lady Helen to Duke of Leinster, quoted in Dooley, *The Decline and Fall*, p.92.
6 Mary to Balfour, 30 October 1912, Ridley and Percy (eds), *Letters of Arthur Balfour & Lady Elcho.*
7 Pamela to Ettie, 2 January 1893 (DP, C1179/2).
8 Balfour to Mary, 9 January 1893, Ridley and Percy (eds), *Letters of Arthur Balfour & Lady Elcho.*
9 Mary to Balfour, 13 August 1890, Ridley and Percy (eds), *Letters of Arthur Balfour & Lady Elcho.*
10 *Northampton Mercury*, 15 January 1892.
11 Blunt diary, 20 August and 24 August 1892 (S.M.Vol.XVI, Fitzwilliam Museum, Cambridge).
12 Balfour to Mary Elcho, 20 February 1892, Ridley and Percy (eds), *Letters of Arthur Balfour & Lady Elcho.*

13 Pamela to Mary, 16 August 1892 (SP).
14 Pamela to Mary 31 August 1892 (SP).
15 *Ibid.*
16 *Glasgow Herald*, 26 November 1892.
17 Robertson Scott, *The Life and Death of a Newspaper*, p.376.
18 *The Sketch*, 10 May 1893.
19 Lewis Hind, quoted in Robertson Scott, *The Life and Death of a Newspaper*, p.385.
20 J.B. Atkins, a journalist at the *Pall Mall Gazette*, quoted in Robertson Scott, *The Life and Death of a Newspaper*, p.375.
21 Robertson Scott, *The Life and Death of a Newspaper.*
22 All quotes from Robertson Scott, *The Life and Death of a Newspaper.*
23 *The Winter's Tale*, 4.3.25.
24 *Pall Mall Gazette*, 16 January 1894.
25 H.G. Wells, *Experiment in Autobiography.*
26 Best known for his poem 'Invictus'.
27 Harry, speaking at Henley's memorial service, 1908.
28 Quoted in Davenport-Hines, *Ettie*, p.83.
29 Katharine Tynan, *The Middle Years.*
30 Davenport-Hines, *Ettie.*
31 George Wyndham to Ettie Grenfell, 14 April 1893, quoted in Davenport-Hines, *Ettie*, pp.83–84.
32 Blunt diary, 5 June 1893 (S.M.Vol. XVI, Fitzwilliam Museum, Cambridge).
33 *Lincolnshire Echo*, 17 August 1893.
34 It is not possible to ascertain exactly when Harry spoke to Pamela of marriage this time. This date is deduced from other known dates.
35 Pamela to Mary, 25 August 1893 (SP).
36 Blunt diary, 16 October 1893 (S.M.Vol. XVI, Fitzwilliam Museum, Cambridge).
37 Blunt, 9 November 1893 (S.M.Vol. XVI, Fitzwilliam Museum, Cambridge).

Chapter 9: Panic

1 Blunt Diary, 16 October 1893 (S.M.Vol. XVI, Fitzwilliam Museum, Cambridge). Nina's relations say they remain none the wiser.
2 Whittingehame Papers (WP) (GD 433/2/482, National Records of Scotland).
3 Violet Granby to Balfour, undated except 'Tuesday night', certainly 1893, probably September (WP).
4 George Wyndham to Ettie Grenfell, 27 September 1893 (SP).
5 30 September 1893 (DP).
6 *Southern Reporter*, 26 October 1893.
7 Harry to Balfour, 15 October 1893 (WP).
8 Quoted in Caroline Dakers, *Clouds: The Biography of a Country House*, p.161.
9 Lady Welby to Balfour, 16 October 1893 (WP).
10 In July 1882, their brother Francis Balfour, aged 30, a brilliant biologist, was killed while climbing Mont Blanc. He appears in psychical research literature as a communicator in an important case investigated by the SPR, 'The Palm Sunday Case', which focussed on Arthur and his dead lover, May Lyttelton.

11 Leveson Gower to Lady Wenlock, 17 November 1893, *Years of Endeavour.*
12 George Pembroke to Violet Maxse, 12 October 1893, Cecil-Maxse Papers 345, quoted in Ellenberger, *Balfour's World: Aristocracy and Political Culture at the Fin de Siècle.*
13 Harry to Balfour from Fontainebleau, undated except 'Saturday', clearly 1893 (WP).
14 Curzon to Balfour, 16 October 1893 (WP).
15 Curzon seems to have overlooked the fact that the marriage took place in England.
16 Charles Welby to Balfour, 16 October 1893 (WP).
17 Nina Cust to Balfour, 24 October 1893 (WP).
18 Charles Welby to Balfour, 31 October 1893 (WP).
19 Charles Welby to Balfour, 3 November 1893 (WP).
20 Harry to Sibell Grosvenor, quoted in Egremont, *The Cousins*, pp.163–64.
21 Margot to Lady Frances Balfour, 13 December 1893 (WP).
22 Margot to Balfour, undated except '28th', from The Glen, probably November/ December 1893 (WP, GD 433/2/482/29).
23 Born 1858, a daughter of the 8th Duke of Argyll and Lady Elizabeth Sutherland Leveson Gower, both social campaigners.
24 Letter Frances Balfour to Betty Balfour (née Lytton, married to Gerald Balfour), 10 November 1893 (WP).
25 Frances Balfour to Betty Balfour, 18 November 1893 (WP).
26 Margot to Balfour, undated except '28th', from The Glen, probably November/ December 1893 (WP, GD 433/2/482/29).
27 DD to Kathleen Lyttelton, 10 February 1894, Chandos Papers 11:3/14, quoted in Ellenberger, *Balfour's World.*
28 Betty Balfour to Frances Balfour, no day given, December 1893 (WP).
29 The Reverend Edward Stuart Talbot had been the first Warden of Keble College, Oxford and from 1893 was on its council.
30 Talbot to Balfour, 31 October 1893 (WP).
31 Talbot to Balfour, 3 November 1893 (WP).
32 Arthur Balfour, quoted in letter from Betty Balfour to Frances Balfour, no day given, December 1893 (WP).
33 *Pall Mall Gazette*, 28 January 1895.
34 *Lincolnshire Chronicle*, 6 February 1894.
35 *The Gentlewoman*, 17 February 1894.
36 *Ibid.*
37 Wells, *Experiment.*
38 Henley to Charles Baxter, 22 February 1894, in Damian Atkinson (ed.), *The Letters of W.E. Henley to Charles Whibley.*
39 John Connell in Robertson Scott, *The Life and Death of a Newspaper.*
40 Hermione to Evelyn, quoted in Dooley, *The Decline and Fall*, p.98.
41 Countess of Fingall, *Seventy Years Young.*
42 Quoted in Davenport-Hines, *Ettie*, p.77.
43 Margot to Blunt, quoted in Lambert, *Unquiet Souls*, p.83.
44 Quoted in Crathorne, *Tennant's Stalk*, p.196.
45 Blunt, 27 June 1894 (S.M. Vol. XVI, Fitzwilliam Museum, Cambridge).

Chapter 10: Fallout

1 Millicent Garrett Fawcett to Arthur Balfour, 19 March 1894 (Millicent Garrett Fawcett Papers (MGF), Women's Library London School of Economics, GB 106 7MGF/A/2/123). A shortened version of this source reference will be used for further notes, prefaced by 'MGF' and followed by the specific document number.
2 Kathleen Lyttelton (KL) to Millicent Garrett Fawcett, 19 February 1894 (MGF/003).
3 Statement of Millicent Garrett Fawcett as sent to the Hon. Secretary of the Manchester Women's Liberal Unionist Association, then to Leigh Maclachlan and others, and replicated in Millicent Garrett Fawcett's letter to Arthur Balfour, 19 March 1894.
4 Leigh Maclachlan to Millicent Garrett Fawcett, 20 February 1894 (MGF/004).
5 Mary Forster to Millicent Garrett Fawcett, 18 February 1894 (MGF/010).
6 Charles Hurst to Isabella Tod, 28 February 1894 (MGF/013b).
7 Harry to Millicent Garrett Fawcett, 5 March 1894 (MGF/014).
8 Millicent Garrett Fawcett to Harry, 6 March 1894 (MGF/018).
9 Harry to Millicent Garrett Fawcett, 8 March 1894 (MGF/021).
10 Millicent Garrett Fawcett to Harry, 9 March 1894 (MGF/023).
11 Dr William Armstrong to Millicent Garrett Fawcett, 12 March 1894 (MGF/028).
12 Talbot to Balfour, undated but probably March 1894 (WP, GD 433/2/482/22).
13 Talbot to Balfour, undated but probably March 1894 (WP, GD 433/2/482/30).
14 Balfour to Mary Elcho, 14 March 1894, Ridley and Percy (eds), *Letters of Arthur Balfour & Lady Elcho*.
15 Frances Balfour to Millicent Garrett Fawcett, 15 March 1894 (MGF/037).
16 Letter within MGF/121.
17 Balfour to Millicent Garrett Fawcett, 22 March 1894 (MGF/122b).
18 Millicent Garrett Fawcett to Balfour, 26 March 1894 (MGF/123).
19 He killed himself in 1922, before his arrest for sexually abusing a boy.
20 Millicent Garrett Fawcett to Haldane in notes of meeting, 12 May 1894 (MGF/083).
21 Balfour to Millicent Garrett Fawcett, 5 April 1894 (MGF/062).
22 J. Edward Mercer to Millicent Garrett Fawcett, 29 March 1894 (MGF/056).
23 Mercer to Balfour, 7 April 1894 (WP, GD 433/2/482/36).
24 Iwan-Müller to Balfour, 10 April 1894 (WP, GD 433/2/482/39).
25 Armstrong to Millicent Garrett Fawcett, 21 April 1894 (MGF/075).
26 Reverend Arthur Lyttelton to Sir William Houldsworth, 30 March 1894 (WP, GD 433/2/482/34).
27 Arthur Lyttelton to Sir W. Houldsworth, 1 April 1894 (WP, GD 433/2/482/35).
28 Millicent Garrett Fawcett to George Needham, 24 April 1894 (MGF/079).
29 Millicent Garrett Fawcett's note of meeting with Haldane, 12 May 1894 (MGF/083).
30 Blunt Diaries, 4 May 1894 (S.M. Vol. XVI, Fitzwilliam Museum, Cambridge).
31 Kathleen Lyttelton to Millicent Garrett Fawcett, 13 May 1894 (MGF/084).

Chapter 11: For Love's Sake

1 John Connell, *W.E. Henley*.
2 Robertson Scott, *The Life and Death of a Newspaper*.
3 Letter from Lucy Clifford to Millicent Garrett Fawcett, 23 May 1894 (MGF/089).
4 Lucy Clifford notes, 25 May 1894 (MGF/090).
5 Millicent Garrett Fawcett's notes, 20 May 1894 (MGF/142). They refer to Mrs Clifford as 'Mrs K', as she did not want her name revealed.
6 Lucy Clifford to Millicent Garrett Fawcett, 25 May 1894 (MGF/092).
7 Lucy Clifford to Millicent Garrett Fawcett, 25 May 1894 (MGF/093).
8 Millicent Garrett Fawcett notes of meeting, 27 May 1894 (MGF/143).
9 Nina to Millicent Garrett Fawcett, 28 May 1894 (MGF/96(a)).
10 Nina to Millicent Garrett Fawcett, 28 May 1894 (MGF/96(b)).
11 Millicent Garrett Fawcett to Nina, 29 May 1894 (MGF//96(d)).
12 Crathorne, *Tennant's Stalk*.
13 Blunt, 20 May 1894, from his secret diaries, quoted in Lambert, *Unquiet Souls*, p.81.
14 Frances Balfour to Lady Salisbury, 29 March 1894, quoted in Jehanne Wake, *Princess Louise* (London: Collins, 1988) p.308.
15 Balfour to Harry, 1 June 1894 (WP, GD 433/2/482/41).
16 Kathleen Lyttelton to Millicent Garrett Fawcett, 12 June 1894 (MGF/102(1)).
17 Millicent Garrett Fawcett notes, 20 July 1894 (MGF/108).
18 From Shakespeare's *Hamlet*.
19 Kathleen Lyttelton to Millicent Garrett Fawcett, 22 September 1894 (MGF/112).
20 Letter from Harry, quoted in Lucy Graham Smith's diary, Thursday, 27 December 1894, collection of Lord Crathorne (LC).
21 Letter Harry to Lucy, referred to in her diary for Saturday, 29 December 1894 (LC).
22 Lucy's diary, Saturday, 29 December 1894 (LC).
23 'Twelfth Night on the Moors', *Pall Mall Gazette*, 8 January 1895.
24 Leveson Gower, *Years of Endeavour*, p.124.
25 *Ibid.*, p.84.
26 *Grantham Journal*, 3 August 1895.
27 Frances Balfour to Millicent Garrett Fawcett, 19 March 1895 (MGF/114).
28 Millicent Garrett Fawcett to Frances Balfour, 22 March 1895 (MGF/116).
29 Frances Balfour to Millicent Garrett Fawcett, undated but clearly March 1895 (MGF/117).
30 Frances Balfour to Millicent Garrett Fawcett, 25 March 1895 (MGF/119).
31 Kathleen Lyttelton to Millicent Garrett Fawcett, 2 April 1895 (MGF/120).
32 Henley to Whibley, 22 November 1895 in Atkinson, *Letters of W.E. Henley*.
33 *Ibid.*
34 *The Sketch*, 24 July 1895.

Chapter 12: Crises

1 Pamela to Sibell, Countess Grosvenor, 29 September 1894, quoted in Renton, *Those Wild Wyndhams*, p.189.
2 Lady Paget, *In My Tower*, Vol.1, entry for 25 April 1895.
3 Quoted in Dakers, *Clouds*, p.161.
4 Quoted in Elizabeth Longford, *A Pilgrimage of Passion*, pp.264–65.
5 Harris, *Oscar Wilde: His Life and Confessions*.
6 Longford, *A Pilgrimage of Passion*, p.286.
7 Quoted in Egremont, *The Cousins*, p.39.
8 Quoted in Longford, *A Pilgrimage of Passion*, p.310.
9 11 February 1895, Blunt Papers (Fitzwilliam Museum, Cambridge).
10 Quoted in Longford, *A Pilgrimage of Passion*, p.312.
11 Quoted in Dooley, *The Decline and Fall*, p.109.
12 *Ibid.*, p.315.
13 Beauman, *Cynthia Asquith*, p.30.
14 Sybil Cust in 1898, Abdy and Gere, *The Souls*, p.79.
15 Henley to Charles Whibley, 24 June 1897, Atkinson, *Letters of W.E. Henley*.
16 Edith Wharton, *A Backward Glance*.
17 Robertson Scott, *The Life and Death of a Newspaper*.
18 *Ibid.*, p.380.
19 *Ibid.*, p.383.
20 Katharine Tynan, *The Middle Years*.
21 Note from Harry, 8 February 1896, in Lucy's diary, Sunday, 9 February 1896 (LC).
22 Lucy's diary, Friday, 14 February 1896 (LC).
23 David Lindsay, *The Crawford Papers*, 20 March 1896.
24 1 October 1896, Ridley and Percy, *Letters of Arthur Balfour*.
25 Paget, *In My Tower*.
26 Countess of Fingall, *Seventy Years Young*.
27 Lady Eden's notes for her autobiography, Avon Collection (AC), University of Birmingham (AP/22/14/12).
28 Eden notes, (AC – AP/22/14/12).
29 *The Gentlewoman*, 30 January 1897.
30 Eden notes (AC).
31 Quoted in Eden notes (AC).
32 Henley to Whibley, 19 January 1897, Atkinson, *Letters of W.E. Henley*.
33 *West London Observer*, 4 June 1897.
34 Henley to Whibley, 24 June 1897, Atkinson, *Letters of W.E. Henley*.

Chapter 13: Acceptance

1 Hugo to Ettie, 31 — (month illegible) 1896, sent from 62 Cadogan Street (DP).
2 Paget, *In My Tower*, 12 December 1895.
3 Blunt in Longford, *A Pilgrimage of Passion*, p.288.

4 Paget, *In My Tower*, August 1897.
5 Lady Windsor in Longford, *A Pilgrimage of Passion*, p.332.
6 Blunt, 12 August 1897, in Longford, *A Pilgrimage of Passion*, p.332.
7 Blunt in Longford, *A Pilgrimage of Passion*, p.333.
8 Paget, *In My Tower*, 28 April 1900.
9 *Ibid.*, August 1897.
10 *The World*, 13 May 1891.
11 Letter 1898, Atkinson, *Letters of W.E. Henley*, p.584.
12 Salisbury in Egremont, *The Cousins*, p.196.
13 Lambert, *Unquiet Souls*, p.117.
14 Conseulo Vanderbilt Balsan, *The Glitter & the Gold*.
15 *Ibid.*
16 Blow, *Broken Blood*, and to the author, 2018.
17 Quoted in Egremont, *The Cousins*, p.284.
18 Lambert, *Unquiet Souls*, p.116.
19 *Ibid.*, pp.116–17.
20 Lindsay, *The Crawford Papers*, 6 May 1898.
21 Lady Welby to Nina, 26 June 1899 (CT).
22 Lady Welby to Harry, 10 July 1899 (CT).
23 Letter to Whibley, 30 July 1899, Atkinson, *Letters of W.E. Henley*.
24 *Luton Times & Advertiser*, 16 June 1899.
25 Mary to Hugo, Lambert, *Unquiet Souls*, p.215.
26 Mary to Balfour, 30 August 1899, Ridley & Percy, *Letters of Arthur Balfour & Lady Elcho*.
27 Balfour to Mary, Lambert, *Unquiet Souls*, p.214.
28 *The Sphere*, 7 July 1900.
29 19 July 1900, Ridley & Percy, *Letters of Arthur Balfour & Lady Elcho*.
30 *The South London Press*, 28 July 1900.

Chapter 14: Tensions

1 15 September 1900 (CT).
2 William Manchester includes Harry in a list of Jennie's lovers in *The Last Lion, Vol. I*. She married Lord Randolph Churchill in 1874 and married again in July 1900.
3 Storrs, *Orientations*, p.34.
4 *South London Press*, 6 October 1900.
5 *South London Press*, 24 November 1900.
6 Paget, *In My Tower*, 2 February 1901.
7 *Batley Reporter*, 22 February 1901.
8 Paget, *In My Tower*, 28 September 1902.
9 Jean Hamilton in Davenport-Hines, *Ettie*, p.123.
10 12 July 1902, Ridley and Percy, *Letters of Arthur Balfour & Lady Elcho*.
11 Dakers, *Clouds*, p.155.
12 12 July 1902, Ridley and Percy, *Letters of Arthur Balfour & Lady Elcho*.
13 Balfour to Mary, 30 August 1897, Beauman, *Cynthia Asquith*, p.17.

14 29 July 1898 (SP).
15 It was sold in May 1902 to a Canadian financier.
16 Harry to Mary Elcho, undated except 1902 (SP).
17 *Ibid.*
18 *Grantham Journal*, 27 June 1903.
19 Harry to Balfour, 23 September 1903 (AP).
20 Marie Mallet, 3 November 1900, Victor Mallet (ed.), *Life with Queen Victoria.*
21 Haldane's letter to *The Times*, 17 January 1929 (SP).
22 Recorded by J.S. Sandars in Egremont, *Balfour*, p.152.
23 *Derby Daily Telegraph*, 22 February 1904.
24 Rennell Rodd, *Social and Diplomatic Memories.*
25 Henley to Whibley, 27 November 1901, Atkinson, *Letters of W.E. Henley.* They had been friends but became embroiled in a literary dispute.
26 Henley to Whibley, 20 October 1902, *ibid.*
27 Cynthia Asquith, *Remember and be Glad.*
28 *The Sphere*, 1 April 1905.
29 Lady Welby to Nina, 17 December 1905 (CT).
30 *South London Chronicle*, 24 November 1905.
31 *South London Chronicle*, 29 December 1905.
32 Egremont, *The Cousins*, p.243.
33 Mark Sykes to his wife in Egremont, *The Cousins*, p.244.
34 Paget, *In My Tower*, 19 September 1904.
35 Wyndham to his mother, 7 April 1905, J.W. Mackail and Guy Wyndham (eds), *Life and Letters of George Wyndham.*
36 Paget, *In My Tower*, 14 April 1905.

Chapter 15: The Young Ones

1 Davenport-Hines, *Ettie*, p.116.
2 15 January 1906, Ridley and Percy, *Letters of Arthur Balfour & Lady Elcho.*
3 *South London Chronicle*, 12 January 1906.
4 One effect of the Act was seen by opponents to exclude most working-class children.
5 27 January 1906.
6 Quoted in *South London Chronicle*, 2 February 1906.
7 *South London Chronicle*, 26 January 1906.
8 Lady Welby to Nina, 17 October 1906 (CT).
9 Storrs, *Orientations.*
10 Michael Waterhouse, *Edwardian Requiem: A Life of Sir Edward Grey.*
11 Simon Blow to the author, 18 July 2018.
12 Blow, *Broken Blood.*
13 Letter from Ettie to Mary, quoted in Davenport-Hines, *Ettie*, p.142.
14 Archie Gordon to Lady Desborough, *ibid.*, p.144.
15 *Ibid.*, p.146.
16 12 September 1906, Ridley and Percy, *Letters of Arthur Balfour & Lady Elcho.*

17 Violet Bonham Carter (as she became), Beauman, *Cynthia Asquith*, p.183.
18 Dorothy Carleton, a cousin of the Wyndham siblings.
19 Lindsay, *The Crawford Papers*, 17 October 1895.
20 *Ibid.*, 24 May 1908.
21 Diana Cooper, *The Rainbow Comes and Goes.*
22 *Ibid.*
23 *Harrow Observer*, 17 May 1907.
24 Leveson Gower, *Years of Endeavour.*
25 *The Bystander*, 1 April 1908.
26 Lindsay, *The Crawford Papers*, 27 May 1905.
27 *The Bystander*, 1 April 1908.
28 Lady Diana Cooper, quoted in Sir Oliver Popplewell, *The Prime Minister and His Mistress*, p.82.
29 Margot Asquith, *Autobiography.*
30 Lady Diana Cooper in 1983, quoted in Lambert, *Unquiet Souls*, p.164.
31 Wyndham to his father, 14 April 1908, Mackail and Wyndham, *Life and Letters.*
32 Diary entry for February 1908, R.D. Blumenfeld, *In the Days of Bicycles and Bustles.*

Chapter 16: New Horizons

1 Prince Lichnowsky, *My Mission to London 1912–1914.*
2 *Illustrated London News*, 24 April 1909.
3 Letter Lady Welby to Nina, 19 April 1909 (CT).
4 From *The Essays of Virginia Woolf, Vol. I, 1904–1912*, quoted by Stanley Weintraub in 'Miss Stephen Reviews' for *The Washington Post* online, 8 March 1987.
5 Harry to Margot, 1 November 1909 (AP).
6 Blunt's diary, October 1909, quoted in Anita Leslie, *Edwardians in Love*, p.279.
7 Blunt's diary, October 1909, quoted in Longford, *A Pilgrimage of Passion*, p.387.
8 Paget, *In My Tower*, 29 November 1905.
9 *Ibid.*, 10 November 1905.
10 Letter from Wyndham to Lady Paget, 9 November 1905.
11 Hon. Percy Scawen Wyndham, quoted in Egremont, *The Cousins*, p.265.
12 Wyndham to John Tweed, 21 February 1909, Tweed Archive, Reading Museum.
13 Wyndham to Madeline Wyndham, 23 December 1908, Mackail and Wyndham, *The Life and Letters.*
14 Charteris, *A Family Record.*
15 Ettie to Balfour, quoted in Davenport-Hines, *Ettie*, p.151.
16 Mary to Balfour, 15 December 1909, Ridley and Percy, *Letters of Arthur Balfour & Lady Elcho.* The poem was 'A Shropshire Lad' by A.E. Housman.
17 Lady Welby to Nina, 4 August 1911 (CT).
18 The election was called in the middle of the crisis caused by the rejection of the People's Budget by the Conservative-dominated House of Lords in order to get a mandate to pass the Budget. It resulted in a hung Parliament. Asquith formed a government with the Irish Parliamentary Party.
19 T.E. Lawrence, *Seven Pillars of Wisdom.*

20 Storrs, *Orientations*.
21 Harry, quoted in Storrs, *Orientations*.
22 Almost certainly a reference to Thomas Cook & Son.
23 Lady Welby to Nina, 22 February 1910 (CT).
24 *Western Times*, 9 February 1910.
25 22 February 1910 (CT).
26 Galton's definition.
27 The book was written in 1913 and published in 1914. Dedication quoted in Storrs, *Orientations*.
28 Arnold Bennett, 31 December 1912, quoted in G.D. Perkin, 'Arnold Bennett and Medicine', *British Medical Journal*, Vol. 283, December 1981. The doctor was Reginald Chetham-Strode.
29 28 April 1910 (CT).
30 2 May 1910 (CT).
31 Harry to Mary, undated but probably late May 1910, when they got back, and Cynthia's engagement was announced.
32 Harry to Mary, undated but probably after 1906, as Curzon's wife died that year (SP).
33 Books in Eton College Collections, Nos B25843 and B25835.
34 National Trust Collections, Belton House, ref. 434695.
35 Undated, sent from the Beach Hotel, Littlehampton, but must be 1912, because Harry mentions the death of Lady Savile, who died in October 1912 (SP).

Chapter 17: Love and War

1 Mary to Balfour, 7 November 1911, Ridley and Percy, *Letters of Arthur Balfour & Lady Elcho*.
2 *The Sketch*, 9 April 1913.
3 Simon Blow to the author, July 2018.
4 As confirmed by Blow.
5 Quoted in Renton, *Those Wild Wyndhams*, p.297.
6 Quoted in Joan Wyndham, *Dawn Chorus*, p.13.
7 Wyndham to Lady Eden, 23 January 1913, notes for her autobiography (AC).
8 Anthony to Lady Eden, 15 June 1913 (AC).
9 Family friend Cynthia Gladwyn was one of those who held this view.
10 Cooper, *The Rainbow Comes and Goes*.
11 'It's not exactly a wedding.' Letter undated but probably October 1913, National Library of Scotland.
12 Harry to Lady Desborough, 23 January 1914 (DP, C630/8).
13 4 September 1914, Margot Asquith, *Great War Diary 1914–1916*.
14 Quoted in Lambert, *Unquiet Souls*, p.164.
15 Quoted in Renton, *Those Wild Wyndhams*, p.299.
16 Nina to Mary, sent from Sandwich, undated except 1914 (SP).
17 Storrs, *Orientations*.
18 Douglas Coult, *A Prospect of Ashridge*. This says the date of Kitchener's visit to Ashridge was 3 August, but this cannot have been right: see Storrs, *Orientations*.

19 Storrs, *Orientations*.
20 Balfour to Mary, 17 September 1914, Ridley and Percy, *Letters of Arthur Balfour*.
21 Letter to *The Times*, 5 September 1914, from Harry and his co-founder, Sir George Walter Prothero.
22 Wells's articles formed his book of that name published in 1916.
23 Baroness Orczy to the Secretary of the CCNPO, 21 November 1914, Brownlow Papers (BP), (Lincolnshire archives BNLW/4/9/1/3/35(i)).
24 G.B. Shaw to Nina, 30 November 1914 (BP, 4/9/1/3/42).
25 Charles Beresford to Harry, 21 July 1915 (BP, 4/9/1/3/7).
26 London, W. Heinemann.
27 Letter from G. de Wesselitsky to Nina, 8 September 1915 (BP, 4/9/1/3/50/viii.)
28 Letter 10 August 1916 (BP, 4/9/1/3/1).
29 Quoted in Abdy and Gere, *The Souls*, p.79
30 From Violet's notebook in 1914, quoted in Catherine Bailey, *The Secret Rooms*, p.253.
31 *Ibid.*, p.256.
32 Cooper, *The Rainbow Comes and Goes*.
33 Cynthia Charteris, quoted in Renton, *Those Wild Wyndhams*, p.326.
34 Diary entry 11 November 1915, quoted in Beauman, *Cynthia Asquith*, p.158.
35 Letter Balfour to Mary (Countess of Wemyss), 28 December 1915, Ridley and Percy, *Letters of Arthur Balfour & Lady Elcho*.
36 Letter 10 July 1915 (DP).
37 Letter 22 October 1915 (DP).
38 Letter 4 July 1916 (DP).
39 Quoted in Davenport-Hines, *Ettie*, p.196.
40 Blow, *Broken Blood*.
41 Simon Blow was made acutely aware of his mother's emotional wounds as a result of her rejection.
42 Letter 3 August 1916 (AP).
43 Letter from Stanley E. Bunn to the *Daily Telegraph*, 3 August 1918.
44 Nina Cust, 'My Prayer', from *Dilectissimo*, in *Not All the Suns*.

Epilogue

1 Echoing Lord Curzon in his appreciation of Harry in *The Times*, 6 March 1917.
2 Rennell Rodd, *Social and Diplomatic Memories*.
3 Margot Asquith, *Autobiography*.
4 T.P. O'Connor.
5 Nina to Leonie Leslie, quoted in Leslie, *Edwardians in Love*, p.277.
6 Nina Cust, from 'A Thanksgiving', in *Dilectissimo*.
7 *Revelations of Divine Love,* Julian of Norwich, fourteenth century.
8 As of April 2021, the most recent lecture was to have been delivered in June 2020 by Professor John Beckett but was postponed.
9 Nina's prose includes *Wanderers* (1928), an account of the travels of her grandmother and mother. Her sculpture is at Belton House.
10 Quoted in Margot Asquith, *Off the Record*.

11 Quoted in Mary, Countess of Wemyss, essay on the Souls (SP).
12 Wemyss essay (SP).

Appendix 1

1 Michael Thornton, 'Did True Blue Blood run in Lady Thatcher's veins?', *Sunday Express* online, 21 April 2013.
2 John Julius Cooper, 2nd Viscount Norwich (1929–2018). He inherited his title from his father, Alfred Duff Cooper, 1st Viscount Norwich, who served as Secretary of State for War (22 November 1935–28 May 1937) and as First Lord of the Admiralty (28 October 1937–27 October 1938). Lady Diana Cooper, author, actress, socialite died on 16 June 1986.
3 Quoted in Charles Moore, *Margaret Thatcher, The Authorised Biography, Vol. 1: Not for Turning*, p.14.
4 Margaret Thatcher, *The Path to Power*. Peregrine Brownlow had long been a friend of the Prince of Wales and when he became Edward VIII, he became involved in the abdication crisis of 1936.
5 As Moore points out, the dates are incompatible.
6 The 7th Baron Brownlow gave Belton to the National Trust in 1984.
7 Moore, *Margaret Thatcher, The Authorised Biography, Vol. 1: Not for Turning*, p.14.
8 As Lord Brownlow told the author.
9 Thatcher, quoted in John Campbell, *Margaret Thatcher: Volume One, The Grocer's Daughter*, p.18.

Index

Note: *italicised* references indicate photographs

YOU MAY ALSO ENJOY …

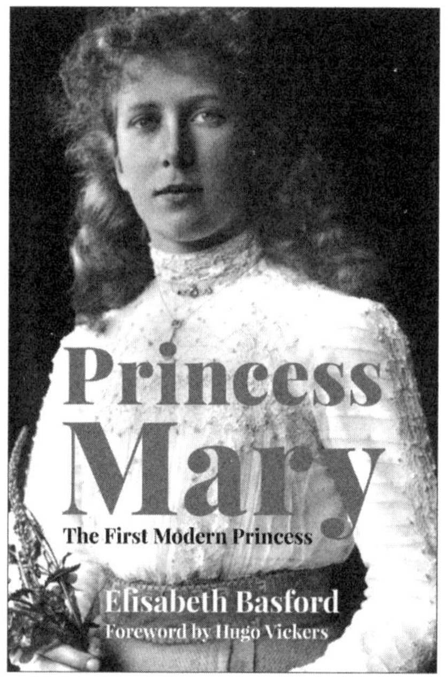

978 0 7509 9261 9

'Filled with never previously known information, this first full biography is the definitive read for this refreshingly forward-looking, eternally good-willed and relatively little-known Princess.'

Annabel Sampson, *Tatler*

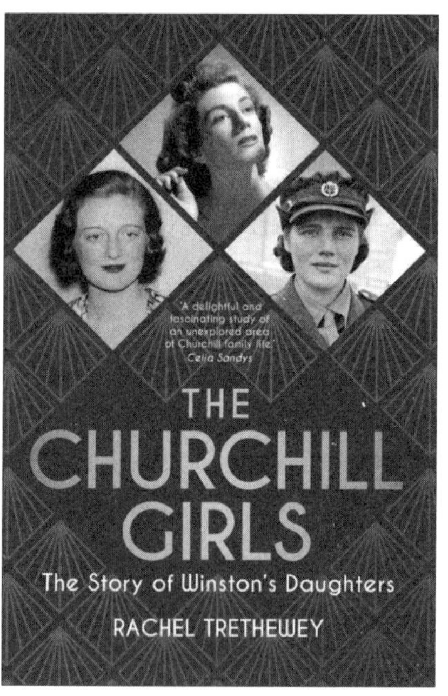

978 0 7509 9324 1

'This fascinating book brings the lives of [Churchill's] daughters out of the shadows for the first time. There is sadness and tragedy, but in the end it's the extraordinary talents and resilience of these remarkable women that shine through.'

Andrew Wilson, author of *Beautiful Shadow: A Life of Patricia Highsmith*